THE BATTLE-FIELDS OF IRELAND, FROM 1688 TO 1691

THE BATTLE-FIELDS OF IRELAND, FROM 1688 TO 1691

JOHN BOYLE

ISBN: 978-93-90387-00-7

Published: 1867

LECTOR HOUSE LLP
E-MAIL: lectorpublishing@gmail.com

THE BATTLE-FIELDS OF IRELAND, FROM 1688 TO 1691:

INCLUDING LIMERICK AND ATHLONE, AUGHRIM AND THE BOYNE.

BY

JOHN BOYLE

BEING AN OUTLINE HISTORY OF THE JACOBITE WAR IN IRELAND, AND THE CAUSES WHICH LED TO IT.

"And as they tread the ruined Isle,
Where rest, at length, the lord and slave,
They'll wondering ask, how hands so vile
Could conquer hearts so brave?"

MOORE

1867.

CONTENTS

INTRODUCTION.

Most of the following chapters were written some time since, at the request of the publisher, whose intention it was to present the readers of Irish history with a portable volume, which, while removing the necessity of wading through many tomes, would give an authentic account of the two leading events of a very important period,—the battles of the Boyne and Aughrim.

Having undertaken the task, and performed it to the extent of his information, it appeared to the writer that, without some allusion to antecedent causes and intermediate events, the book, though it should be acceptable to some, would be quite unsatisfactory to others; and it was concluded to make such interpolation as, without overburdening, would render the offering more clear and comprehensive.

After collecting much matter bearing on the subject, and finding it impossible to compress it methodically within the limits assigned, such selections were made, from historians of every shade of opinion, as would suffice, without distorting the parts already arranged, to give a consecutive view of the Jacobite war in Ireland, from its inception to its close.

As it was almost exclusively a war for religious ascendency on the one side, and for complete civil and religious liberty on the other, continually presenting a politico-religious aspect, it was chosen to leave the ethological bearing to other mediums, and confine this principally to the leading military events of the time. Hence, no allusion whatever is made to the interior merits of either faith dependent on the issue; nor to its exterior action, only so far as to preserve the order of an unbroken narrative.

Having followed the war down to the battle of Aughrim, inclusive, and reached the limit prescribed, the writer stops short of the final event—the last siege of Limerick; and he does so as well from motive as necessity, for he thinks that event could be more appropriately connected with a history of "The Brigade." But whether the subject is ever resumed by him or not, will greatly depend on the reception of this little volume, which is now submitted to the public.

THE AUTHOR.

THE BATTLE-FIELDS OF IRELAND.

CHAPTER I.

A CURSORY VIEW OF ENGLAND AND IRELAND ANTERIOR TO THE ACCESSION OF JAMES II.

Few monarchs ever ascended the English throne under more unfavorable auspices than James II. Though he reached it in the order of legitimate right, it was at a time when the monarchy of England was well-nigh divested of its most vital prerogatives, and when the voice of the sovereign had little more weight in the national councils than that of any ordinarily dissentient member; and to this were superadded rivalries, jealousies, and hatreds, which having their sources in remoter times, gathered strength like the rivers, and grew deeper and darker in their course.

As a representative of Scottish royalty, he inherited many a bitter memory from Bannockburn to Flodden, and as a descendant of the unfortunate Mary, he was an object of hatred to the old reform families of England, with whom her persecutor, Elizabeth, was still a hallowed memory; he was a grandson of James I., whom neither the acquisition of a kingdom, nor the confiscation of Ireland,—so grateful to every English adventurer,—could redeem from national contempt; a son of Charles I., whom the revolutionary elements evoked in Church and State by the pedantry of his father, had brought to the scaffold; and brother to the second Charles, one of the most indolent and dissolute monarchs that ever disgraced a throne. Through the last three reigns, the name of Stuart had been a term of distrust or hatred, both to the High Church party of England, and the fanatics of Scotland; but through some unaccountable cause, it had one, and only one, abiding-place,—the heart of Catholic Ireland,—whose people, through every phase of that dynasty, had experienced nothing but treachery, confiscation, and proscription.

Other circumstances, too, though of a domestic nature, tended to establish the unpopularity of James, and to raise up difficulties in his road to royalty. In 1671, his wife, the Duchess of York, though nominally a Protestant, died in communion with the Catholic Church, and from that time forward he himself made open profession of Catholicity. Towards the beginning of 1673 he was married to Mary of Modena, a Catholic, and the daughter of a royal house then in close alliance with France. The Parliament, which met shortly after, expressed great indignation at this event, and gave practical effect to its resentment. A declaration of indulgence which had been issued by Charles in 1671, granting to dissenters from the High Church the public observance of their religion, and to Roman Catholics the right to hear Mass in private houses, was censured, and repealed in its application to the Catholics. In this session was also passed the "Test Act," which continued in full legal force down to the reign of George IV., and which, with some modifications, is virtually observed at the present day. By the passage of this act, every Catholic official in the realm was removed, and the Duke of York lost the command of the British navy, in which he had won high distinction, and which he had brought to a greater degree of efficiency than it had hitherto known. These and similar marks of disapprobation were specially meant for James, who was then heir-presumptive, and showed him the dangers that beset his way to the throne. He, however, continued on unwavering in his principles, while every exercise of conscience on his part was met by a check on the king's prerogative, or a direct censure on himself. But when it became known, after the demise of Charles, that he, too, had received the last sacraments at the hands of a Catholic priest, and that James had been instrumental in the conversion of his reprobate brother, the rage of the High Church party knew no bounds, and their denunciations were echoed through every recusant party in the land. Comfort they knew none; their forbearance was stretched to the utmost tension; their cup of hatred was filled to the last drop; and even that drop was pendent, as from a leaf; the next wind might shake the branch, and then——

But still they had one hope. James was a good round age; as yet he had no issue male by his Catholic queen; his daughters, by his former wife, were educated in the Protestant faith, and had each been espoused to a Protestant prince; and in a few years, the throne would apparently revert to a Protestant sovereign.

William, Prince of Orange, the husband of the elder, was the ostensible head of the Protestant Alliance, and a devoted enemy to France. This was a relief in their present misfortunes, and a little forbearance was thought better than much blood-letting. The Duke of Monmouth, too, the natural son of Charles, was a great favorite with a large portion of the English people, and had even, during the life of his father, struck for the crown; and though banished the realm for that offence, he was still a centre to rally round, in case of necessity. These were the considerations which alleviated the misfortunes of James's enemies, and made his accession, even for a moment, tolerable.

The reign of James I., commonly called the "Pedant," from his affectation of learning, his uncouth appearance, and slovenly habits, was not marked by any act that elevates a people, or adorns a crown. It was chiefly employed in religious disquisition, which, giving rise to innumerable sects, greatly disturbed the interior spirit of the nation. That part of his time not so devoted, was spent in securing to the reform party the lands, lay and cleric, which had been confiscated during the reign of his immediate predecessors. But he was never popular. Though his low garrulity and set apothegms were hailed by the vile minions by whom he was constantly surrounded, as the sublimation of wisdom, they never failed to plant a thorn in the breast of the nobles, and with them he was an object of unmitigated contempt—deeply felt, but not openly expressed. Still the courtiers and the king got along pretty well, and each improved after a mutual acquaintance. He knew their instincts and their passions, and they secured his favor by sacrificing to his egotism. In them he discovered an inordinate appetite for plunder, and in him they saw an obtusity of honor, and an unscrupulousness of conscience, that could be made sure instruments in securing the spoils of an incomplete reformation. He resolved to cater to their appetite, and they determined to obey his rule, though they did not at all reverence his majesty.

The death of Elizabeth had left England in a profound peace, which was scarcely disturbed during his reign; and this fortuitous circumstance, more than his innate cowardice, won for him the name of "the peaceful monarch." He has had many satirists and many eulogists, and some who were both as occasion answered. Among the latter may be reckoned Sir Walter Scott, by whom we are told that the restless spirits of the former reign might calmly enjoy "the peace which James the peaceful gave." But, then, this was only in poetic *romaunt*, and by one who greatly despised him in romantic prose. Such eulogiums, however, had only reference to the influence of his reign on England and Scotland; the tyranny of an English king towards Ireland had been, in all times, his surest passport to popularity, and there his reign was one of terror, vengeance, persecution, and spoliation.

The prince who connived at the murder of his royal mother, could lay little claim to the respect of the good or high-minded in any age or nation, and so he lived an object of contempt and loathing to all that was good or honorable in the land. But though men of honor shunned his court, the venal there held high jubilee. The king's natural avarice was keen, and it was still further whetted by Scotch self-seekers, who thronged lobby and vestibule in all their greedy officiousness. Their rapacity had to be appeased. The people of England, too, were grown sullen and discontented; a spiritual madness had lately overspread the land, and produced a state of society always ominous of evil to the monarch; hence the public mind should be diverted from its sombre broodings. To secure himself on the throne, he saw the necessity of opening a way to the enterprise of the incongruous elements by which he was surrounded, and many precedents pointed to Ireland as the never-failing outlet for English discontent.

The latter half of Elizabeth's reign had been disturbed by a series of revolutions in Ireland. The first of these was headed by the Earl of Desmond, in defence of religious liberty; it extended all over Munster, and ended in his death and the confiscation of that province. Shortly after it was revived by Hugh O'Neil, Earl of Tyrone, and assuming national proportions, continued with almost unvaried success to the battle of Kinsale, in 1602, and terminated in a treaty which was wantonly violated after the queen's death. These wars extended through a period of more than twenty years, and left Ireland greatly prostrated on the accession of James I.; but the country was beginning to revive, and, under a fostering hand, it would soon have been content and prosperous. It was hoped, too, that as James, while king of Scotland, had contributed much to foment the uprising of O'Neil, he would be as instrumental in allaying the causes that led to it. The English "Undertakers," however, looked on an Irish war as a prelude to a general confiscation, and felt bitter disappointment at the terms accorded to the Irish rebels by the late queen. The apportionment of one province, which took place after the death of Desmond, did not satisfy them, while Ulster, a wealthy and populous one, was still left in the possession of the natives. The Scotch followers of James could not understand the thing at all, and attributed it to the dotage of the queen. In this state of affairs, the king saw an opportunity of rendering himself acceptable alike to his English and Scotch subjects. It was an age fruitful in plots and expedients, when plunder took the name of civilization, and avarice stalked forth under the cloak of religion. "The artful Cecil," the contriver and discoverer of many plots, was consulted by the king, and a scheme was laid for the violation of the compact of Mellifont, and the confiscation of Ulster. Lord Chichester was then deputy for Ireland;—but the words of Dr. Jones, the king's bishop of Meath, will tell the matter with sufficient brevity:[1] "Anno 1607, there was a providential discovery of another rebellion in Ireland, the Lord Chichester being deputy; *the discoverer not being willing to appear,* a letter from him, *not subscribed,* was superscribed to Sir William Usher, clerk of the council, and dropt in the council-chamber, then held in Dublin Castle, in which was mentioned a design for seizing the Castle and murdering the deputy, with a general revolt and dependence on Spanish forces; and this also for religion; for particulars whereof I refer to that letter, dated March the 19th, 1607."—This letter was read, and O'Neil, the late leader of the Irish, was singled out as the head and front of the supposed conspiracy.

O'Neil, who had been educated at the English court with a view to the advancement of the English interest in Ireland, was apprised of the conspiracy designed for his ruin, and at once detected the master-spirit—"The artful Cecil." From this he knew that his doom was sealed should he abide the action of the council, before which he had been summoned. He accordingly notified the chiefs of Ulster of the impending blow, and advised flight as the only means of safety. Most of them followed this advice, and he himself, collecting his household, retired to Rome, where he died in 1616.

The flight of O'Neil accomplished all that the conspirators wished, and with far less trouble than they anticipated. Wholesale confiscation, without resistance, was out of their calculation, even in a country borne down by the protracted strife of nearly twenty years. There still remained an element in Ulster, which, though it could not work the deliverance of the nation, could wreak summary vengeance on many a hungry Undertaker; but this settled all at once, to the great "joyousness" of the king: and he lost no time in proclaiming his satisfaction, in words of which the following is an extract: "Wee doe professe, that it is both known to us and our council here, and to our deputie and state there, and so shall it appeare to the world (as cleare as the sunne) by evident proofes, that the only ground and motive of this high contempt, in these men's departure, hath been the private knowledge and inward terrour of their own guiltinesse," etc. "But," says Mitchell, "no attempt to give these proofs was ever made," and never will be. The very manner of their departure is a proof of innocence. Had there been a conspiracy, they would have abided the result, and sold their lives with their lands at a price dear enough to the English enemy. But they went in the belief that their lives and lands alone were what the king sought, and that by quitting the country, they would save the minor chieftains and their clansmen from the greed of England. They calculated erroneously, for this did not accord with the design of the infamous king, and the whole

---

[1] Mitchell's Life of Hugh O'Neil, pp. 236, 237.

province soon became the spoil of the "Undertakers." An act of Parliament—the English Parliament—immediately followed the king's proclamation, declaring that "Whereas the divine justice hath lately cast out of the province of Ulster divers wicked and ungratefull traytors, who practised to interrupt those blessed courses begun and continued by your majestie for the general good of this whole realm, by whose defection and attainders great scopes of land in those parts have been reduced to your majestie's hands and possession," etc.—and of course awaited but the royal pleasure to be transferred to his loyal subjects of the realm. Nor was the royal assent long withheld, for the royal coffers were always open, even to smaller windfalls than the revenues arising from a confiscated province.

The work of settlement was soon commenced, under the supervision of the king, privy council, committees of conference, committees of inquiry, contractors, undertakers, speculators, and commissioners names of ominous import in Ireland and so often revived there that her people can rehearse them like a catechism. "In the six counties of Donegal, Tyrone, Derry, Farmanagh, Cavan, and Armagh, a tract of country containing 500,000 acres, was seized upon by the king and parcelled out in lots to Undertakers."[2] The "domains" of the attainted lords were assumed to include all the lands inhabited by their clans, and so far were the king's new arrangements from respecting the rights of the ancient natives, that "the fundamental ground of this *plantation* was the avoiding of natives and planting only with British."

That this cruel policy was carried out to the letter, would seem scarcely credible. But let the authority already quoted settle that matter. "It is true," says Sir Thomas Phillips, in "Harris's Hibernia," "that after the prescribed number of freeholders and leaseholders were settled on every townland, and the rents therein set down, *they might let the remainder to natives, for lives, so as they were conformable in religion, and for the favor* to DOUBLE THEIR RENTS!" Even so, to double their rents, if natives, though conformable in religion. A *high favor*, and all for the love of God!

This is but a very imperfect outline of the plantation of Ulster, and the manner of effecting it; and it is alluded to in these pages, only in so far as it illustrates the subject-matter of them, on which that settlement has a direct bearing. Its immediate and subsequent effects on the Irish race, though the theme of many a commentator, have never been told, and never will be. Even its remoter consequence at the present day can scarcely be alluded to without opening up wounds but imperfectly healed, and memories too bitter for wholesome reflection. It renewed, by one dash of the royal pen, all the wrongs of the preceding centuries, and filled the last stronghold of the Irish race with a people inimical to their interests, and who, with the exception of one short epoch in the country's history, have remained a cancer on the body politic, and, as if by a special providence, though meant to strengthen the dynasty of the Stuarts, were mainly instrumental in causing its extinction.

The reign of Charles I. was an eventful and a bloody one. In 1625 he ascended the throne; in 1649 he ascended the scaffold; and through the intervening period of twenty-four years, it was a continual struggle for the preservation of the royal prerogatives. These prerogatives were yielded, one by one, to the fanatical spirit

[2] Mitchell's Hugh O'Neil, p. 241.

of the age, and the last royal prerogative, that of life—for it is held a standing apothegm, that the king can do no wrong—terminated in a disastrous civil war which drenched the three kingdoms in blood.

England had been in a state of transition since the reign of Henry VIII. The religion of the country had undergone a change which had left more than one-half of its population—and that the more powerful one—adherents of the new faith. New manners and new morals had kept pace with the change of religion. The lands, too, had undergone as great a change as the people. Most of the old manors were possessed by new lords; and as for the Church, its glebes had passed to the early conformists, and its cash to the royal coffers. Hatred on the one hand, and revenge on the other, the usual concomitants of all violent changes in civil or ecclesiastical bodies, were the order of the day. Among those who had become recipients of the spoils, a feeling of insecurity was predominant. These changes had all been wrought through the will of the sovereigns—the royal prerogative, and it required no prophetic ken to know, that while that prerogative remained unimpaired, some future sovereign might undo all that his predecessors had accomplished; and this continual apprehension was the parent of each successive reform: and self-preservation the object.

The reign of James I. sowed the seed of religious discontent; that of Charles I. reaped the harvest. The old faith had been too closely drawn towards the political arena, and had suffered by the contact; the new one whirled in its vortex, and the result was the worst state of human society—civil and religious anarchy. A church had been established by law, and richly endowed by the spoils of the old one, antecedent to the accession of Charles, and its followers were called the "High Church" people. But outside its communion, innumerable sects overspread the land, known by the general name of "Nonconformists." The highways and by-ways of England and Scotland resounded with their religious disquisitions; every man had become an interpreter and a prophet. The most powerful of those sects were the Puritans of England, and the Covenanters of Scotland, who, though differing in religious principles, closely assimilated in their hatred of all monarchical government, and of the outward ceremonies of divine worship. Practising greater simplicity, they laid claim to greater purity of religion, until they at length believed themselves invested with a divine mission to eradicate "popery," "prelacy," and monarchy. The materials of combustion had been long preparing, and nothing was wanting but some partisan more daring or fanatical than the rest to apply the match, and he was at last found in Oliver Cromwell, a great king-hater, and one of the most daring military spirits of that or of any other age. Putting on "the armor of the Lord," and the "Shield of Righteousness," they seized the "besom of destruction," and went forth under his banner to complete the purgation of the land.

How this war, between the King and Parliament, progressed and terminated, forms a bloody chapter in English history, but it can be noticed in this place no further than its effect on Ireland; there it helped to swell the tide of oppression; it brought another war, another defeat, another confiscation, and another wholesale expatriation of the native race.

Since the plantation of Ulster, religious persecution had been aggravated by an established system of confiscation, under the name of the "Irish Titles Act." In the mean time the "Nonconformists" of England and Scotland having taken up arms against King Charles, made a solemn vow to exterminate the Catholics of Ireland, and the apprehensions of the latter were soon alive to the emergency. Groaning so long under civil and religious exactions, they looked on the king's difficulty as a most suitable event to petition for a removal of their grievances. But their action was anticipated, and while their leaders were considering a course of procedure, a series of outrages was perpetrated in the province of Ulster which precipitated them at once into the vortex of rebellion. A garrison of Scotch soldiers, stationed at Carrickfergus, in the dead of night, and without premonition, made a descent on Island Magee, a peninsula in the neighborhood, and drove all its inhabitants, to the number of 3,000, over the cliffs into the sea; scarce a soul escaping to tell their cruel fate. The Catholic inhabitants of the surrounding counties flew to arms, and the flames of rebellion were soon lit throughout the province. The Protestants rose to oppose them, and excesses were perpetrated on both sides. This hastened the action of the Catholic leaders. The Irish chiefs, the Catholic Lords of the English Pale, and the bishops of the Catholic Church convened at Kilkenny for mutual protection and right, under the name of the "Confederation of Kilkenny," and inaugurated one of the boldest efforts for civil and religious liberty known in the country's history.

In the mean time, the war between the king and the Parliamentarians progressed in England. The king's affairs grew desperate, and overtures were made to the Irish Confederates by the king's adherents in Ireland, the principal of whom were the Earls of Clanricarde and Ormond. The Confederates held out with great tenacity for their stipulated measures of redress; yet these the king, even in his direst extremity, refused to concede. But through the intrigues of the two royal agents, the councils of the Confederation were at last distracted; two parties, one for the king, and one for Catholic right, were formed; the soldiers took sides with their respective leaders, and made war against each other. So they fought for some time, the latter being generally successful, and the king at last offered concessions, but too late to redeem his fallen cause. The result is history; the king lost his head; Cromwell invaded Ireland; O'Neil, the only soldier capable of opposing him, is said to have been poisoned, and after his death Cromwell met with but futile opposition. The son of the decapitated king, after a few abortive attempts to secure the crown, became a refugee until the death of Cromwell, when he was recalled, through a popular reaction, and crowned as Charles II.:—and this is called the Restoration. It is called the Restoration, because it restored the throne to its lawful successor; because it restored the High Church party its privileges; and because it restored some of the lands confiscated in England during the Commonwealth to their former owners. But it was ushered in by an odious concession. It left the English rebels in full enjoyment of their lands and immunities, both in England and Ireland. In the latter country the confiscations of Cromwell were legalized, nor was the property of those who joined the late king's cause ever restored to them! But then, in England, it was a Parliament that rebelled against a sovereign; in Ireland, it was a people that demanded rights older than sovereign or Parliament,—that made all the difference.

Under the Protectorate of Cromwell 5,000,000 acres of arable land were confiscated, and the Restoration continued the robbery, by searches into titles which produced litigations, generally settled in English courts, to which all Irish questions were then transferable. It is needless to say that those suits terminated in establishing defective titles in the natives: the lands became the prey of the crown or its cormorants, and expatriation or slavish dependence was the award of the complainant. Five-sixths of the land passed away from the native race, and the population became dependents, without law or appeal, on the soil which had been theirs from time immemorial.

These confiscations had great effect in satisfying the vulture appetite of England. But as this business approached completion, the national mind reverted to the one great question—that of Protestant succession. The days of Charles drew towards a close. As yet the British Constitution had not debarred the heir-presumptive, though he should be a Catholic; and this was a thorn in the national heart. The fears of "popery" became again the national theme, and nobles and people alike brooded on this impending calamity. The hostility to James, always bitter, grew more open and violent as the king declined. In 1680, the Earl of Shaftesbury had him indicted in Westminster Hall, as a popish recusant; but the Chief-Justice dismissed the suit. In 1681, during a temporary illness of the king, a rebellion was set on foot by Shaftesbury, the Duke of Argyle, Lord William Russell, and others. The avowed object was the restoration of The Protectorate, but the covert design, to supplant the Duke of York, and place Monmouth, the natural son of Charles, on the throne. The king recovered; the plot exploded, Monmouth was banished the court, and retired to the Continent, and Argyle and Shaftesbury were attainted, but fled to Holland, to concoct new schemes for barring the succession of James. On the 6th of February, 1685, Charles died, unhonored and unlamented, save in so far as his death opened the way to an unwelcome successor, and all looked in fearful boding to that dreaded event.

The reign of Charles was a weak and inglorious one. His was a kind of passive existence, spent in connivance at the treason of a corrupt court, and the regicides of the last reign, while they connived at his secret carousals and studied profligacy. His youth was one of promise, and it is even asserted by some of his biographers that his indifference to all the great ends that excite the ambition of princes was an exemplification of practical wisdom. That such a reign was the only one that could have secured his permanency on the throne is now a matter of speculation. The received opinion is, that he believed it was, and acted in accordance with that belief. His well-known repartee to the Duke of York, who endeavored to rouse him from his apathy, would more than indicate this—that "he was too old to go again upon his travels." Yet it scarcely serves as an excuse for a long life wasted, and the noble ends of government neglected. But this much is well known in Ireland,—too well to be forgotten,—that he mulcted his English subjects to carry on his debaucheries; that he despoiled the Irish Catholics to remunerate his English creditors, and when both sources failed, he became a stipendiary on the bounty of the French king, bequeathing to his successor an exhausted exchequer, a turbulent people, a crown pawned for many a debt, and yet with many an heir-expectant. It required but a short time for James to establish facts which were patent to all minds but his: that the nobles by whom he was surrounded were irreconcilable to his views; that a time-server might wield and direct them if he pandered to their passions; but a king could not rule in peace, and retain the faith *he* had chosen. Yet, with all the evidence of the three last reigns before him to the contrary, he had an abiding faith in the justice of the English people. He knew that he was the choice of the Irish, and believed the native pride of the Scotch would not admit of the alienation of their crown; but above all, he trusted in the justice of his views, and he came to the throne with a fixed resolve to harmonize the conflicting elements of the State, and to make England, what he believed it ought to have been—a really free and happy nation.

CHAPTER II.

THE REIGN OF JAMES II. IN ENGLAND—THE INVASION OF WILLIAM, PRINCE OF ORANGE. FROM 1685 TO 1688.

The accession of James was not met by any overt act of opposition. On the contrary, it was hailed by the rejoicings of the people, and the parliamentary leaders of the High Church party, at that moment plotting his expulsion, received him with the usual congratulations and addresses of loyalty. The Catholics of England and Scotland, who were still a respectable minority, felt their long-suppressed hopes kindle anew, and by their Irish brethren the event was hailed with undisguised satisfaction. Nothing could shake the loyalty of this oppressed people to the house of Stuart. The cruel exactions, broken pledges, and studied persecutions of the last three reigns were at once forgotten. The advent of each false king after the other, had been represented as sure to redress the grievances which the former one had inflicted, and after every outrage they became more steadfast in their devotion. If, during the rebellion of 1641, their attachment to this house was sufficient to withdraw a large portion of them from the standard of their native chiefs, then battling for their lands and religious liberty, how then must they have felt when the house of Stuart presented them a Catholic king, and one who gave unmistakable signs that justice and toleration should at last be extended to them; that persecution for conscience sake was at an end, and that the exiled of many years might again return to their native land!

That James knew the dangers that beset him in England, there can scarcely be a doubt; but the measures of redress which he contemplated being just and beneficent, he believed they would in a short time harmonize all interests. He had faith in his own justice, but miscalculated in attributing so noble a sense to the dominant and intolerant nobles by whom he was surrounded, and was still more mistaken when he expressed an abiding faith in the justice of the English people. Yet filled with the hope of marking a glorious page in the annals of England, he assumed the sceptre with a bold and kingly hand. His speech before the assembled council of the nation was all that a generous or magnanimous people could desire, and all his subsequent acts are marked by a strict adherence to the principles which he then enunciated. "I will endeavor," said he, "to preserve the government of Church and State in the manner by law established. I know that the Church of England is favorable to monarchy, and those who are members of it have made it appear on various occasions that they were faithful subjects. I will take particular care to defend and support it. I know likewise that the laws of the kingdom are sufficient to make the king as great as I could wish. As I am determined to preserve the prerogative of my crown, so I will never deprive others of what belongs to them. I have often hazarded my life in defence of the nation; I am still ready to expose it to preserve its rights."

He eschewed the tendency to despotic power which his enemies had circulated, or any design to call in question the titles or hereditaments of such as acquired lands through the Reformation. His object was not to disrupt but to harmonize and adjust, and blend all interests for an onward movement in civilization. He declared civil liberty to be the right of Catholics and Protestants alike. He proclaimed liberty of conscience, and took immediate action to secure it by liberating several thousand Catholics confined in the prisons of Ireland for non-attendance on Protestant worship, and also twelve hundred Quakers who had been imprisoned for a like offence. He declared the abolition of all penal laws, all religious test-oaths, and even oaths of allegiance on the assumption of civil office. He extended the same rights to the people of Ireland and Scotland as to those of England, and enjoined the bishops to announce in their churches that liberty of conscience was henceforth the law of the land. Here, 'tis said, he made his first royal blunder. Proclaiming liberty of conscience from a pulpit is hardly in accordance with that right of denouncing heresy and schism, which every church, whether founded on human will or divine right, has asserted from the days of Abram. But, then, on the other hand, the Church of England, which had been proclaiming that and every thing else the royal reformers of the last century chose to dictate, might have announced this liberal measure of a king, the goodness of whose motives were well understood. But they denounced the innovation as a license to sin, though he intended only to have it announced that persecution for conscience sake had ceased in his dominions. The order was obeyed by some of the bishops, but by the majority it was stubbornly resisted. The king prosecuted for contumacy. The judges in some cases executed the royal mandate and the bishops were imprisoned; in others they refused, and bishops and judges joined issue in a passive resistance. Still the king bated not a tittle of the principle laid down. The establishment of civil and religious liberty for all classes and denominations had been the great object of his life, and he was not to be driven from his purpose. He believed that the majority of the nobles were tired of persecution for conscience sake, and wished for a restoration of social harmony. He believed that the masses yearned for it, and he calculated on their loyalty. He believed that the Restoration was a proof that legitimacy would never again be assailed, and he took no precautions against conspiracy; nay, he scouted the warnings of his friends, that one was ripening among the members of his council, and that even his own children were spies upon his actions, and plotting his destruction. But an event soon transpired that removed his incredulity, and awakened him to a sense of the difficulties and dangers that beset him.

The first rebellion of the Duke of Monmouth and its result have already been noticed. On its suppression, the chief conspirators, Shaftesbury and Argyle, fled to the continent. The former died shortly after, but the latter linked his fortune to that of Monmouth, plotted on, and gave direction to the ambition of this English favorite. Repairing to Holland, it is said that they received both counsel and a promise of aid from the Prince of Orange to attempt another invasion. After the death of Charles, William detached himself from this conspiracy, for his own pretensions to the British throne had become greater than those of Monmouth, and indeed it is hard to reconcile the conduct of William unless we accept a charge, which is not without supporters, and which is greatly to that Prince's discredit:—that of urging the wayward Duke to his destruction, and thus removing an obstacle to his own ambition. However that be, William disconnected himself from the conspiracy, and Monmouth soon after retired to Brussels, where he was joined by Argyle and continued his preparations for an invasion. Getting counsel and assistance from his partisans in England and Scotland, he prepared for a descent at the earliest opportunity; and the excitement created by the troubles between King James and the bishops gave him at once both a hope and a pretext. With a fleet of three ships and one hundred followers, he landed at Lyme, in Dorsetshire, and in a few days he had a following of above two thousand men. He proclaimed the king a traitor and a popish usurper, and called on the country to rise in opposition to his rule. At Taunton he was presented with a pair of colors and a copy of the Bible, by twenty young ladies, and assumed the title of king. Here his army increased to six thousand. At Sedgemoor he attacked the royal forces under Feversham and Churchill, and was completely overthrown; and, flying for shelter through the country, he was taken and finally executed. His evil genius, Argyle, met with a similar fate; the greatest rigor was exercised against the scattered refugees of this ill-advised rebellion, and many of the nobles of the land were attainted of treason.

This event opened the eyes of the king to the dangers by which he was surrounded. The army had shown signs of disaffection. Many of the leaders of the Protestant party in Ireland and Scotland were known to be connected with this conspiracy; even the members of his council were more than suspected of complicity; and he saw that his rule could only be established by the introduction of a Catholic element into the army. Since the passage of the "Test Act," nearly all the Catholic officers of the army and navy had been removed. Many of these were men of distinguished ability, and he now determined to recall them to the service. Accordingly, in his speech to Parliament on the 9th of November, 1685, in allusion to the rebellion of Monmouth, he introduced the proposition in the following words: "Let no man take exception, that there are some officers in the army not qualified, according to the *late Test,* for their employments; the gentlemen, I must tell you, are most of them well-known to me, and having formerly served me on several occasions (and always approved the loyalty of their principles by their practice), I think them now fit to be employed under me; and will deal plainly with you, that after having the benefit of their services in such time of need and danger, I will neither expose them to disgrace, nor myself to the want of them, if there should be another rebellion to make them necessary to me. I am afraid some men may be so wicked, to hope and expect that a difference may happen between you and me upon this occasion. * * * I will not apprehend that such a misfortune can befall us as a division, or even a coldness between me and you; nor that any thing can shake you in your steadiness and loyalty to me, who, by God's blessing, will ever make you all returns of kindness and protection, with a resolution to venture even my own life in the defence of the true interests of this kingdom."

It is scarcely necessary to say that this met the opposition of Parliament; and so far from being received in the liberal and loyal spirit which the king seems to have anticipated, it was denounced as a measure for the abolition of the Protestant religion. The revocation of the *"Edict of Nantes,"* by Louis XIV., occurring about the same time, had filled England with Protestant refugees, which gave strength to the arguments of the opposition, and excited a spirit of retaliation in the English people. The king, however, persevered, and tested the legality of the "Test," in the person of Sir Edward Hales, who had held the commission of colonel in the army, and who had lately become a Catholic. The judges decided in his favor, but the king was accused of intimidation. This opened the way to reform in the army, and gratified the Catholics, but it raised the spirit of opposition among the bishops and leaders of the High Church party in a corresponding degree. Not deterred by this opposition, the king persevered in his measures of redress; and called Dissenters and Catholics to office wherever opportunity occurred; and, says Hume, "Not content with this violent and dangerous innovation, he appointed certain regulators to examine the qualifications of electors, and directions were given them to exclude all such as adhered to the test and penal statutes." In all of which one fails to see, notwithstanding the exaggeration of Hume, any attempt at injustice, or proscription. It was in fact, from beginning to end, an effort to establish equality and right on the one part, and to preserve and perpetuate an odious ascendency on the other. That many of the steps taken by the king to reach his object may have been imprudent, and must, from the surrounding circumstances, have met with bitter opposition, is not to be wondered at; but that his views were right, and his object wise and magnanimous, cannot be denied. The exclusion of Nonconformists, from social and legal equality, in a former reign, produced a civil war, which most Protestant writers vindicate as necessary, and it is hard to see why the same writers advocate the permanent exclusion of the Catholics, who were certainly entitled to equal consideration. Meanwhile the opposition ran high, and the High Church party being now united by the death of Monmouth, took council throughout the three kingdoms, and determined to call in William Henry, Prince of Orange, as their last hope to preserve their cherished and glorious ascendency.

The title—Prince of Orange—is derived from the town of Orange (ancient Awrasio), in the southeast of France, department of Vaucluse. In the middle ages this town was the capital of a principality, which for a considerable period belonged to the house of Nassau; and William Henry was then the incumbent both of the title and the domain. After his death the title passed to his heir, the King of Prussia, and is still retained in the royal family of Holland; but the principality whence the title is derived, has been since ceded to France. The father of William, who was Stadtholder of the Dutch provinces, died in 1650, and the office, which was not inherent, but elective, remained in abeyance, under the management of the brothers De Witt, until 1672, when England and France declared war against Holland. William laid claim to the office of his father, but was opposed by the De Witts. The emergency pointed out William as the choice of those opposed to the claims of France, and the De Witts, still opposing, became the victims of an assassination, said to have been concocted by William. This placed William at the head both of civil and military affairs, which, however unscrupulous were the means of attainment, he conducted with great ability, and saved Holland from subjugation to the French king. From 1672 to 1677, the war continued with various success. At the close of that year's campaign, William visited England by invitation, and Charles, in order to terminate a war which was unpopular with the majority of his nobles, acceded to the proposal of his counsellors, to pave the way for an alliance with Holland, by espousing Mary, the eldest daughter of James, then Duke of York, to the Stadtholder. This marriage, which took place shortly after, gave William, who was then both nephew and son-in-law to James, the right of heir-presumptive; and, the immediate result of it was a peace between England and Holland, at Nimeguen, in 1678.

William was a very ill-favored prince, weak of body, ungraceful in gait and manner, and of a forbidding countenance at once expressive of cruelty and unscrupulousness. He was not a statesman, nor yet an able diplomatist, but possessed a keenness of perception, that enabled him to see through the motives of men, a reticence of habit, which protected him from importunity, and a will subservient to the call of ambition. Yet though he was the acknowledged head of the Protestant league, and conformed to the ceremonies of exterior worship, he was a most confirmed sceptic, and averse to all religious disquisition. He, however, possessed those qualities which the enemies of James most desired. He was ambitious of power, an able soldier, the ostensible champion of Protestantism, and the irreconcilable enemy of the French monarch.

From the time of his marriage with Mary, he was ambitious of the English throne, chiefly, 'tis said, that he might check the power of his detested enemy, Louis, and the connection gave him a valid title, should the king, his father-in-law, die without legitimate male issue. The Duke of Monmouth, who was an English favorite, being removed, and the Duke of Berwick, the natural son of James, and nephew of Lord Churchill, afterwards Duke of Marlborough, cherishing no such pretensions, William's fears were quieted, and it is even said that he received the first advances of the High Church party with indifference. But rumors of the queen's pregnancy excited the fears of William; he became apprehensive, listened to their appeals, a conspiracy was set on foot through the agency of Bishop Burnet, Sydney, Peyton, and Gwynne, and he began to organize a military force for the invasion of England. The materials were ready to his hand. "The Thirty Years' War" had overspread Europe with adventurers from every nation, and he soon gathered to his standard an army of the most daring spirits of the age, consisting of Dutch, Danes, Swedes, Huguenots, and Germans, always ready and eager for any enterprise that offered fame or fortune to their arms.

On the 10th of June, 1688, while these preparations were carried stealthily forward, the Queen of England gave birth to a son. This event removed all hesitation on the part of the Prince of Orange, and precipitated "the Revolution." From this time forward negotiations between the Prince and the English conspirators were pressed with earnestness and vigor; every concession demanded by the Prince was yielded without question by the agents of the Church party, and he bound himself to the invasion and the maintenance of Protestant supremacy. Still the utmost secrecy was observed on both sides, and the Earl of Sunderland, who was in the king's confidence, and at the same time in league with William, kept the one impressed with a sense of security, and apprised the other of all that transpired in the national councils.

An incident which occurred at this time may serve to show the animus of party spirit, and illustrate the intriguing and unscrupulous character of William. It had been prearranged between the Prince and his English partisans, that in case the queen gave birth to a son it should be declared supposititious. Accordingly, William prepared an instrument to that effect, to be published on his arrival in England; and yet, with characteristic duplicity, he dispatched Zuylestein, ostensibly to congratulate the king on the birth of his son,—the Prince of Wales,—but covertly to complete arrangements with the heads of the conspiracy in England.[3] By such artifices the king was kept in complete ignorance of the storm gathering around him, until the summer had nearly passed, when Talbot, Earl of Tyrconnell,—then deputy for Ireland,—received information from the captain of a Dutch trading vessel, of the extensive preparations going on in Holland, and of the designs of the Prince of Orange on the English throne.[4] Tyrconnell lost no time in communicating this intelligence to the king; and a letter which he received shortly after from his minister at the Hague, informing him that a powerful invasion must be soon expected, followed by private information from the French king to the same effect, at last opened his eyes to his real situation. M. Bonrepos, the envoy of Louis, who brought this intelligence, accompanied it with the offer of 30,000 French troops, to suppress the invasion before it could make head; but as the evil counsel of Sunderland still prevailed, on the ground that such an armament from France would excite the indignation of his English soldiers, and precipitate the catastrophe which he wished to avoid, the generous offer of Louis was declined. James continued in a state of the greatest bewilderment. All the boldness and decision of his earlier years seemed to have deserted him; and at a time when only men of approved loyalty should be trusted, he recalled to his service the contumacious officials of the late reign, and so paved the way for the success of the impending Revolution.

Preliminaries being arranged between William and his English adherents, by the beginning of October, 1688, he collected his forces at Holvoetsluys, a port in the south of Holland, lying over against the eastern coast of England, and, under the advice of Bishop Burnet, put to sea toward the end of the same month. His armament consisted of fifty ships of war, twenty frigates, four hundred transports, and some smaller craft, carrying 14,000 men, with arms and equipments for 20,000 more. The van and rear of this fleet were commanded by Admiral Herbert and Vice-Admiral Evertzen, respectively, having the Prince of Orange and his military adherents in the centre. All the ships carried the English flag, having the arms of the Prince emblazoned at the top, with the words:

"RELIGION AND LIBERTY,"

[3] For a further insight to the court intrigue of that period, the reader is referred to the Memoirs of the Duke of Berwick, vol. i., pp. 20 to 30.

[4] The Popular History of Ireland, vol. ii., p. 571.

and at the bottom with the device of the house of Nassau,

"I WILL MAINTAIN."

In his train were many English, Irish, and Scotch refugees, and three hundred Huguenot officers, the principal of whom were Marshal Schomberg; his son, Count Schomberg; Caillemotte and his brother Ruvigny; Mellioneire, Cambon, Tettau, and others of approved valor and of great military experience.

During the voyage a storm arose, the whole fleet was scattered, some of the ships foundered at sea, and the rest had to put back for several days. William, however, continued his course, and arrived safe at Torbay, in the county of Devon, on the 5th of November, 1688, with about 700 followers. It being the anniversary of the Gunpowder Plot, he availed himself of the circumstance, and appealing to the passions and prejudices of the people, stated the object of his invasion to be the protection of the Protestant religion from the machinations of "Popery." But this not having the desired effect, he felt somewhat disconcerted, and after spending a few days in the exercise of his marines and being joined by the remainder of his forces, he made the necessary disposition and took up his march for Exeter. Here, finding that the country gentlemen and clergy of the Established Church fled at his approach, and that none of the leading conspirators came to meet him, he began to think that he had been deceived by false promises; and with a presence of mind that rarely deserted him, he at once had recourse to intimidation. Accusing them of their twofold treachery, he apprised them of his intention of furnishing the king with a list of their names, and of then returning to Holland and abandoning them to their fate. This soon aroused them to a sense of their position. Lords Colchester and Godfrey fled from London in the night and joined his standard; others came in after these, and with a force continually increasing as he went, he continued his march towards London.

Upon receiving information of William's descent upon the English coast, King James mustered an army of 30,000 men, and marched towards Salisbury to oppose him. On the way, Lord Cornbury, under pretence of attacking an outpost of the enemy, took his own regiment and three others and abandoned the royal cause: further on, the Duke of Grafton, Colonel Barclay, and Lord Churchill, Lieutenant-General of the Guards, openly deserted. Seeing the defection continue, the king retired to Andover, whence Prince George of Denmark, the young Duke of Ormond, and other distinguished personages, fled in the night, and joined the standard of the invader. Overwhelmed with shame and confusion he returned to London, but here he found that his daughter, Anne, under pretence of fearing his anger on account of her husband's defection, had left the palace and taken refuge with his enemies. He had always been a most affectionate and indulgent father. The ingratitude of his elder daughter, though it pressed heavily on his heart, was borne with becoming fortitude, but that of the younger, not having the same extenuating causes, outraged all the dearest sensibilities of the father; his spirit was broken, and, weeping in his bereavement, he exclaimed: "God help me, my own children have forsaken me!" His queen and infant son demanding his first attention, he committed them to the care of the Count de Lausun, by whom they were conveyed in safety to France, and dispatching Lord Feversham with a letter of remonstrance to William, he determined to remain in London himself, and bide the issue of events. But contrary to honorable usage, Feversham was imprisoned, the palace was surrounded by Dutch guards, in the night, and the king was notified that he should quit London by 12 o'clock next day. Accordingly, he was sent under arrest to Rochester, whence he escaped to Picardy, and arrived at St. Germains on the 25th of December, deserted by all his family but the Duke of Berwick, and the Grand Prior Fitzjames.

The departure of the king was a signal for the uprising of the London mob; the Catholic inhabitants were forced to seek refuge in flight; their property was marked out for destruction; the houses of the Spanish and Florentine envoys were rifled, and William entered the city by the blaze of the few religious houses which had been erected during the short reign of the expatriate king. He lost no time in arranging his terms of settlement with his new subjects and in opening negotiations with the leaders of the Church party in Ireland and Scotland. On the 12th of February, the Princess Mary joined him in England, and they were proclaimed king and queen; the Prince of Wales was debarred the right of succession, William was invested in the administration, and his children by Mary—should he be blessed with any—were to be endowed with the right of succession.

CHAPTER III.

EVENTS PRECEDING HOSTILITIES IN IRELAND—THE PREPARATORY MEASURES OF TYRCONNEL.

Leaving William of Orange in undisputed possession of the English throne, and King James a suppliant at the French court for the support which he had so unwisely declined previous to the invasion, it is necessary to reconsider the condition of Ireland before presenting her part in this great politico-religious drama.

Of the three generations which had passed, antecedent to the events under consideration, each had witnessed a war more protracted and devastating than any which marked her history since the invasion. These were the wars of Desmond and Tyrone, and the war of the Irish Confederates of 1641; each of which was followed by a wholesale confiscation and plantation of the country with a population antagonistic to every interest of the native race. Through these violent changes four-fifths of the ancient chieftainries had changed proprietors, and those which were undisturbed by each successive military convulsion, the court of claims and the acts of attainder and settlement that continued down to the death of Charles II., had well-nigh sequestrated. The surface of the country is computed at ten millions and a half of acres; and of these, says Newenham, "Upon the final execution of the acts of settlement and explanation, it appears that 7,800,000 acres were set out by the court of claims, principally if not wholly, in the exclusion of the old Irish proprietors." It is scarce necessary to remark that if the above estimate of the island—which is taken from Dr. Petty's survey—includes the waste and water, the arable land had passed to the undertakers, and the waste and water were the portion of the old Irish proprietors.

The loss of liberty, too, had outstripped the loss of lands, for liberty and law had first to be silenced that these wholesale robberies might go unquestioned. Education had been proscribed, and ignorance had increased exceedingly. True, those of the "better sort" might have received an education at the hands of the Establishment, by forswearing their religious convictions and pandering to the spirit of the times, but the Catholic schools and colleges of the land had been suppressed; expatriation was the consequence of all attempts at the education of youth in the religious principles of their fathers, and death the penalty of return after banishment. Nearly all those who still retained any vestige of their patrimonial estates, had purchased them at the sacrifice of their religious convictions, and those who haply retained both, had done so through the friendly interference of some powerful minions of the English court, who were few and far between. There were still a few other exceptions to this general rule, which deserve a casual notice. The descendants of the early settlers of the Pale, though still adhering to the Catholic faith, had been held by the English Government as a distinct element from the native race. On questions pertaining to the English tenure of the island they had antagonistic interests. Through each successive convulsion they had been treated with greater leniency, and had received much more consideration on the adjustment and final settlement. Their condition was, therefore, less intolerable than that of the *native* chiefs; they had privileges without rights, while the latter had neither rights nor privileges. But then there was a counterbalancing influence; the native gentry had local popularity; while the Palesmen had Government consideration;—both felt their religious grievances in common, and between them there was a mutual forbearance, and an exchange of kindly offices.

Such was the condition of the descendants of the Normans, and of the fast waning septs of the ancient race; but, the people!—they had no consideration, national nor local; no protection but their poverty and their native tongue: no right but that of animal existence, and that only on sufferance! Yet, through all, they had retained the noblest characteristics of manhood; tenacious memory, stubborn will, unselfish love of country, unshaken fidelity to their faith; and who could doubt that they would now—true to their instincts—be the last refuge of a just king in adversity.

When James ascended the throne, on the 16th of February, 1685, the Earl of Ormond was deputy for Ireland. He had taken a leading part in the most exciting scenes of the last fifty years. Gifted with the highest graces of mind and person, he had figured, in early life, as one of the most important personages of the English court, and had won the highest favors of Charles I., and his queen, Henrietta. His powers of diplomacy and statesmanship were kept in continual exercise during the latter years of that reign; but though gifted with talents to excel in each, in each he was signally unsuccessful; and all the evils that befell that king and eventuated in the extinction of his house, may be fairly traced to the one leading passion of Ormond,—an implacable hatred of the Irish Catholics. It would seem as if all the enmity of all the reformers, from Elizabeth to Cromwell, had in him found an exponent, and in directing his deadly malice against them, he was over-successful: he accomplished their ruin, but virtually consigned his patron and sovereign to the scaffold.

His after life was ignoble and inglorious. He became prodigal of honor, tenacious of power, and served as trimmer and timeserver in turn, to Royalists and Parliamentarians alike. But whether in the service of his king or in complicity with his enemies, he held his political principles subservient to his worldly interest, and was consistent only in one passion, his religious intolerance. The character of this statesman had become odious to James long before his accession to the throne; and believing that no wholesome measures of redress could be introduced into Ireland, while one so notorious for his duplicity and hatred of its people remained at the head of affairs, he lost no time in recalling him. He then deputed the government to two Lords-Justices: Boyle, the Protestant primate, and Forbes, Earl of Granard, each of whom had attained a high degree of popularity with the people of all religious denominations. He had reason to believe that these appointments would be received in the spirit which dictated them, and prove a measure of general satisfaction. Upon the Catholic population it had the desired effect; but with the High Church party and the Nonconformists it was quite different. The hatred and jealousy that existed between them was only secondary to their mutual hatred of the Catholics, and these appointments kindled anew the ire of each party against the other. The Puritans were dissatisfied with Boyle, alleging that his Protestant-ism savored of "Popery;" and the Churchmen averred that Granard was a favorer of the sectaries, and an enemy to the "Establishment."

In order to harmonize all interests and carry out his measures of redress, James sent over the Earl of Clarendon as deputy, and with him Colonel Richard Talbot, an Irishman and a Catholic, as Lieutenant-General of the militia. But whether it was that Clarendon was opposed to the policy of the king, or that he felt unable to give effect to his measures of redress in a country so divided in sentiment, he retired shortly after, and Talbot was created Earl of Tyrconnell and appointed deputy in his stead. In Tyrconnell were then united the civil and military power, and of all the king's subjects who at that time accorded with his religious and political views, there could scarcely be chosen one better adapted to give practical effect to the reforms which he had extended to Ireland.

Richard Talbot, Earl, and afterwards Duke of Tyrconnell, is one of the noblest characters in Irish history. He was a loyal subject of the king, whom he served with characteristic loyalty, and though of Norman descent, he was as national in heart as the most devoted of the native race. Of noble presence,[5] courtly manners, untarnished honor, unshrinking courage, indomitable will, and fervid patriotism, he was old enough to remember the Revolution of 1641, had been a sympathetic observer of the sufferings that succeeded, and all the energies of his mind, from his first introduction to royal favor to the end of his career, were directed to effect the civil and religious liberty of his country. Had James been a timeserving king, from Tyrconnell he would have received no adulation; as he was sincere and steadfast in his pledges to the Catholics, Tyrconnell was his devoted servant. As deputy and commander-in-chief, his powers for good were more than ordinary, and he stretched them to the utmost tension that justice permitted. His task was delicate and dangerous; but he discarded the delicacy and braved the danger, as though he alone felt the awakened energy of a whole people. Imprudent they term him; but looking through his chequered life, and reviewing the scenes he had witnessed in youth, we cannot acquiesce in the decision. The circumstances by which he was surrounded brooked no delay, and what is termed imprudence by our recent annalists, would, if viewed in the light of his time, appear the wisest statesman-ship; and it must be generally conceded, that if the king was as bold and intrepid as Tyrconnell, the usurpation of William would have been as abortive as that of Monmouth.

I have turned aside from the course of direct narrative to dedicate a page to the memory of this much-maligned statesman. It is deemed a duty obligatory, be-

---

[5] There is a very fine engraving of him given in the second volume of Story's Impar-tial History.

cause there is a tendency, even among Irish nationalists, to offer him as a sacrifice on the altar of conciliation. Truth may be unpalatable, but it is always wholesome, and without due reverence for it, there will be no incentive to do and suffer for noble ends. The religious martyr finds his reward above, but the patriot's reward is the blessing of posterity, and history should never divert a people's heart from those who labored for their good, albeit their efforts were unsuccessful. Richard Talbot, Duke of Tyrconnell, is a name to be on the tongue of every Irish child, and his deeds a memory in the heart of every Irish patriot. He survived the battle of Aughrim, at which he was present, but a short time; and he should have died there, and gone to rest on that mournfully historic field, where rest some of the best and bravest that Ireland ever nurtured on her bosom. His character would then be complete. He labored for them through life; they were worthy of his companionship in death.

Of the parliament which he assembled in Dublin, after the removal of religious disabilities, the majority in the lower house were of the Catholic faith, and as the measures which were introduced during that session afford ample testimony that they were keenly alive to the higher duties of legislation, a brief outline of them is here submitted in the order of their political importance:

First.—An act removing all political disabilities from the natives of Ireland.

Second.—An act against removing writs of error from the Irish to the English courts.

Third.—An act of indemnity to Catholics who had been declared innocent by the Court of Claims.

Fourth.—An act to encourage strangers to settle and plant in the kingdom of Ireland.

Fifth.—An act investing in his majesty the goods of absentees.

Sixth.—An act for the advancement and improvement of trade, and the encouragement of ship-building.

Seventh.—An act declaring that the Parliament of England cannot bind Ireland.

The last was a virtual repeal of "Poyning's Law," an act passed during the reign of Henry VII. in a parliament convoked at Drogheda by Sir Edward Poyning, in 1494, and which provided "that no parliament could be held in Ireland until the chief governor and council had first certified to the king under the great seal of the land, as well the causes and considerations, as the acts designed to pass, and until the same should be approved by the king and council of England."

All these acts were known to be so just and salutary, that it was hoped they would at once meet the unanimous approval of the English king and his council. But they were all, or nearly all, negatived by the council; and the king himself, though he gave his assent to all the others, rejected that repealing the law of Poyning. It had met with great opposition in the upper house of the Irish Parliament, for though it was a law which placed Ireland under the complete legislative control of England, there was in the "higher estate" then, as to-day, a spirit of subserviency to the English interest, and the king was as jealous of his royal prerogatives as any of his predecessors. But this act was afterwards repealed, when nearly one hundred years more of bitter experience had proved its ruinous effect on the country, and eighteen years of unparalleled prosperity was the consequence. This subject is, however, out of the course of our narrative, and is only referred to as showing that the repeal of Poyning's law did not originate with Grattan or the volunteers of 1782, but had been the principal object of the statesmen of ante-Jacobite times, as the repeal of the Union has been in our own days.

No body of legislators ever understood the wants of a country better than that parliament did the necessities of Ireland. And well might they understand them, for their impoverished country and broken fortunes bore striking and melancholy evidence of the evil effects of foreign legislation aided by a subsidized native oligarchy inimical to every interest but their own. For three generations the people had known no respite from robbery and proscription. Over two hundred thousand of them had passed into exile, or had been consigned to penal servitude in the colonies within the last fifty years. Then, as to-day, the population, though small, was deemed "surplus," while outlawry and banishment suppressed all manifestations of a national spirit. The chiefs were detached from their clans, and the clans, in losing their former protectors, had found but deadly enemies in their new taskmasters. The old feudal system was nearly extinct, even in the districts least visited by English adventure, and this Parliament had realized the stern necessity of reconstructing a nation out of the elements at its disposal. The troubles that surrounded the king gave it a temporary power, which it wielded for the removal of grievances becoming chronic in the land, but "no act of a proscriptive or retaliatory character stains the parliamentary records of that period."[6]

Measures of redress now followed in quick succession. Political and religious disabilities were removed from all denominations, without distinction; and the people were not slow in availing themselves of their long-lost privileges. Catholic churches were once more opened to the service of God, and local schools began to appear throughout the country. Catholic judges, mayors, and sheriffs took their places wherever opportunity offered, and the people felt a gratification corresponding to their altered condition. But, throughout all, they acted with a forbearance and dignity worthy of a people long tried in adversity; they expressed no exultation at their sudden emancipation, and no spirit of retaliation was manifested that might give alarm to their Protestant countrymen.

The Protestant officials of that day, who held the liberty of the country, as it were, in lien, threw many obstructions in the way of these reforms. Among the foremost of these were Topham and Coghill, masters-in-chancery, and the Chancellor himself, and they were removed for open contumacy, and on what then appeared "good and sufficient reasons," — throwing the legal technicalities of an odious system in the way of a people's emancipation from the penal servitude of ages.

Early in 1686, Tyrconnell issued a proclamation in accordance with that of the king, that all classes of his majesty's subjects were allowed to serve in the army,

[6] Dolby's History of Ireland.

accompanied by an order that the arms which had hitherto been given out should be returned to the king's stores, preparatory to a reorganization of the militia. The militia of the country, which at that time must have numbered about 20,000, were exclusively Protestant, and were officered by men of the most proscriptive tendencies, and apart from those regularly enrolled, the whole Protestant population were under arms, subject to the call of local leaders at a moment's notice. Being, almost to a man, opposed to the measures of Catholic redress then being instituted by the king, would appear sufficient motive for this action on the part of the deputy. For the last generation they had been the rigorous executors of the acts of attainder and settlement; the memories they awakened could scarcely be conducive to good order or a feeling of public security: not being national, they were regarded with distrust, and were held as unsafe guardians of the liberty which they openly denounced. Many of their leaders were known to be implicated in Monmouth's rebellion, and as a precautionary measure, it became necessary to infuse a spirit of loyalty among them by the introduction of a Catholic element. To accomplish this seems to have been the great trouble of the deputy. Men there were, to any number, ready at his call, but arms were wanting, and the revenue of the country was scarce sufficient to defray the expenses of the civil government. There was, therefore, no other resource but to call in the arms for a redistribution, and to organize a body of native troops from whom exclusion would be excluded. This measure created great alarm, among a party who had been so long dominant; and, if in its accomplishment, any denomination were excluded who felt a liberal sentiment towards the great body of the people, there would have been cause for just apprehension, but such does not appear on the record of the period. All test oaths were abolished according to the proclamation of the king, and all denominations, without distinction, were invited to join the new organization. The Catholic people responded with promptitude and alacrity, and an army of about 8,000 men, was soon enrolled from the old royalist corps scattered through the country; a few regiments more sprang up from the remnants of the native clans, and with these the deputy felt able to execute the laws, and garrison a few of the most important military stations in the kingdom.

On the other hand, the Protestant militia, feeling jealous that men so long outside the pale of all law, should at once be endowed with the high privilege of freemen, shunned the organizations, and many of their prominent officers, retiring to Holland, took service under the Prince of Orange, then conspiring for the overthrow of their rightful sovereign.

In this age and clime, such intolerance may seem greatly exaggerated, if not altogether incredible. But stepping down through the successive changes of ninety years, we find that the Volunteers of 1782, with the light of the American Revolution before them, were quite as exclusive. Up to the day when, on Essex-Bridge, the regiment of Lord Altamont held its way through the ranks of his Britannic majesty,[7] and a revolution appeared imminent, the proposition to allow Catholics to bear arms in the native militia, even as private soldiers, had been scouted with contempt. The provisions of Catholic Emancipation are not yet accepted there, for

---

[7] See Barrington's Rise and Fall of the Irish Nation.

we have seen the "Test Act" revived as late as 1864, in Dublin, to the exclusion of a Catholic alderman. Before such evidences, doubt vanishes, and we are able to appreciate the position of Tyrconnell, and the necessity for intrepid action in the premises. No man had a greater share of praise and censure from contemporary historians than he, and he is still a subject of each as the minds of men incline to either side in the issues that then distracted the country. His precipitancy in removing the restraints on religion, and in giving too active an impulse to the popular will, has come in for its share of condemnation. He is also criticized for a too pompous display of his dual power, as Viceroy and Commander-in-Chief: but we should remember that they who censure his hasty measures of redress, are those who persistently oppose all redress; that his manner of life as Viceroy was simple and unostentatious as compared with that of his successors in office, and that his dual power was conferred on him, when the king's brother-in-law, Clarendon, had deserted him, and there was no other man capable and at the same time willing to assume that critical position.

Tyrconnell, however, was not a man to be diverted from his purpose by either threat or criticism, and so he pursued his course unshrinking. His country demanded redress and he hearkened to her call. The emancipation of his co-religionists was necessary, and he endeavored to effect it: but in doing so he infringed no civil or religious right of others: none were denied equality before the law, and none were removed from office except for open contumacy or covert treason. No doubt he had to brave obloquy and opposition; but who could serve that country and that king at that particular crisis, and escape the shafts of malignity?

In the summer of 1688, when the conspiracy of the Prince of Orange became known to Tyrconnell, in the manner already indicated, he lost no time in communicating his intelligence to the king. It was received with incredulity, for the evil counsel of Earl Sunderland still held sway over every other representation. How could he believe that his affectionate son-in-law, who had made him a prompt tender of military assistance to suppress the rebellion of Monmouth, could have been prompted by any but the most honorable and filial motives? Had he not offered to lead his forces in person, and to protect the capital and the inmates of the royal palace?

But the urgency of the occasion emboldened Tyrconnell, and he at last succeeded in arousing the king's suspicions. He urged the necessity of an immediate alliance with France, and though in this he was not able to move the fixed impression left by the wily secretary, he prevailed so far on the king as to accept the greater part of the forces he had raised for the protection of Ireland; and so they were immediately sent over and placed at the royal service.

Tyrconnell then formed the bold design, without the knowledge of the king, of placing Ireland under the protection of France. The proposition was well received by Louis, but events culminated with such rapidity during the autumn of 1688, that no time was left for diplomacy, for it required the undivided attention of Tyrconnell to repress the spirit of disaffection throughout Ulster as the winter approached. The leaders of the Protestant party in Ireland were alive to all that was taking place, and premonitory symptoms of open revolt were apparent to all. In Ulster, Lord Blaney, Rawdon, Skeffington, Keames, Kelso, and Walker, who had kept a close correspondence with the Prince of Orange since the death of Monmouth, sounded the alarm, and called their followers to arms. Every action or word of the deputy was seized on to excite the passions and fears of their people, and every counter-effort on his part to allay the growing excitement was futile. The time was propitious, and they seized on every event to magnify their danger. The alarm became wide-spread, and the old hatred that so often left the country a prey to foreign adventure was revived in all its bitterness. Fanaticism overruled common sense, and the people were divided.

A report was industriously circulated that a massacre of the entire Protestant population of the country was arranged for the 9th of December, with a minuteness of detail that convinced the most incredulous. This was about the date that was to usher in the Prince of Orange. The conspirators knew it, but the people were ignorant. The utmost consternation prevailed; the Protestant people in considerable numbers abandoned their homes, flocked to the sea-shore, and stowing themselves away in the hold of every available craft that presented, passed over to England, while the boldest of them fled to the North to join the standard of William's adherents. Those who reached England awakened the liveliest sympathy for the condition of their Irish brethren, and the most bitter indignation against "the murdering Irish." The arrival of William at Whitehall was the signal for a general onslaught on the English Catholics, and the Irish residents there had to take refuge in immediate flight. The regiments imprudently sent there at the suggestion of Tyrconnell, being placed in small detachments throughout the country, were forced into the usurper's service, or, trying to make their way home, were set upon in detail, and slaughtered mercilessly in the streets and by-ways wherever they passed. Some few fought or forced their way to the seaboard, and through the kindly offices of the English Jacobites, made their way back in the most wretched condition.[8]

The news of William's arrival soon spread throughout Ireland and Scotland. In the former country this event had been anticipated: the people had already arrayed themselves into two parties known through succeeding times as Williamites and Jacobites. In the latter a convention was called, and after much angry opposition, the covenanters declared that James's flight was a virtual abdication, and that he had consequently "forefaulted" his right to the throne and the allegiance of his subjects of Scotland, which they tendered to William. A respectable portion, however, headed by the Archbishop of Glasgow, the Duke of Gordon, the Earl of Balcarras, and Graham of Claverhouse (Viscount Dundee) supported the Jacobite cause and took up arms in defence of their lawful king.

On the 7th of December the gates of Derry were closed against the Earl of Antrim's regiment of Highlanders sent thither by Tyrconnell on the invitation of its governor, and the call to arms was sounded through all the province of Ulster. Blaney, Walker, Keames, Kelso, Skeffington, and Rawdon called a convention, and assuming their right to dispose of the country, tendered its allegiance to William. They then entered into a league "for the maintenance of the Protestant religion

---

[8] Popular History of Ireland, vol. ii, p. 572.

and the dependency of Ireland upon England," and placed themselves at the head of the military organizations formed throughout the province: and Enniskillen, Culmore, Sligo, Coleraine—nearly all the important posts from Down to Donegal, and from Cavan to Antrim—were seized on and garrisoned in the name of the Prince of Orange.

It is scarcely necessary to say, that the 9th of December came and passed without any manifestation of that murderous design attributed to the Catholics. The conspiracy was on the other side, and manifested itself in the following manner. Major Poor, who had served in a dragoon regiment under Cromwell, had got the command of two companies of cavalry, from "The League." With this force he commenced a series of raids on the inhabitants of Louth, and levied a tax of £500 on the tenantry of Lord Bellew. Hearing of this, Bellew sent his son, a youth of eighteen, with a company of dragoons, to assist the farmers in resisting the tax. These troops met and fought for some time with the most determined bravery, until Bellew, closing with the Major, killed him with a blow of his pistol on the head, when the troops of the Major took flight, leaving their dead and wounded behind them. This was the first act of open hostility: it aroused the Catholic people to the necessity of defensive measures, and quickened that martial spirit, never extinguished; their hearts responded to the war-note of the times; but what could the spirit do, but chafe at delay? Their country was impoverished, and they had neither arms nor organization.

CHAPTER IV.

FROM THE COMMENCEMENT OF HOSTILITIES TO THE LANDING OF KING JAMES IN IRELAND.

Tyrconnell, seeing that a civil war could no longer be averted in Ireland, bitterly regretted the loss of those troops that he had sent to England. A few well-equipped regiments: those of Mountcashel, Clancarty, Lord Antrim, Lord Bellew, and his own, about three thousand,—were all that remained in the country. Men by thousands daily presented themselves for enrollment, but they were destitute of every thing that constitutes the soldier, "excepting courage and good will," and he had neither money nor arms to equip them. The Williamite organization grew more powerful and extended, day by day. Along with the province of Ulster, it soon embraced the counties of Longford, Meath, and Dublin; its leaders, in the mean time, feigning to treat with Tyrconnell, while privately soliciting arms and succors from the Prince of Orange. Tyrconnell at last determined to make a final appeal to the country, and for this purpose issued colonels' commissions to the heads of the old Catholic houses and the loyal Palesmen of Leinster. The effect was electric. With a common impulse they rushed to his standard, and threw the wrecks of their former fortunes in the balance. In a short time, the regiments of McMahon, O'Reilley, MacDonnell, Maguinness, Maguire, O'Donnell, Nugent, Loutrell, Fitzgerald, Felix O'Neil, Gordon O'Neil, Cormac O'Neil, Bryan O'Neil, Sir Neale O'Neil, Clare, Galway, O'Moore, O'Dempsey, and others were in the field, to the number of 20,000, nearly all recruited from their respective households.

But the people having been long deprived of the right to bear arms, were necessarily unprovided with them, and the state to which the country had been reduced by the misgovernment and oppression of the last forty years, rendered them unable to provide any other than the rudest weapons, hastily improvised. They had, therefore, to be armed and provisioned at the individual expense of their leaders, and it was found impossible to equip and sustain the multitudes that presented themselves for service. The murmurs of the people were loud and deep, but there was no remedy. The organizations of the Council, all well armed, and supplied with the necessaries of war, were wide-spread throughout the country, and were levying, in the name of the Prince of Orange, on the Catholic people of Ulster, and even the eastern and southern provinces had to yield to their exactions. Notwithstanding all this, thousands had to be dismissed to their unprotected homes, with promises that a little time would remove those difficulties. It was represented, as it was indeed believed by all, that an immense armament was fitting out in France, to accompany the king, who was daily expected to arrive; that his presence would rectify every thing, and afford them the means and opportunity of giving active proof of their patriotism; and with these promises, though chafing at delay, they retired to watch the current of events, and bide the arrival of their king. The new regiments were reduced to a limited standard of about 250 each, so that 12,000 men, including those already enrolled, were rendered fit for service, and with this force Tyrconnell opened the campaign of 1689.

Carrickfergus and Charlemont in the north, and all the forts on the Shannon, from Lough Allen to the estuary, were still in the possession of the Irish, and each had to be reinforced and put in a better state of defence: the town of Kilkenny, and the cities of Cork and Waterford, had each to receive its quota of troops; Dundalk, an important seaport, had to be secured against the excursions of the insurgents of Monaghan and Armagh; and the metropolis could not dispense with the few veteran regiments that had been stationed there since the inauguration of the deputy. After the distribution of his forces among these posts, Tyrconnell found at his disposal a small army of 6,000 men available for the field, and, dividing it into three corps, he gave the command of one to Lieutenant-General Justin Mc-Carthy, to operate in Munster, where Inchiquin had raised the standard of revolt; one to Lieutenant-General Richard Hamilton, for the reduction of the rebel garrisons from Dundalk to Derry; and another, a co-operative force of about 1,000 men, was placed under Lord Galmoy, to give countenance to the outlying posts around Cavan and Enniskillen.—The limits prescribed these pages preclude a detailed account of these expeditions, although each presents some of the most striking and agreeable events of that period. McCarthy, at the head of 2,000 regulars and a few hundred followers, reduced, in a few days, the rebels of Castle-Martyr and Bandon, and turning his attention to Inchiquin, who was plundering and laying waste the country, from the Shannon to the Blackwater, he drove him back on his stronghold in Clare, and marched uncontrolled from the Fergus to the Barrow. The Williamites of Munster, surprised by these events and the rapidity of their execution, laid down their arms, returned to their homes, and all apprehension of future trouble in that quarter was at an end:—for this important service McCarthy henceforth received the title of "Pacificator of Munster."

When the rumor of William's conspiracy first became known to the Earl of Tyrconnell in the preceding year, he sent General Hamilton, as already indicated, with about four thousand men, for the service of James in England. After the invasion of William this force was either slain, dispersed, or forced into his service, and their general, contrary to the usages of war, and to the terms accorded to the other adherents of the king, was detained a prisoner. Being an Irish gentleman by birth, of great family influence, and one of the best cavalry officers of his time, William saw in him one who, if weaned from his allegiance to the king, would be a powerful agent of success to his designs on Ireland, and accordingly, 'tis said, made overtures to that effect. History, however, is not clear as to the nature of these proposals, nor of the manner in which they were met by Hamilton. This much at least is known, that he was released from captivity, was sent with proposals of an accommodation to Tyrconnell, but on arriving in Ireland he urged the most determined opposition to William, and was appointed to lead the expedition against the rebellion in Ulster.

Leaving Drogheda on the 8th of March, with a force of about two thousand men, he marched through Dundalk and Newry, and on the 13th took up a position between Loughbrickland and the river Bann, and sent out Colonel Butler to take a reconnoissance of the enemy, said to be in force between him and the Laggan. The service was one of extreme peril, and required the utmost courage and address:— he was in the midst of a mountainous country, surrounded by a wary foe, and the slightest misconduct on his part, was sure to result in the capture or destruction of the main body.

The task was, however, performed to the satisfaction of the general: the enemy were found strongly intrenched at Dromore-Iveagh, on the north side of the Laggan, to the number of 8,000 men, under the command of Hugh Montgomery, Lord Mount Alexander. It was soon decided to attack them; so breaking camp with the dawn, on the morning of the 14th, Hamilton crossed the Bann and advanced boldly on their position. The cavalry regiment of Montgomery advanced to meet him, but after the first charge of Hamilton's dragoons they fell back in confusion on the main body, and his infantry having also crossed the river, a general attack was ordered. The enemy, however, did not wait the assault, for Montgomery himself running away, his men followed the example, and a complete rout succeeded. The Irish remained masters of the encampment. Montgomery continued his flight to Hillsborough, into which he threw a few companies, and ordering the bulk of his forces to Coleraine, embarked at Donaghadee, and sailed for England. This was the first time the forces of "The Council" met the Irish in the field. They had been organizing and levying on the country for months; they were well armed; had an intrenched position of their own selection, behind a deep and rapid river, and the result was the loss of their camp equipage, four hundred slain, and that disgraceful flight known in the history of the period as "The Break of Dromore."

After stopping here for a day to rest his men and secure the advantages of his victory, Hamilton pushed on to Hillsborough, the headquarters of the Council, while Sir Arthur Rawdon advanced rapidly from Lisburn to its relief, at the head of 4,000 men. Rawdon, however, only arrived in the vicinity to find the place in the possession of Hamilton, and to see its paroled garrison making their way home across the country. On learning that Rawdon was in the neighborhood, the Irish troops advanced to meet him, but he, ordering his men to make the best of their way towards Coleraine, abandoned them to their fate, and, like Mount Alexander, embarked for England.

The capture of Hillsborough was of great service to the Irish cause. It had been the headquarters of the "Council" since its formation, and was the repository of its papers, plans, and secret correspondence with William; but, above all, it contained immense stores of provisions, wrung from the inhabitants of the surrounding country since the preceding winter. The evacuation of Dungannon, on the west side of Lough Neagh, a fine central position of the Williamites, and one of their chief depots for provisions and military stores, followed closely on that of Hillsborough; and Hamilton, pursuing the retreating insurgents through Belfast,

Antrim, and Ballymena, drove them in on Coleraine, and halted to recruit his little army in the town of Ballymoney, within a few miles of their only remaining stronghold in Antrim. While here, he was assailed by a strong force sent out to cover the movements of a foraging party, but he attacked them so vigorously that he drove them within the gates of the town, inflicting a severe loss, and capturing all the booty collected in their excursion.

Thus, in less than a fortnight after his departure from Drogheda, all the eastern counties of Ulster—Armagh, Down, Antrim, and the greater part of Tyrone—were reduced to obedience; but, as he was now about to approach the walled town of Derry, he halted for a few days in his career, to await artillery and reinforcements from the capital.

In whatever light this campaign is considered—whether from a Williamite or a Jacobite point of view—it confers immortal honor on Hamilton and his little band, for it can scarcely be dignified by the name of an army. In a season of unusual severity, in the face of a vigilant foe, four times his number, and established in the strongest positions that could be selected, he, by vigilance and audacity, baffled all attempts at surprise, and with an insignificant loss, and without a single repulse, cleared the greater part of the province from the grasp of an enemy that a few days before had uttered defiance before the gates of Dundalk, and bore away their booty undisturbed within sight of the capital.

The co-operative force, under Galmoy, was scarce less successful. The scene of his operations embraced Monaghan, Cavan, and Fermanagh, where the leading rebels, Lord Blaney and Gustavus Hamilton, carried fire and sword wherever they went. The first to arouse the infatuated people, by the cry of religion, they were the persistent violators of all religious precepts. The total extirpation of the Catholics could alone appease them, and to this end they kept the minds of their followers inflamed by every species of misrepresentation and calumny. The people were driven from their homes, and wholesale murder and rapine, with crimes too revolting for detail, marked their course among the doomed fugitives. In the few months that had elapsed since the advent of the Prince of Orange in England, this section of country had become almost desolate. Few were to be seen but the destroyers let loose over it, or the stealthy Rapparees, that tracked their steps, to wreak a deadly revenge for the crimes that rendered them at once both homeless and merciless. But the contest was unequal; the unarmed people were forced to give way before the trained-bands of Hamilton and Blaney, when Galmoy entered on the scene, to add fresh fuel to the flame. He soon roused the flagging spirit of the Jacobites. Blaney and Hamilton, now joined by Wolseley, put forth all their strength to oppose him, but they were met by measures as arbitrary and effective as their own. "No quarter" became the cry on both sides; but the military skill of Galmoy proclaimed him the master-spirit, and after a few reverses, and a rigorous retaliation, they fell back wherever he advanced; all opposition in the open country soon ceased, and they were forced to take refuge within the walls of Enniskillen.

The poor countenance shown by the rebels in the field, now emboldened Galmoy to attempt the reduction of Enniskillen, which was their chief rendezvous in the south-western portion of the province; and for that purpose he approached the Castle of Crom, one of its principal defences, and having driven in its outposts, invested it about the middle of March. This fortress, which stands on a peninsula in the waters of the Lower Erne, being impregnable to his light-armed infantry, he now had recourse to stratagem. He got some tin cannon constructed, and giving out that artillery had reached him from Dublin, placed them in battery within musket range of the castle. On the 21st he summoned it to surrender, but the garrison, having been apprised of the *ruse* intended for them, provided themselves with the long guns used in duck-shooting on the lake, and answered his summons with a well-directed fire that killed about forty of his men, and compelled him to retire to a safer distance, leaving his mock cannon behind him. They were soon conveyed into the fort, and were exhibited as trophies at many a succeeding celebration of "the glorious and pious, etc.," furnishing the Enniskilleners with a theme of boastful merriment.[9]

The name "Enniskilleners," has now become nearly obsolete, and is only applied to a regiment of dragoons in the English army, kept up in perpetuation of the part they took in the ruin of their country; but at the time of the Revolution it was applied without distinction to the partisans of William, who, when driven before the Jacobites, took refuge within the town of Enniskillen, and held out until the relief of Derry, to which it was next in importance. It is a place of great natural strength, and has many historic memories dating farther back than the unhappy events that have given it such unenviable notoriety. It was originally the stronghold of the Maguires, who held it for centuries against each successive invasion, but had passed into the hands of Sir William Cole, after the civil war of 1641. It stands on a river connecting the upper and lower waters of Lough-Erne, which, lying from the north-west to the south-east of the County Fermanagh, and connecting with Lough-Oughter on the south, extends over a distance of more than forty miles. These lakes and their tributaries, studded with islands innumerable, render the country for several miles a labyrinth almost impassable to all but the natives. There is not, perhaps, in the world, for the same extent of country, a place so well adapted to insurgent warfare. In such a country the people of La Vendée would have exhausted all the resources of the French Directory; and the wonder is, not why Galmoy could not take it, but how he even approached it, in the face of such overwhelming odds.

Meanwhile the exiled king was keenly alive to all that was passing in his late dominions. Assured of the strenuous support of Louis, on the first demonstration of popular will in his favor in England, his agents there were active in their endeavors to effect a change of public sentiment; nor did their efforts seem barren of good results. The way of William, since his accession, was not strewn with flowers. Signs of reaction manifested themselves daily, and it required all the efforts of his Dutch and German mercenaries, to check the spirit of disaffection. The people had been taken by surprise. Their subjugation to the arms of Holland had been effected by a conspiracy between a few of the nobles and William, in which they

[9] It is necessary to remark that Taylor, who relates this incident, confounds the name of Galmoy with Galway. They were two distinct characters: the latter, whose family patronymic was Burke, was killed at Aughrim; the former accompanied the "Brigade" to France. His family name was Butler.

had no part, and many of the moderate nobles had begun to regret an action by which they intended only a change of the royal policy, but which had terminated in a change of sovereigns. Nor was the result, in any light, very flattering to their vanity; nor a comparison between the sovereigns favorable to the new incumbent. It was, however, from the dignitaries of the Established Church that William experienced the greatest opposition. The Archbishop of Canterbury and six others, though active in their opposition to the reforms introduced by James, would never acknowledge any other king, and continued to pray publicly for his welfare and protection. Mary sent to the Archbishop to ask his blessing, but received for answer: "When she has obtained her father's blessing, I shall be very ready to give her mine." The Prince of Orange was outraged by such perverseness of spirit, and as an example of the religious liberty that he had established in England, deprived them of their bishoprics. Throughout the country a reaction had really set in. The Dutch guards and the English soldiers came frequently into collision, and the insolence of the former, being generally overlooked by William, he became an object of popular disfavor. To silence this disaffection he determined to send the malcontent regiments to Holland, and supply their place with Dutch soldiers. A Scotch regiment mutinied, and marched northward "with drums beating and colors flying," but were overwhelmed by three regiments of Dutch dragoons, under Ginkle, and sent off to the continent. This revolt caused the passage of the famous "Mutiny Bill," which deprives the British soldier of the right of citizenship, shuts him off from the benefit of civil law, and makes him an alien in his own country.

The Jacobite cause in Scotland was still hopeful, for there, Viscount Dundee kept the field, and refused all terms of compromise, while in Ireland three provinces remained steadfast in their allegiance, and the adherents of William in the other province, though still obstinate in the course they had adopted, were unable to keep the field. The Earl of Tyrconnell, faithful to his trust, animated the people by word and example, and "retained," says the Duke of Berwick, "all the kingdom in obedience;" so James, at last, rousing himself from his apathy, determined to assume the management of affairs in his Kingdom of Ireland. The state of the country demanded his presence; the people clamored for it; and the French king hastened it by his counsel, and gave promise of adequate military support. Accordingly, James set sail from France, under an escort of thirty-three war-ships, and arrived at Kinsale on the 12th of March, 1689. He was accompanied by his son, the Duke of Berwick, M. de Rosen, M. de Momont, M. de Pusignan, de Lery, Boïsselau, Lestrade, Guidon, and about one hundred French officers of different grades, and twelve hundred of his guards, who had joined him in his exile.

The people, who expected to see this imposing array of ships pour out its thousands of armed men on their shores, were greatly disappointed; but the arrival of the king banished every other consideration. His adversity awakened all the sympathies of their nature, and he had an abiding-place in every heart. From Kinsale he proceeded to Cork, which he entered amid the greatest rejoicings. After the usual formalities, of which religious ceremonies formed the most solemn and imposing part, he received from the deputy an account of his stewardship. It exceeded even what he had been led to expect, and as a mark of his approval,

Tyrconnell was raised to the rank of Duke, and McCarthy, *"The Pacificater of Munster,"* was created Lord Mountcashel, and honored with a seat in his cabinet. After a short delay here, the king proceeded to the metropolis. His route through the country was one continued ovation. Crowds of people lined the wayside, invoking blessings on his cause, while religious ceremonies, pledges, and addresses of loyalty, arrested his way at every step of his route. The city of Dublin, proverbial in all times for taste and elegance, and which had never witnessed the advent of a king since the days of Henry II., exhausted every effort that art or fancy could suggest, to grace the royal pageantry. The corporation, headed by the mayor, in all the pomp of office, went forth to meet him, and tender him the keys of the city. Farther on, and near the portals of the castle, the Primate, crowned with the triple tiara, and holding in his hand the emblem of redemption, awaited to receive his obeisance, and bestow the benediction. As he approached the august dignitary, a general halt of the procession took place, and even the multitude, that surged like a closing sea behind, hushed their acclamations, and bent in lowly reverence, until the king, rising from his genuflection before the cross, and, bareheaded, offered them his parting acknowledgments. Then, as the national flag, standing out above the castle-gate, revealed to him the terse and significant motto:

"Now or Never; Now and Forever,"

one wild and prolonged cheer, deep and fervid, burst from the hearts of the multitude. The die was cast, and their adherence to the discrowned monarch was sealed and irrevocable.

Immediately after his arrival in Dublin,[10] James proceeded to the construction of his cabinet, the leading members of which were Tyrconnell, Mountcashel, General Nugent, and some of the French officers that formed his escort. He at once issued a proclamation, offering pardon and protection to all who would retire peaceably to their homes, and again announced his unalterable determination to maintain the civil and religious liberty of all religious denominations. The army, however, demanded his earliest attention, for, whatever was its enthusiasm, its real condition was far from encouraging. The gentlemen who bore the expense of the first levy were unable to continue the drain on their slender means, and the soldiers were suffering much privation. It was necessary also to organize a force sufficient to meet events that might now be daily expected, and accordingly the king at once appealed to the country. More than one hundred thousand men, almost simultaneously, offered their services; "but," says Hume, "not two in every hundred were provided with muskets fit for service; the rest were armed with clubs and sticks tipped with iron," and he found himself compelled to decline the service of all but about twenty thousand.[11]

These, together with those already in the service, constituted an army short of thirty thousand men, the whole artillery in the country was twelve field-pieces and four mortars; and with this force, in the weakest period it had known since the first invasion, Ireland resolved to measure strength with England, its army

---

[10] March 24th, 1689.

[11] The Student's Hume, page 550. More than one hundred thousand were on foot, and he found himself compelled to disband the greater part of them.

of mercenaries, and the most powerful of her own provinces now arrayed on the side of the usurper. The king had unbounded confidence in the timely assistance of France; but the people had realized the purport of this war; for them it was to be a struggle for national life or total extinction, and though many retired to their homes wherever it was practicable, thousands who had already been rendered homeless, seized on every rude weapon that presented, and, determined to wring a subsistence from the enemy, took up the bold and reckless life of the Rappar-ee. Tyrconnell was now appointed commander-in-chief of the army; M. de Rosen was raised to the rank of lieutenant-general, and appointed second in command; M. de Momont was raised to the same rank; de Pusignan and de Lery to that of major-general; Boïsselau was appointed adjutant-general, Guidon master-general of cavalry, and a reinforcement of about three thousand troops, then the best in the country, was sent to Lieutenant-General, the Viscount of Dundee, who was making head against Mackey, the commander of the Williamite forces in Scotland.

The condition of affairs now brooked of no delay; the English Parliament was convened for an early day; William had expressed his intention of sending an expedition into Ireland, and only waited its assent: the suppression of the Ulster rebellion before such an event should take place, was a matter of vital importance to the Jacobite cause, and an active campaign was at once determined on. Accordingly, Major-General, the Duke of Berwick, was dispatched to the assistance of Hamilton, now lying before the fortified town of Coleraine, while de Pusignan, with a select body of horse and foot, and two pieces of artillery, was to march through Charlemont and Dungannon, and passing to the west of Lough Neagh, unite with Berwick and Hamilton, and proceed against Derry, the chief stronghold of the rebellion.[12]

---

[12] The Duke of Berwick was then in his nineteenth year, having been born on the 21st of August, 1670. He had already been raised to the rank of major-general by the Emperor of Austria, for honorable service under the great Duke of Lorrain; he was a son of James II., and nephew of John Churchill, Duke of Marlborough.

CHAPTER V.

THE BATTLE OF CLADIFORD—THE INVESTMENT OF DERRY—PROCEEDINGS OF PARLIAMENT.

Lying impatiently before Coleraine since the affair of Dromore, Hamilton, on being joined by the Duke of Berwick, determined to renew hostilities, and immediately proceeded against that important position. Its garrison consisted of 3,000 effective men, who were expected to make a determined resistance; but on the approach of the royal troops they destroyed the bridge on their front, and, abandoning the fort, retreated in the direction of Derry. Hamilton soon occupied the place, and, leaving a regiment there under Colonel O'Morra, and being joined by de Pusignan, who had captured Moneymore, Magherafelt, Dawson's Bridge, and, in short, all the places on the left of the Bann, marched to Strabane, which he reached on the 15th of April, without meeting any opposition. Here he halted to rest his troops, and having ascertained that the enemy to the number of 12,000 men, from Enniskillen and Derry, under the command of General Lundy, were drawn up at Cladiford, behind the river Finn, determined to offer battle. On receipt of this intelligence, Hamilton and Berwick, leaving their main body at Strabane, took 600 horse and 350 foot, and advanced to reconnoitre; but on their appearance the town was evacuated, and the enemy, destroying the bridge, drew up in a fortified camp on the western side of the river.

Neither their force nor the strength of their position had been exaggerated: the river, which was of considerable volume, was found to be unfordable, while their right and left, beyond it, were protected by morasses impassable to cavalry; a strong breastwork had been thrown up in front of the bridge, behind which, in advance of their main body, 2,000 men were arrayed in order of battle. Hamilton, however, determined to attack them, without apprising De Pusignan, and setting a party to work on the bridge under cover of his infantry, he marched the cavalry along the river, determined to cross at the opportune moment. The infantry approached the bridge and opened a fire which dislodged the enemy from the trenches, and the planks being laid, they dashed over, and making a lodgment in the abandoned works, drove them back in confusion to the camp. Taking advantage of this diversion, the horse swam the river on their right, and forming on the opposite side, charged the entire body of the rebels, now drawn up on the high grounds to receive them. But the bold front assumed by Hamilton disconcerted them, and observing, at the same time, a squadron of dragoons, which had just arrived under De Rosen, crossing the river to their left, their whole force became panic-stricken, and fled in confusion. Their cavalry was followed up and driven furiously through Raphoe, a distance of five miles; "As for their infantry," says Berwick, "we killed about four hundred of them on the spot, but the rest, being favored by the morasses, found means to escape." The loss of the royal troops in this affair was one officer and two men, drowned in crossing the river.

Hamilton found abundance of provisions and some war materials at Raphoe, where, waiting to rest his troops, he was joined by Lord Galmoy with eight hundred men, and determined to advance on Derry, when his progress was arrested by the arrival of a deputation that came to treat for its surrender. The party were well received, and a conference being arranged to take place within two days, on condition that he should approach no nearer than St. Johnstown, they departed highly satisfied with their reception. Hamilton proceeded to the appointed place, and being impressed with the importance of Derry to the Jacobite cause, offered them the most liberal terms:—"Life, liberty, property, and protection, on condition that the town would be surrendered at twelve o'clock next day. The terms were accepted, and awaited but ratification on both sides."

In the mean time, the king had left Dublin on the 8th of April, to take a view of the country. Hearing of the victory at Cladiford, he directed his course to that place, and arrived at the camp on the 18th, on the very hour that Hamilton was in conference with the delegates from Derry. De Rosen, perhaps, jealous of Hamilton's success, or wishing to gain credit with the king, represented to him that his presence before Derry would cause its gates to be at once thrown open, and prevent unnecessary delay, so he prevailed on him to make the experiment. Avoiding the place of conference, he took a circuitous route, and appearing before the town, summoned it to surrender. The "defenders," taking this sudden appearance of the king at such a time as an act of treachery on the part of Hamilton, answered the demand by a cannon-shot, which killed an officer by his side, and caused him to retire in shame and confusion. The consequence is easily foreseen. The treaty about to be ratified was broken off; the alarm was sounded throughout the rebel ranks; the "defenders" determined on more stern resistance; a siege was ordered by the king, and under escort of De Rosen, he returned to Dublin to meet his Parliament, which had been convoked for the 7th of May.

The consequences of this ill-advised interference on the part of the king are generally attributed to the Count de Rosen, whose appointment to the command of the army was one of the many unwise proceedings attributed to this very weak or very imprudent monarch. Speaking of the affair just narrated, the Duke of Berwick says: "M. de Rosen was the more to blame in persuading the king to the step I have just mentioned with regard to Derry, as he knew and had approved the agreement of M. Hamilton." But, with due respect for established authority, there is ground for a deduction different to that drawn by the Duke and other learned contemporaries. From the beginning of this revolution the "defenders" had practised the art of duplicity to a very considerable extent. In the winter of 1688, they sent delegations to Dublin and London at the same time with very different objects:—that to Dublin was meant to delay any action on the part of the deputy, while the other went to expedite an invasion by the Prince of Orange. Notwithstanding the short time that had elapsed from their defeat at Cladiford until the conference with Hamilton, they had received a large supply of arms and ammunition from England, and had gathered their scattered forces into the town; and there is reason to surmise, that while the king was outraged before their walls, Hamilton was outwitted by their delegation.

But however this may have been, we think that if Hamilton, with his characteristic promptitude, had marched boldly on Derry from Cladiford, he could have dictated his terms within its walls. Most of the "regimented men" spoken of by M. Walker in his history of the siege that succeeded, were still outlying in the "far north;" the fugitives from the late defeat would have been cut off from any hope of entering the place; and the supplies received during the interval would have been intercepted. There was not then within the town, a force capable of offering any protracted resistance, and a surrender would be the probable, nay, the almost certain consequence. Fewer lives, also, would have been sacrificed on each side, and the whole country would have been reduced to the arms of the king before the arrival of the Duke of Schomberg. But, then, the army was under the command of De Rosen, and whether this delay was occasioned by that general or not, it is now hard to determine.

The success of the royal arms in Monaghan, Leitrim, and Fermanagh, kept pace with the progress of Hamilton and Berwick. The insurgents were everywhere driven from the open country, and compelled to take refuge in Crom and Enniskillen. The garrison of Sligo, consisting of 3,000 foot and 1,000 horse, under Lord Kingston, withdrew to Ballyshannon, which commands the entrance to Lough-Erne; and towards the beginning of May, there remained no place of any significance in their possession but the fortified towns of Enniskillen and Derry. But the defenders of the latter place had made good use of the temporary cessation of hostilities after the battle of Cladiford. Their outlying posts were immediately abandoned, and troops came in daily from all quarters. Culmore, a strong post which guarded the entrance of the Foyle, and which they had held through the winter, was evacuated on the approach of the Jacobite army, and its garrison of 1,500 men, under Captain Murray, after a hazardous march through the mountainous country to the west of the river, succeeded in getting safely within its walls. The accession of these forces gave a new impulse to the flagging spirit of the defenders. Governor Lundy, being suspected of Jacobite tendencies, was at once deposed, and a military council was constituted, of which Murray, the Reverend George Walker, and Colonel Baker, were the ruling spirits.

The town of Derry stands on the western bank of the river Foyle, about five miles above its expansion into a lough of the same name. It is situated on an oval-shaped hill; the houses, rising tier over tier, look very picturesque to one approaching it from an eastern direction; but to the west it is overlooked by an irregular line of hills, stretching far back into the County of Donegal. Since the time of the Revolution, it has been greatly extended in all directions, but was then confined to the hill already mentioned, and was encompassed by a wall of immense strength, and about a mile in circuit. It was founded by King James I., in 1607, as a refuge to the settlers, whom he sent from England and Scotland, to the exclusion of the native race; and, by a sort of retributive justice, it helped to complete the ruin of his house, in the person of his grandson, but eighty years later. After the departure of the king for Dublin, the Irish generals proceeded to invest this important position, and, by the 20th of April, had made the following disposition of their forces: The fort of Culmore, which stands about five miles below the town, was occupied by a small garrison after its evacuation by Captain Murray, and the river was obstructed by a boom a little higher up. Hamilton, with about one thousand horse and foot, established his camp some two miles from the walls of the garrison; General Ramsay, with four battalions, took up a position at Hollywell Hill, nearly the same distance to the west; Brigadier Wauchop, with two battalions, a squadron of horse and two field-pieces—their only artillery—made a lodgment on the eastern bank of the river, at a place known as the "Waterside;" while a reserve of three battalions of infantry and nine squadron of cavalry was stationed at Johnstown, about six miles farther up the river, in the direction of Strabane.

The "defenders," from their walls, saw the gradual approach of the Jacobite army, and felt the necessity of prompt and determined action. Every consideration that impels men to deeds of daring was heightened by the fiery appeals of their leaders. The fall of so many important posts, in such quick succession, had deprived them of the vast stores which they had collected through the preceding winter; the population of the town had increased to twenty thousand within the last month, and famine, at no distant day, would do the work of war, should William fail to succor them in the interval. On the other hand, they still outnumbered the beleaguering army three to one; were better supplied, and much better armed; they had their city as a last refuge, in case of defeat, and one successful battle before its walls might save them from the horrors of a protracted siege. All these considerations awakened them to a consciousness of their true position, and nerved them to action, while it was yet possible to dislodge the enemy; and from this time, until the town was completely invested, they exhibited a courage and determination worthy of a better cause.

On the 21st of April, Colonel Hamilton was ordered from General Ramsay's headquarters to occupy the village of Pennyburn, about a mile below the town, in the direction of Culmore; and taking with him a guard of 200 men, he proceeded to the execution of his order. As he passed within sight of the town, he was assailed by the enemy, amounting to 1,500 foot and 300 horse; but he gained the village, and occupying the houses and adjacent cover, he kept up a fire, while he dispatched a messenger to de Momont's quarters for assistance. It happened that the Irish cavalry were out on a foraging expedition; there being only a guard of forty troopers and the same number of horse dragoons in the camp; and with this force de Momont and Major Taaf rode at once to the rescue. On reaching the scene of action, they found Hamilton still disputing the possession of the town with the enemy's foot, while their horse were drawn up with their right resting on the river to receive them. A fierce conflict ensued; the enemy broke and fled into the town, but de Momont, Major Taaf, and seven of their command, were killed, and "there was not a man left who was not either wounded or had his horse shot under him."[13] The loss of the enemy is not stated, but judging from the vast superiority

---

[13] Memoirs of the Duke of Berwick, page 50, vol. i.

of their force, and its hasty retreat, it must have been much greater.

Pennyburn was then occupied by the royalists, and reinforced from the encampment at Boom Hall[14] to the number of 500 men, and a second attack, after such a signal defeat, was little apprehended. But as that position brought them within cannon range of the city, the enemy, conscious of its importance, determined to risk another effort to dislodge them before it could be secured by intrenchments. Accordingly, on the 25th, they sallied out with a force of 8,000 men, and endeavored to surround this detachment. The Irish disputed every inch of the ground, but were forced back to the last houses in the village, and were on the point of retreat, when Ramsay appeared in the rear of the enemy, and assailed them with great vigor. Other reinforcements arrived; the action continued from nine o'clock in the morning until seven o'clock in the evening, when the enemy retreated in confusion. In this sally de Pusignan was killed, Brigadier Pointy was wounded, and Berwick received a contusion, which he tells us was the only hurt he ever had, though his after years were spent in continual warfare.

As the next attack was the last of that series of "brilliant assaults" so greatly extolled by the eulogists of the Williamite cause, it is here transcribed entire from the Memoirs of the Duke of Berwick, who was himself an actor in the affair which he so simply, yet so graphically, describes:

"They sent us word from Dublin that they were dispatching artillery to us; for which reason we thought it right to possess ourselves immediately of such posts near the town as might be of use in pressing the siege. With this view, Ramsay, with his troops, on the 6th of May, attacked a windmill, which stood on an eminence at half-cannon shot from the town, and behind it was a bottom in which he meant to encamp. The enemy defended themselves with great bravery; and, at last, the whole town sallying out upon him, he was driven from his post and obliged to retire. Ramsay himself was killed, with about 200 men; several officers of distinction were made prisoners. Wauchop took the command of Ramsay's troops, and resolved upon another attempt to make himself master of the mill; but the enemy, apprised of the importance of it, had covered it with a great intrenchment, which our troops could never force, and we sustained a further loss of several officers, and at least a hundred men." * * * "After this experience, we assembled all our troops, consisting of twelve battalions and fifteen or sixteen squadrons (about 2,800 men), and encamped opposite the front of the place, behind a rising ground, at the distance of a long musket-shot; and we left on the other side of the river two battalions that had been stationed there. A few days after, six large pieces of cannon—four guns and two mortars—arrived: there were thirty in the town. We had, in all, not more than five or six thousand men; the besieged had ten thousand, well armed. About the same time arrived M. de Rosen, with some French engineers and matrosses to begin the attack. As I was not pleased with the business, any more than with the new general, * * I asked for the command against Enniskillen, and obtained it, and left the camp on the 21st of June, with four hundred horse dra-

---

[14] This is the present name of the position then occupied by Hamilton, and seems to have been since given it, in consequence of the "Boom" that was there thrown across the river to prevent the ships of William from ascending it.

goons, and marched to Cavan Park."

The Parliament which assembled in Dublin, in obedience to the king's call, had high and solemn duties to perform, and seems to have been fully impressed with their importance. The country was impoverished; its treasury was empty; its banking-system was completely unhinged; and, as money was the great necessity of the hour, little could be done towards the support of the army until the financial system of the country was established on a satisfactory basis. Though the Williamites of Ulster had fallen away before the national troops, they had still two very important strongholds, Enniskillen and Derry, in their possession; and hostilities might be protracted until the arrival of an invading army, which the king's English agents apprised him might be soon expected, and to raise and equip an army able to cope with it was the real business of the session.

But the Parliament was not constituted for that expeditious legislation that the king expected. In the Upper House there were no Catholic prelates, and the Protestant lords, spiritual and temporal, greatly outnumbered the Catholic peers.

In the Lower House the Catholic element greatly preponderated, and conflicting opinions are never slow to arise in the greatest emergencies. The Protestant representatives very naturally wished to know whither the king's reforms tended; and the Catholic members, with a desire quite as reasonable, wanted to have their rights secured by constitutional guarantees. The discussions arising in consequence of these different views were long, and not free from religious rancor, and so, much of the time—short enough for the pressing duty of the hour—was wasted on questions that might have been better left for future deliberation. Grattan, in alluding to this Parliament eighty years later, says: "Though Papists, they were not slaves; they wrung a constitution from King James before they accompanied him to the field."[15] This was the view of a great statesman; but yet we think that the first and only duty of that Parliament should have been to grant, even to wring, money from the country, to remove their king's dependence on the bounty of France, and enable him to support an army equal to the necessity of the time; and this it undoubtedly could have done, had the Catholic members been as liberal in voting supplies to James, as their Protestant colleagues were afterwards in casting the wealth of the country at the feet of William. These rights that Grattan appreciated so much—the rights he won himself—where are they? The great duty was to beat the enemy and leave the rest to time.

The speech of the king to the assembled Parliament was all that could be desired, and went far to secure that general accord so necessary to success. His principles were unaltered. Pardon and protection were again offered to all who, within a certain day, would return to their homes. He pledged himself to secure social harmony through the establishment of civil and religious liberty; to elevate the social condition of the people, and advance the interests of trade and commerce. The address met the approval of both Houses, and, under the best auspices, they entered on their important duty.... With the exception of the following acts, which appear supplementary, the measures introduced into this Parliament were the same as those already noticed:

[15] Popular History of Ireland, vol. ii, p. 557.

First: An act declaring that all persons should pay tithes only to the clergymen of their own communion.

Second: An act repealing the act of settlement, and indemnifying Catholics who had been declared innocent by the Court of Claims.

Third: An act of attainder against all persons bearing arms for William, declaring their property, real and personal, forfeited, unless they surrendered before a certain day.[16]

Fourth: An act increasing the king's subsidy to £20,000 per month.

These acts all received the royal sanction, though the third met with considerable opposition; and the fourth was passed over an earnest protest from the Protestant lords, spiritual and temporal. But the *great* act, the one which concerned the future welfare of the country, far more than all the others, met with the persistent opposition of the king, though strenuously advocated by the majority; and so the act of Poyning remained unchanged until the days of Grattan and the volunteers of '82.

At last, and towards the end of June, they reached the great, important business of the session—the ways and means of supporting the army. The Catholic gentry had maintained the war up to the present time, and their means were totally exhausted. The Protestant gentry seemed unwilling to risk fortune or credit on the issue as between the king and the Prince of Orange. The king's condition was desperate, and called for extraordinary remedies; there was no alternative between exaction and abdication, and he overstepped the limitations of trade for the higher law of preservation. He doubled his subsidy by proclamation; established a bank restriction act by the same authority; issued a million and a half of copper coin, and gave it a nominal value. These measures were declared arbitrary, but they were also measures of the direst necessity; he pledged himself to revoke them when the necessity had passed, and also to redeem the coin issued in sterling money. The traders demurred, raised the price of provisions, and rendered the coin almost worthless; the king established a scale of prices, and threatened penalties on those who exacted more. Such was the offence, and such the demand for this "arbitrary assumption." The king in his extremity, the country in the throes of a revolution, the brave men pouring out their life-blood on the battle-field, were as nothing in comparison to the claims of a self-constituted monopoly.

In criticising those "arbitrary assumptions" of the king, we should bear in mind that free trade was then no established principle of either English or Irish legislation; that the corn laws of England, which are somewhat of a kindred character, have been repealed after years of angry agitation, and within a very recent period; that the people, whose rights were of paramount consideration, gave their unqualified approval to those measures; and, even allowing them to have been arbitrary, he could be no patriot who would put the claims of trade in opposition to the liberty of the nation. In one measure alone—his interference with the Dublin University—does the king seem to have acted both unwisely and arbitrarily; and

---

[16] Taylor characterizes this act as *monstrous*; yet, when were such liberal terms accorded by an English king to Catholic rebels?

of this, the following extract from Taylor's history will afford a sufficient exposition:—"The first step taken by King James in his war on the Dublin University, proved that he gave that body more credit for common sense than it merited. He nominated a Roman Catholic to be professor of the Irish language, and was afterwards astounded to hear that no such professorship existed in that venerable institution. Doctor Leland rates James very severely for having committed such a blunder, but, truly, the blunder belongs not to him alone. He could scarcely have credited the existence of such a practical jest as an institution whose professed design was to instruct the Irish in the doctrines of the reformed religion, which yet left the teachers wholly ignorant of the language of those whom they had to instruct. Compared with this, the folly of Goldsmith's attempting to teach English in Holland, without first having learned Dutch, sinks into insignificance."[17] The point is well taken, and the oversight of the primary duty of the founders is, no doubt, of a piece with many others that might be noted; but candor compels the acknowledgment, that neither the king nor the Catholic people should be first to rectify a *mistake* which left the college so harmless in pressing the object of its establishment.

The heads of the institution, alarmed at this interference of the king, endeavored to convert the property of the college into ready money. Tyrconnell ordered the prosecution of the purchaser, and seized on the plate so disposed of. Litigation followed, and after some time the property was restored to the institution, on condition that it should not again be sold. The king next appointed a Catholic to a fellowship of the college, and its authorities demurred; but before the matter was pressed to an issue the candidate's incapacity was discovered, and the affair terminated for the time. Such were the encroachments of the king on that venerable institution, antecedent to the invasion; but now that he had become king regnant in Ireland, he pressed those innovations with more rigor and less cause. He abolished its original charter, expelled the provost for contumacy, and is even accused of a design to convert the college into a Jesuit seminary. This was all inexcusable; the more so, that it was inconsistent with his avowed principles, that it awakened the reasonable apprehensions of the loyal Protestant people, and, above all, that it consumed the time and attention which should have been devoted to the great and pressing demands of the country.

By this unnecessary and ill-timed delay, the military affairs of the nation were allowed to languish; the army, dependent on tardy and forced supplies, had partaken of the general apathy; and were it not for the indefatigable efforts of Tyrconnell, scarcely the semblance of an army could have been maintained to the end of this memorable session. But while the king was engaged in angry discussion with his turbulent Parliament, Tyrconnell was engaged in the organization of the forces. He had already sent 2,500 troops to the army before Derry, had in course of training 9,000 more awaiting arms and equipments from France, and a well-appointed force ready, under Lord Mountcashel, to undertake the reduction of Enniskillen.

---

[17] Vol. ii., page 108.—These troubles commenced while James was yet on the English throne.

CHAPTER VI.

THE BATTLE OF NEWTOWN BUTLER, AND THE RELIEF OF ENNISKILLEN AND DERRY.

The time elapsed since the withdrawal of Galmoy from Enniskillen, on the 24th of March, had not been barren of stirring events; but events of a predatory character, and so differently colored, by the historians of each side, as to leave the mind in a state of uncertainty from the constant succession of almost similar events. This, however, appears distinct enough: that Galmoy, with a small body of troops, continued to check the excursions of the Enniskilleners, and, as the siege of Derry progressed, kept the country open for the passage of the king's trains to and from the metropolis; while, on the other hand, the Enniskilleners, emboldened by his occasional disappearance from their vicinity, renewed their raids under Wolseley, Hamilton, and Blaney, spreading terror wherever they appeared, and supplying their stronghold with the necessary booty of cattle and provender. As their position grew stronger, and their numbers increased, those raids became more frequent and extended, and by the beginning of June were such as to claim immediate and energetic measures for their suppression.

It was therefore resolved that Lord Mountcashel should proceed against Enniskillen from the direction of Dublin, while Berwick and Brigadier Southerland were to approach it from the north and west, and place their commands at his disposal. For this purpose, Berwick was ordered from Derry on the 21st of June. He was to march through Donegal, chastise the outlying insurgents there, and establish his headquarters at Trellick; while Brigadier Southerland, who lay towards Sligo, and under whom Colonel Sarsfield commanded a division of horse, was to move round to Belturbet, and, in his way, scour the country along the south-western side of Lough-Erne. Both were then to drive the enemy within their defences and await the arrival of Mountcashel, who was to proceed from Dublin, through Monaghan and Cavan, when all were to co-operate in a simultaneous movement for the reduction of this rebel stronghold.

On receipt of these orders, Sarsfield, at the head of three troops of horse, one of dragoons, and three battalions of foot,—a force of about five hundred men,—cleared the country along the south-east of the lake, and arrived at Belturbet on the 10th of June. Here he received an order from de Rosen to march forthwith to Omagh, about twenty-five miles north-west of Enniskillen, to protect the Irish besieging army at Derry against rebel attacks from that quarter, and proceeded at once to execute his commission. Southerland, with the remainder of his command—about 1,200 men—advanced through the south of Leitrim, and doubling Lough Oughter, reached the vicinity of Belturbet on the 16th of June. Here he found that Sarsfield had departed for Omagh, and that he was left to cope alone with the united commands of Hamilton, Wolseley, and Lord Blaney. On the 18th, he was informed by one of his spies that the enemy, 15,000 strong, knowing his condition, were about to seize a narrow pass, through which he had advanced, and to attack him in front and rear, with the intention of capturing or annihilating his force before the arrival of Mountcashel.[18]

On receipt of this information, Southerland, leaving Lieutenant-Colonel Scott and two hundred and eighty men in the churchyard of Belturbet to check the pursuit, withdrew in the night, and, by a skilful movement, brought his command in safety to Sligo. The Enniskilleners, baffled in their design, then turned their whole force against Scott, who, after a stubborn contest of two hours, was compelled to surrender: and all the supplies of the garrison, eighty dragoon-horses, seven hundred muskets, and a considerable quantity of gunpowder, fell into the hands of the enemy.

Berwick left Derry on the 21st, and, at the head of his four hundred dragoons, marched rapidly to the town of Donegal, where three hundred of the enemy from Ballyshannon were forming magazines. He approached their position in the night; attacked them at daybreak; killed many, forced the rest to the shelter of the castle; burned the magazines; and marched off with a booty of 1,500 cattle. Being shortly after joined by two regiments of horse and four battalions of foot,[19] which swelled his command to 1,200 men, he advanced, and on the 6th of July formed an encampment at Trellick, about nine miles north-east of Enniskillen.

On the 13th, he advanced with a party to reconnoitre the country and the fortifications of the town, when he was ambushed by a force of two hundred foot and one hundred horse, and attacked with great vigor. But notwithstanding the suddenness of the onset, he turned on them; killed all but six of the infantry; drove the horse within their intrenchments, and returned with a captain, a lieutenant, two pair of colors, and the arms of the slain.

Shortly after this he was raised to the rank of lieutenant-general, and the king ordered that he should have troops and artillery to press the object of the expedition. But de Rosen, whose mission to Ireland seems to have been to disconcert every movement that promised success, again ordered him to Derry, and he abandoned the expedition against Enniskillen with that reluctance which he indicated in after years by the following remark: "It is true, we had few, if any, cannonballs, and scarce any ammunition; but yet, as the Fort of Enniskillen was only a mud fort, we might have carried it; besides, the *town* being entirely unfortified, we should have got possession of it, and by that means have obliged the fort to surrender."

---

[18] There is reason to think that this force is overestimated by about 3,000 men, but there is no actual authority to deny its accuracy. The numbers are taken from the Memoirs of King James, who bases his statement on the report of Southerland.

[19] This must have been Sarsfield's command, for, though it is not so stated in the Memoirs, the contiguity of Trellick to Omagh, to which place Sarsfield had been ordered by de Rosen, would indicate it.

But then it was de Rosen's to command, and Berwick's to obey.

The recall of Berwick left the Enniskilleners again free to renew their excursions and strengthen their fortifications, and they availed themselves abundantly of this temporary advantage. Their forces daily augmented, and they grew more exacting on the country as they increased in power. The garrison of Sligo kept them in check on the western side of the lake, but from Ballyshannon round to Belturbet, a circuit of fifteen miles, all had to quit their homes or yield to their exactions. Their military power towards the end of July was formidable; and, taking the forces of Lord Blaney, Captain Francis Hamilton, Wolseley, and Colonel Creighton (the commandant) into account, must have come up to Southerland's estimate of 15,000 men. Stationed at strong positions around the shores of the Lough; having large depots at Ballyshannon, Enniskillen, and Crom Castle, and acquainted with all the intricacies of the lake and its confluents, they should have been able to cope with an army of twice their number. In addition to this, they had lately received from England ten pieces of cannon, with ball and match to suit; fifty barrels of gunpowder; a large supply of dragoon firelocks and muskets; a corps of engineers and gunners; experienced officers, with commissions to raise new regiments of horse and foot; and eight hundred veterans of Kirke's command, under Colonel Berry.

To drive this force from their network of fortifications, and lay siege to Enniskillen, Mountcashel arrived with about 3,600 men and seven pieces of artillery at Belturbet on the 27th of July.

The town had been abandoned, on his approach, and on the 28th he advanced and invested Crom Castle, on the eastern side. By the 30th he had carried the outer works, and driven the enemy within the walls, though not without considerable loss, and at once opened a cannonade upon the castle. While here, he received word that Colonel Berry was advancing on him by way of Lisnaskea, with eight hundred regulars, followed by the united forces of Wolseley and Hamilton. Without discontinuing the operations against the fort, he withdrew a part of his command about two miles to the eastward, and took post at Newtownbutler. Learning that the enemy's forces had all united, and were too powerful to meet in the open country, he sent Colonel Anthony Hamilton, with O'Brien's regiment of dragoons, to hold them in check, while he himself prepared for a retrograde movement to Belturbet. The troops of Hamilton were drawn into an ambush by Berry, near Lisnaskea; their commander was wounded, his next in command killed, and in a retreat which was ordered, two hundred and thirty were slain or taken prisoners. Mountcashel, on hearing of this disaster, advanced with his own regiment of horse; arrested the retreat and repulsed Berry; but seeing Wolseley, with a force of 8,000 men, close in Berry's rear, he took up his retreat to Belturbet. Berry and Wolseley moved forward rapidly; Mountcashel closely pressed, and considering resistance safer than flight, at last drew up his men about a mile to the south of Newtownbutler, and hastily formed in line of battle.

The action which ensued was disastrous to the Irish army. Opposed by more than double their number, and attacked in front and flank, they fought with great bravery, and the battle might have resulted in their favor, but an unfortunate blunder, in carrying out the general's orders, disarranged their lines, created a panic among the soldiers, and a total rout was the consequence. The lake and its tributaries cut them off from escape in any direction, and, being completely hemmed in, they were slaughtered without mercy. Their loss is estimated to be over 2,000 men, of whom 400 only were killed in the battle, the rest being massacred through the night, to the cry of "No popery!" or drowned in the lake into which they had thrown themselves in the vain hope of escaping the general carnage. Mountcashel himself was wounded and taken prisoner, but was saved from death by a captain named Cooper, to whom he had previously rendered a similar service. Sir Stephen Martin and Lord Abercorn, and many officers of distinction, were killed. All that escaped of this unfortunate command fled towards Belturbet, and, after the capture of their general, the expedition was abandoned.

Affairs at Derry were now approaching a crisis. The siege had been pressed with vigor under every disadvantage: minority of force, inadequate artillery, and a season almost unprecedented for heavy rains, which kept the trenches continually filled with water from the beginning to the end of the siege. The besieged, reduced to the last extremity, had become almost passive in their resistance, and were frequently on the point of surrendering, when the appearance of an English fleet would again raise their spirits for a time, but to cause a still greater depression when it had to withdraw without being able to afford relief. Every successive disappointment renewed the murmurs of the people, and cooled the ardor of the soldiers. Several times through the summer they had received fresh supplies of powder and ball; but of provisions, which were as easily smuggled in, they had received little or none.

De Rosen, exasperated by delay, collected the fugitive population of the district, and placing them between the town and his men, gave orders to drive them in on the besieged. The Irish soldiers, though suffering great privations, and eager for the surrender, refused to obey the order, and threatened a mutiny if compelled to enforce it. De Rosen continued unmoved, but Hamilton and the other leaders communicated the circumstance to the king, and received a positive order that the multitude should be allowed to depart unmolested to their homes. The garrison, taking advantage of this circumstance, sent away the most helpless of the citizens, and took in a reinforcement of the young and active in their place, so that de Rosen's cruelty ultimately tended to their advantage.

Yet, notwithstanding the advantage thus gained by the besieged, their suffering had become unendurable, and despair had settled on all, when, towards the middle of July, Kirke again entered Lough Foyle, and displayed his fleet to the wistful eyes of the starving inhabitants, and was again obliged to retire without accomplishing his object. This was the turning-point of the siege. The long-hoped for relief again disappeared; the authorities of Derry determined on a surrender, and demanded a cessation to regulate its provisions. But Kirke managed to convey a note to the governor, concealed in a twisted rope, which he tied round the waist of a country lad, and this note—which may be found in Walker's account of the siege,—apprised him of a plan which he had set on foot to relieve the garrison.

Baffled in his efforts to succor the town from the side of Lough Foyle, Kirke divided his fleet and with one part of it doubled Malin Head, sailed up Lough Swilly, and established a garrison of 800 men near Rathmelton, a few miles west of Derry. The place was well selected for his purpose; which was to attract the attention of the besiegers, and cause them to withdraw some of their forces from the side of the Foyle. This movement was observed by de Rosen, who, instead of drawing his forces from the water-side, ordered Berwick from Enniskillen to check the movements of Kirke, and dislodge him, if possible, without weakening the forces stationed at the obstructions in the river; and Berwick, as already indicated, abandoned Enniskillen, and arrived at Rathmelton, with a force of 1,200 horse, about the 22d of July.

The position occupied by Kirke was one of great natural strength. The inlets of the Lough indented the country in all directions, and extended up to within three or four miles of Derry, presenting almost insuperable difficulties to an attacking force; and, on one of its peninsular mazes, he was found strongly intrenched under the protection of his frigates. Berwick spent a whole day in trying to dislodge him, but without effect, when he retired to an adjacent height, and contented himself with watching his movements, and confining him to his intrenchments.

But Kirke succeeded in his object. Notwithstanding the vigilance of Berwick, he threw both men and munitions into Enniskillen; partially relieved Derry; and conjuring the governor to hold out yet a little longer, sailed out of Lough Swilly, and joined the fleet at the Foyle, while Berwick united his command to the force of the besiegers.

On the 28th of July, the English fleet again appeared in Lough Foyle, and bore up steadily towards the obstructions above Culmore Fort, near the mouth of the river. It consisted of twenty ships of war, 300 transports laden with provisions and military stores, and 6,000 veteran troops under the command of General Kirke.[20] The result may be anticipated. The blockading army, not having cannon of sufficient calibre to sink the approaching vessels, the boom across the river was broken. Derry was partially relieved on that day, and, on the 30th, all attempts of the besiegers to thwart their movements had become futile. The whole fleet rode up the river, and succored the beleaguered town, and the Irish army, after a few days more, raised the siege, and retired towards Dublin, on which Marshal Schomberg was reported to be projecting a descent. On their way they were joined by the remnant of Mountcashel's command; nor was the news that preceded them in Dublin of a more cheering character. Since the siege had commenced, the famous battle of Killicrankie had been fought and won. There, on the 26th of May, Dundee, at the head of 2,000 Irish, and about the same number of Highlanders, defeated General Mackay's army of 8,000 veterans. But with this victory expired the hopes of the Jacobite cause in Scotland. Dundee received a mortal wound in the moment of

---

[20] A name of unenviable notoriety in the history of those times. Hume, at page 526 of his History of England, alluding to the severity of Lord Feversham in suppressing the rebellion of Monmouth, says: "He was outdone by Kirke, a soldier of fortune, who had long served at Tangiers, and had contracted from his intercourse with the Moors, an inhumanity less known in European and free countries." His cruelty in Ireland has become proverbial as that of Cromwell. There he became as distinguished for torturing the loyal subjects of the king, as he had previously been in persecuting the followers of Monmouth.

victory; the Highlanders, dispirited by his death, dispersed after a few unimportant skirmishes, and what was left of the Irish contingent returned to their own country.

So ended the siege of Derry, an affair of little military note, but of great political and religious import. Though its gates were closed against the king's troops on the 7th of December, free access to it from the sea was not obstructed until the surrender of Culmore, on the 21st of April. It had made ample preparation for a siege, and, notwithstanding the blockade, had received 480 barrels of gunpowder, and stores of provisions and clothing, from that time until the end of June. It had not been closely invested until the latter part of May; and, unless from the two light field-pieces of General Wauchop, on the water-side, there was no cannonade whatever before the 21st of June, when Berwick withdrew to Enniskillen. The defenders, during the heat of the siege, had other advantages not generally accorded to an enemy. They were allowed to send away ten thousand of the sick and indigent inhabitants, and, during the armistice that ensued, had managed to admit an equal number "of the young and active." They had thirty siege-guns on their walls, 10,000 "regimented men," and a population, stated at twenty thousand, to supply the casualties of war.

The investing force was 5,000 men, four siege-guns, two mortars, and two field-pieces. From this force 400 dragoons marched with the Duke of Berwick to Enniskillen, and during the siege they received but 2,500 additional troops, making the entire force 7,500 men. The weather was continually unfavorable to siege operations, and, excepting in the amount of rations, the besiegers endured far more suffering than the besieged. The bombardment continued at intervals from the 21st of June to the 28th of July; but during the last week there had been an almost entire cessation of hostilities, to admit of negotiations. On the estimate of the Reverend George Walker, who has left a journal of the siege, the ball and mortar, great and small, thrown into the town up to the 22d of July, was 587. After this there was but an occasional shot until the siege was raised. This fell short of fifteen shots a day, and about one every two hours, admitting them to have been fired in regular succession. During the siege the garrison had been reduced to 3,000 effective men, while the besiegers retired with 3,500 — showing a loss to the defenders of 7,000, and to the assailants of 3,600.

The Duke of Berwick, who was present in all the skirmishing that took place up to the 21st of June, and who afterwards became a prominent character in the great wars of the continent, had certainly no inducement to magnify this episode in his life, by underrating the Jacobite forces; nor is it to be credited that the Reverend George Walker has given an overestimate of the besieged. Whatever were the privations of the non-combatants, — and they must have been great — it does not appear from his journal that the defenders were, for any considerable time, on an allowance much below that of soldiers in ordinary warfare. We find that in two or three instances they were obliged to resort to the boiling of salt hides for a substitute; and to eating "dogs and cats, etc.," now considered a luxury, though thrown in by Williamite writers to shadow a picture dark enough from any perspective.

But if the defenders did not display as great intrepidity as the besiegers, they showed qualities which, in their position, would be considered by many as more important:—wonderful fortitude and great endurance—and their service to England can scarcely be overestimated. They forced this war for religious ascendency; they maintained this stronghold until the landing of Schomberg, which turned the tide of fortune; but in all that transpired before the walls, the Jacobite army exhibited greater courage, and far greater valor and intrepidity. If, then, it should be asked why they were able to withstand, so long, the greater valor claimed for their enemies, the answer is plain:—Stone walls, abundant means, and great numerical odds. If it be true,—and it is so asserted,—that in a moment of desperation they threw open their gates and invited the enemy to enter, and it should be asked, why they were not accommodated?—it should be remembered that there is a wide difference between rashness and valor. But that they were driven from the open country, by a much inferior force, and twice brought to terms, unwisely rejected by an over-punctilious king, are also as certain as the records of the time are reliable. But, when it is asked, why men and appliances sufficient were not brought to bear on them in time; the answer is harrowing, but nevertheless true:—an impoverished country, a ruined exchequer, and the consequent dependence on the bounty of the French king.

CHAPTER VII.

THE LANDING OF MARSHAL SCHOMBERG, AND HIS WINTER CAMPAIGN.

Hitherto, the success of the Jacobite cause in Ireland and Scotland, had rendered the tenure of the English throne by the Prince of Orange a matter of uncertainty both to himself and his English adherents. The state of public feeling in the capital had rendered the presence of his foreign mercenaries continually necessary to his person; and he knew that should James succeed in repressing the rebellion in the other two kingdoms, his restoration to the third would follow as an inevitable consequence. He had already, with the English people, lost all that popularity which immediately succeeded his invasion. By turning the Convention into a Parliament, in order to avoid a popular election, he outraged the first principle of the British Charter, and the people soon learned that his pledges to maintain their liberty and religion were only affected for the time, to establish his own dominion over them. The Conventionists, too, so long subservient to his wishes, had, since erected into a Parliament, inveighed against the Dutch influence in the kingdom, and he, more than once, had threatened to abdicate and leave them to the mercy of their outraged king. This threat never failed of its desired effect on the leaders of the Opposition in Parliament; but the popular discontent had to be suppressed by the strong hand; and the British soldiers who showed any sign of disaffection, were sent to serve as his Dutch contingent to the League, while the followers of Schomberg and Ginckle lived at will in England.

But now that the relief of Derry and Enniskillen put a better face on affairs in Ireland; and the death of Dundee freed him from farther apprehension for the safety of Scotland, he resolved to relieve the English people of the presence of his foreign mercenaries, by employing them in the reduction of the only kingdom that preferred allegiance to King James. He accordingly apprised the Parliament of his intention. The proposition was favorably received, and large subsidies being granted for that purpose, an army consisting of eighteen regiments of foot, and six regiments of horse—about 20,000 men,—was soon organized from among the military adventurers that the higher pay given in England at that time had drawn thither from the Continent. A fleet was soon ready to transport this army to Ireland, and the whole was placed under the command of Marshal, the Duke of Schomberg, and Count Solmes, to make a descent on the eastern coast of Ireland, and, after establishing communications with the rebels, to proceed to the reduction of Dublin. On the 12th of August this fleet appeared off the coast of Down, and, sailing into Belfast Lough, effected a landing at Bangor Bay, between Belfast and Carrickfergus. The next day Schomberg took possession of Belfast, and after strengthening its defences, and giving his troops some rest, he appeared before the Castle of Carrickfergus and summoned it to surrender. The garrison was under the command of Colonel McCarthy-More, and consisted of his own regiment and that of Colonel Cormac O'Neil,—about eight hundred men,—poorly supplied, and greatly embarrassed by the population of the town, who had taken refuge within its walls. Schomberg immediately opened upon it from his ships and land batteries, keeping up a fierce cannonade day and night during the entire period of the siege. The garrison made a stubborn resistance, and visited the besiegers with severe loss, which elicited the praise of Schomberg, and excited a spirit of vengeance among his followers. The walls being breached after the second day, the besieged had resort to a singular stratagem. The cattle within the walls were slaughtered, hauled up and thrown into the breach, and earth and stones being heaped over them, the place was soon as tenable as ever; their balls being spent, they tore the lead from the roof of the castle, and converted it into bullets; and at last, their powder being exhausted, and no succor arriving from the Irish army; after a siege of eight days, they surrendered on terms considered highly honorable. But these conditions were flagrantly violated after the evacuation; the prisoners, whom the English Annalist calls "brave fellows, but poorly clad," were subjected to treatment which darkens the history of the time; crimes too abominable for recital, were perpetrated by the foreign mercenaries on the defenceless inhabitants of the town: and Schomberg, who tried to check their excesses, only succeeded in rendering himself so unpopular as to affect unfavorably the result of the ensuing campaign.... Judging of this army of mercenaries on the authority of the historian, Taylor, they must, indeed, have been a godless host. "They were," says he,[21] "the outcasts of all society, familiar with every crime, abandoned to every excess. Vices for which language scarcely ventures to find a name; abominations that may not be described, and can scarcely be imagined, were constantly practised by these bandits.... The traditions of the Irish Protestants and Catholics contain a horrid catalogue of the enormities practised by this 'black banditti;' and these accounts are fully confirmed by the narratives which the contemporary writers have given of their conduct in other countries. With these were joined some raw English levies, who found it much easier to imitate the debaucheries than to practise the discipline of the foreigners. Indeed, no worse scourge could be sent by an angry Providence than the army which now proceeded against Ireland."

Having repaired the Castle of Carrickfergus, and left English garrisons there and in Belfast, Schomberg drew out his army into the open country, and spent some time in organizing the Enniskilleners, who now flocked to his standard. Nor does it appear that they who now joined him were of a character to check the evil propensities of his foreigners. In allusion to them, the authority just quoted, gives the following not very flattering picture:

"The soldiers of Schomberg were perfectly astounded by the appearance of the men whose fame had been so loudly trumpeted in England.... Every man was armed and equipped after his own fashion, and each was attended by a mounted

----

[21] Vol. II., page 137.

servant bearing his baggage.... Descended from the Levellers and Covenanters, they preserved all the gloomy fanaticism of their fathers, and believed the slaughtering of Papists an act of religious duty. They were robbers and murderers on principle, for they believed themselves commissioned to remove idolatry from the land.... Reeking from the field of battle, they assembled round their preachers, who always accompanied them in their expeditions, and listened with eager delight to their wild effusions, in which the magnificent Orientalisms of the Old Testament were strangely combined with their gross and vulgar sentiments.... William himself despised them most heartily, and subjected them to military execution by the dozen for violating the laws of war. From the moment they joined the regular army, they performed no exploit worthy of their former fame, simply because they could not learn a new mode of fighting. They were aware of this themselves, and frequently declared, with truth, that they could do no good while acting under orders."[22]

Such was the army; discordant in language, in habit—in fine, in every thing but its love of plunder and confiscation, with which Schomberg now undertook the conquest of the country and the eradication of the Catholic faith; and had he moved directly on the capital without delay, there is hardly a doubt that he could have established his winter-quarters in it, for there was then no army on his front capable of offering any protracted opposition. Behind him, and to his right, lay the northern province, lately relieved from the presence of the Jacobite army; with no garrison but Charlemont, on the Blackwater, to concern his movements, and that, in the presence of the Enniskilleners, and in the midst of a population friendly to his cause, might have been safely disregarded. Far off towards its western confines lay a few detached encampments of the Irish, too remote to offer any timely opposition, while the garrison of Belturbet was so straitened and reduced by the late reverse at Newtownbutler, as to be scarcely able to maintain its position against the outlying insurgents of Fermanagh. At this moment he might have safely chosen at once, either to march westward across the whole breadth of the island, or direct upon the capital, without meeting a force capable of disputing his progress. But on his front lay Newry, and there, report said that a large army was encamped under the Count de Rosen and Hamilton, though, in truth, no body of any consequence had as yet left the capital, and these generals were then at Drogheda, engaged in the work of mobilizing and disciplining their raw levies. After spending several days, undecided whether to advance direct against it, or turn northward and undertake the siege of Charlemont, he at last adopted a middle course, which was to detach a force against that stronghold, while with the bulk of his army he felt his way cautiously towards Dublin. Proceeding slowly along the coast for several days, within easy communication of his fleet, he at last turned his steps

---

[22] Taylor adds, that "they never hesitated to encounter any odds, however unequal." But, in no place throughout the whole course of the war, did they meet an equal number of the royal troops in the field. It may be asked, as pertinent to the point, What had become of the militia—from fifteen to twenty thousand—disbanded by Tyrconnell in 1686? They were surely not in the Jacobite army, nor is it to be believed that they were idle spectators. They were in the army of William; and as to *their* discipline, it was that of the English army of that day.

towards Newry, to try the countenance of the enemy. The time lost by this indecision enabled the Duke of Berwick to anticipate him there, and with a force of 1,000 foot and 600 horse dragoons, hastily mustered, he stood prepared to oppose him. Knowing the futility of giving battle with such a small body of men to an army like that led by Schomberg, flushed with its recent success, he endeavored to effect by stratagem that which he could not by force. So, raising intrenchments at Newry, and causing a report to be spread through the enemy's ranks that he was marching forward to give him battle, the movements of the latter became more slow and cautious as he advanced. The country between the two armies was studded with hills favorable for deception, and on these Berwick posted videttes, within sight of the enemy, and took up a central position himself, making as bold a front as possible. Schomberg, on observing this, believed that the whole Irish army was drawn up to dispute his advance, and, halting his army, he encamped at the distance of two miles, and went at the head of fourteen squadrons to reconnoitre the position. Berwick in the centre, with only two troops of horse, caused his videttes to withdraw gradually, and ordered a flourish of trumpets, as if about to charge, when Schomberg hesitated, halted, and finally retired to his camp. He was followed at a safe distance by Berwick, and, the night soon closing, he spent it in hasty preparation; he strengthened his position, delivered ammunition to his troops, and resolved to attack in force the following morning. The morning came, every thing was in requisition for the great issue of arms, but no army appeared on his front, for Berwick had retired during the night, and marched to Drogheda to join the Duke of Tyrconnell, who had assembled an army there, and where the king had arrived to conduct the campaign in person.

The army now assembled at Drogheda, under the command of the king, consisted of about 20,000 men, not more than half of whom were the veterans of the last year, the rest being raw levies, indifferently clad, and armed with such weapons as could be hastily improvised for the occasion; with a park of artillery, generally estimated at twelve light field-pieces. Here a council of war was held, in which the king was earnestly besought to abandon the capital and fall back towards the centre of the island; but, after much deliberation, he determined to offer battle, and advanced to Dundalk, where Schomberg lay intrenched with an army greatly augmented by accessions from Derry and Enniskillen, and vastly superior in every thing that could render an army effective.

It is hard to account for the indecision of Schomberg at this period; for several days the Irish army hovered in his vicinity, but no challenge could induce him to quit his intrenchments. His well-known gallantry made this the more remarkable, and his continual persistence in declining an engagement, daily offered, led de Rosen to believe that "he wanted something," and to urge the king to assail him in his encampment. But this proposition was declined by the latter, on the ground that, as "he wanted something," winter would do the work of war on his army of foreigners without hazarding a battle, and leave him completely powerless to continue his campaign in the ensuing season. Elated with the belief that Schomberg was afraid to meet him in the field, after issuing a manifesto offering rewards to such as would desert to his standard, he took leave of his army and returned to the capital. The army soon retired to winter-quarters at Drogheda, and Schomberg, after an inglorious campaign of four months, spent in advancing about thirty miles, withdrew from Dundalk, and encamped in the low country to the north of it, where he passed the remainder of the winter. Here a loathsome disease attacked his troops. Thousands of them fell victims to it, and the whole army became so enfeebled, that the living were scarcely able to bury the dead. Others, principally of the French troops, under the inducement held out by King James, deserted to the Irish army, though many were retaken and executed: until disease, demoralization, and desertion had actually reduced his army to four or five thousand men at all capable of service. Cognizant of this, the Irish generals again appealed to the king, to attack him while in this condition, and rid the country effectually of his presence; but with his characteristic dogmatism, he still persevered in a policy that seemed to work so well, lost an opportunity which seems to have been offered by Providence for the success of his cause, and hugged his illusion till too late. De Rosen and d'Avaux were soon after recalled to France; the Irish generals had become disgusted with their leadership; the army felt relieved by the event, and higher hopes were felt for the campaign of 1690.

CHAPTER VIII.

SCHOMBERG'S CAMPAIGN CONTINUED—THE ARRIVAL OF THE PRINCE OF ORANGE.

The winter, and the advantages it offered to the Irish army, passed away, and the Duke of Schomberg, who, for several months, could have offered but an ineffectual opposition, was, through the vacillating policy of the king, and the factious opposition of the Lords, spiritual and temporal, in his Parliament, allowed to take the initiative in the renewal of hostilities. While he pressed the siege of Charlemont with renewed vigor, he dispatched 3,300 English and Enniskilleners, under the command of Brigadier Wolseley, to seize on Belturbet and Cavan, which were occupied through the winter by a small force under General Wauchop, and to the relief of these positions, which were considered of much importance, the Duke of Berwick was ordered with a force of 1,500 foot and 200 horse. Belturbet had been the scene of many bitter conflicts since the commencement of the rebellion, and had been taken and retaken by the troops of each army in turn, as the tide of war fluctuated. Situated in the midst of a fertile district, it was of much advantage in the way of supply. By its possession, through the previous year, the Irish had been enabled to hold the Enniskilleners in check even after the disaster of Newtownbutler; and it was still hoped that, by holding it, they could confine them to the more northern counties, and prevent their concentration round the Duke of Schomberg, or divert his attention from the capital.

Berwick, on receipt of the order, proceeded by rapid marches, and arrived at Cavan, which is about five miles from Belturbet, late in the evening, whence he sent orders to General Wauchop to throw out pickets in the direction of the enemy, and notify him of their earliest appearance. Owing to the heavy rains that had fallen through the night, this order was either totally neglected, or but carelessly observed; and early in the morning, while Berwick took up his march from Cavan, Wolseley approached as rapidly from the direction of Monaghan; each with the intention of occupying a mud fort which commanded the town. Both forces, each unapprised of the design of the other, met in the intrenchments, and a fierce conflict followed. Wolseley was driven from the fort and through the adjoining coppice in great confusion, but Colonel MacGeoghaghen being killed, and General Nugent and several officers wounded, their troops became panic-stricken, "and, in a moment," says Berwick, "from being conquerors, we became conquered." Wolseley lost 300 men, and Berwick 500; the fort was evacuated as a consequence; the Irish fell back to Cavan, which they shortly after abandoned; and Schomberg, being relieved of further apprehension from that direction, and being strength-

ened by his native auxiliaries, turned his undivided attention to the siege of Charlemont.

Believing that the fall of Belturbet, and the isolation of his position, must have
dampened the ardor of Colonel O'Regan, the commandant of the Castle of Charlemont, Schomberg offered him honorable conditions in case he agreed to surrender the fort, but he found the spirit of this indomitable old chieftain as hopeful and
defiant as ever. Since the arrival of Schomberg, he had succeeded in baffling all
efforts to reduce the place; and, though now surrounded, and cut off on all sides
from hope of succor, he thanked the duke for his offer, but replied that he would
never surrender "his castle," and was determined to hold it for his king, or die in
its ruins. He was, however, placed in a very embarrassing situation. Within the last
few days a body of five hundred soldiers, bearing a scanty supply of ammunition
and provisions, had forced their way into the garrison, and, having thus partially
relieved it, were ordered unceremoniously to fight their way out again, but, in
making the attempt, were driven back under the guns of the fort. The governor
refused them admittance. He said that he was ordered to defend the place, and
would do it, and looked on them as much his enemies as the troops of Schomberg.
They were, therefore, placed on the counterscarp of the fort, where they were exposed to the fire of the enemy, and many of them were actually killed during the
bombardment that followed. But, though in appearance, and in many of his characteristics, he affected the ogre, his heart relented; and, while he could bear to see
them shot from the walls, he could not see them die of starvation, and so doled out
his scanty provisions until they were consumed, and the garrison was reduced to
all the horrors of a famine-siege. Every means of supporting life was now resorted
to, and every effort for the reduction of the fort was in vain, until on the 14th of
May, when, literally starved out, after a siege of nine, months from the landing of
Schomberg, he capitulated, and marched out with what remained of his famished
garrison. The terms granted him by Schomberg, who was impatient of delay, were
highly honorable: the garrison was allowed to retire with arms and baggage, and
the king, who neglected to succor him during this protracted siege, raised him to
the order of knighthood, and he was henceforth known as Sir Teague O'Regan,
and intrusted with the defence of Sligo, which he held until the last tocsin summoned him to Limerick.

This was the only event worthy of the military fame of Schomberg since his
arrival in the kingdom. From the first to the last, the Castle of Charlemont and its
commandant were as thorns in the side of this unfortunate soldier of fortune. It
would seem as if the old chief had him under a spell; for once he set eyes on him
and his stronghold, they were in his thoughts day and night, and he would not depart until the place was rendered to his arms. Yet, 'tis said that he had an immense
liking for that quaint old soldier, and was even sorry when he saw him depart
from his seemingly enchanted castle. A soldier himself, and an accomplished one,
he could appreciate soldierly qualities even in an enemy; and O'Regan, notwithstanding his grotesque appearance and eccentric habits, was a rare military genius. Of this siege it may be said, that, unless in so far as that of Derry affected the
final issue of the war, it loses in comparison with that of Charlemont, both in the

duration of the contest, and in the spirit, hardihood, and valor of the besieged. Its fall may be said to have put an end to the Jacobite power in Ulster, and also to the military career of Schomberg. He frittered away his time in its reduction, when it might have been safely left in his rear; and the stubborn old chief that commanded it, after having diverted his purpose so long from the real object of his campaign, offered him his grateful acknowledgments, and laughed at his folly when departing. The delay occasioned by this event was a matter of vital importance to the Jacobite cause; for it had enabled King James to make more ample preparations for the opening campaign, and saved Dublin, which, up to that time, could have made but slight resistance, if any, to the veteran army of Schomberg.

Knowing, through his English agents, that the earliest possible attention of the Prince of Orange would be directed to his affairs in Ireland, King James was now making active preparations. While the levies lately made were undergoing that hasty discipline which the duty of the hour made obligatory, he sent Tyrconnell to the French court to solicit the assistance so long promised, and so unaccountably delayed. Men there were at his call for any purpose, and to any amount, but he lacked money, small-arms, artillery — in short, every thing that could render their service available. Through the exertions of Tyrconnell, a French contingent was immediately put in readiness, and, towards the end of April, a force of six thousand men, with a park of artillery, consisting of ten pieces, under the command of the Duc de Lausun, arrived in Ireland. But this was the extent of the French king's bounty, for the money, clothing, provisions and arms, on which James had calculated so long, and which alone could enable him to put the requisite number of troops into the field, were still withheld. Had the troops now sent been of the regular French army, and given in good faith, they would have been a great acquisition to King James. But the French king did not allow his generosity to outrun his discretion. He was then engaged in a war with the allies, which severely taxed the population of his own kingdom, and so the troops sent to Ireland were a heterogeneous body consisting of French Huguenots, Germans, and even English Protestants, taken prisoners on the Continent, and offered pardon on condition that they would serve under the standard of King James. It is said that at least one-third of de Lausun's force was so constituted, and of this, the number of desertions that took place while they remained in Ireland, and the unwilling service performed by the rest, would afford ample corroboration. Nor were the discordant elements of which this force was composed, nor its want of devotion to the Irish cause, nor the eccentricities of its general, the only drawbacks consequent on this accession. Ireland had been represented, as indeed it would seem to be, inexhaustible in men who wanted but arms and discipline to become excellent soldiers. Louis wanted men at the time, and, taking advantage of this information, stipulated for an equivalent to the force which he sent over with de Lausun. On the other hand, King James thought that he would engage the French king and nation more earnestly in his cause, by the introduction of French troops into Ireland, and, as a matter of course, the terms were accepted. All things considered, it did not seem an unwise act, and might even be an advantage to his cause, had he not been as poor a diplomatist as he had lately proved himself a statesman. Any number of armed men would have been better than the same number without arms; and 'tis said that it was optional with him to send his equivalent either in disciplined soldiers or in raw recruits. But his pride prevailed over his judgment; and, perhaps ashamed to make a poor display in the eyes of the French king and people, he resolved to send over Lord Mountcashel and his command in exchange. This general, who had escaped from Enniskillen in December, was now at the head of six thousand troops, designated by the annalists of the period as "the flower of the Irish army," and had all seen service in the events of the preceding years. They were accordingly marched to Cork, where, embarking on board the fleet of Chateaurenaud, which brought over the brigade of de Lausun, they bade adieu to their own country, and arrived in France early in May.

We therefore hear no more of Mountcashel in the last struggle for the liberty of his country; but his name was occasionally borne from another land, in whose service he fought and bled, like the gallant men so soon to follow. During the remaining year, he received an accession of four thousand troops to swell this force, which formed the nucleus of that "brigade," still the theme of the warrior and poet, but who have left no other memorial to Ireland than their wrongs, and their reckless valor in foreign lands. The year after his arrival in France, Mountcashel, while fighting against the allies in Savoy, received a wound from the effects of which he subsequently died at Barège, in the Hautes Pyrénées, and the highest military honors were decreed by the French king to his memory.

The Convention Parliament of England had been dissolved on the 6th of February, and a new one, more in the interest of William, had been convened in March. To this Parliament he signified his intention of taking the command of the forces in Ireland. The proposition was highly satisfactory, and a supply of £1,200,000 was granted him for that purpose; a presentation of £100,000 was also voted to Marshal, the Duke de Schomberg; and large supplies of provisions, clothing and military stores were soon got in requisition.

The report that de Lausun had landed in Ireland with a French army, tended to hasten these preparations, and to swell the proportions of the designed armament. Pending the prince's departure, large bodies of English troops were shipped to the garrisons of Ulster, and as Schomberg had expressed dissatisfaction with the conduct of his English and Anglo-Irish troops in the field, a new army, consisting of foreign adventurers—Dutch Danes, Scandinavians, Swiss, and French Huguenots; some, no doubt, induced by religious fanaticism, but many by the higher pay in the English army, and the promise of subsequent plunder, flocked to his standard. On the 6th of June, William's grand park of artillery and ordnance stores arrived at Carrickfergus, and on the 14th he himself, accompanied by Prince George of Denmark, the Prince of Hesse Darmstadt, the Dukes of Ormond and Wortemberg, the Earls of Oxford, Portland and Scarborough, Generals Mackey and Douglas, and other notables, arrived and proceeded to Lisburn, where Schomberg had awaited his arrival since the fall of Charlemont.

No sooner was the news of William's arrival spread abroad, than the clergymen of the Established Church, and the Presbyters and dissenting clergy of all denominations, waited on him, proffering him their allegiance, and embarrassing him with fulsome addresses, indicative of all they had done and would do for the advancement of religion and the eradication of "popery."[23] William, though impatient of delay, received them with grave respect, if not with cordiality. The gentlemen of the establishment were simply told that "he would take care of them," while large sums of money were distributed among the dissenting teachers of the northern province, indicating that, as they had already done more for the cause, more was expected under the government about to be established for their behest. The men of the establishment retired not over-pleased with their new master, and the Covenanters, thanking God that they had a country to sell, and a religion to trade in, also took their departure, and William addressed himself to the real object of his mission; for, as he expressed it, "he did not come into Ireland to let the grass grow under his feet." This was a significant hint to the Duke of Schomberg, that he had fallen under his displeasure through his tardy movements since he came to the country. It was so received by that old veteran, and an estrangement, never after reconciled, was the consequence. The days of Schomberg were nearly numbered; but, short as they were, they were embittered by the ingratitude of the prince in whose service he had spent the better part of an eventful life.

The available force of William in Ireland now numbered over sixty thousand effective men. There were none of these who had not seen active service, and by far the greater portion were veterans long inured to continental warfare. The "Thirty Years' War," which has left its impress on the nations of Europe, down to the present day, had sent afloat a swarm of military adventurers ready for any cause that could offer fame or reward; and to England they flocked as the best market for their services. From this force he selected an army of 38,000 or 40,000 men, and, placing the remainder in the garrisons of Ulster, he struck his tents and turned his steps towards the Irish capital.

If we except those bands of Rapparees that traversed the country at large, and levied on it in the name of the king, or for their own support, the Jacobite force, according to the highest estimate, was now but 30,000 men. And taking into consideration the long sweep of coast from Dublin round by the south and west to Galway, and the defences of the Shannon from Lanesborough to Limerick, there could not have been then in garrison less than 10,000. This would leave him an available force for active service of about 20,000, and of these 6,000 were French, the only well-appointed infantry in the service; and about 9,000 Irish infantry, indifferently armed with muskets and short pikes; but the cavalry were a superb body, long inured to service under Hamilton, Berwick, and Sarsfield, and numbered about 5,000 men. When with these is taken into consideration a train of twelve field-pieces, lately brought over from France by the Duke de Lausun, the reader will have a reliable estimate of the force which King James now assembled to dispute the possession of the country with the Prince of Orange.

On the 16th of June King James arrived at Castletown Bellow, near Dundalk, where part of his army occupied an advanced position under the command of M.

[23] Addresses of the same import were presented to James on his arrival, by the established clergy. But Taylor says their addresses to William were "probably more sincere," and instances this fact:—"James was regularly prayed for by all the churches within his lines. When William advanced his name was substituted, and when he retreated, his rival again became 'our most religious and gracious king.'"—Vol. ii., p. 145.

Girardin, a French officer; and thither also the rest of his forces soon repaired from their winter-quarters at Drogheda. Here, drawn up on the heights, behind a river, with their right resting towards Dundalk and the lowlands, where Schomberg had passed the preceding winter, stretching before them to the north, they awaited the appearance of the enemy.

From the 16th to the 22d William was at Newry and James at Dundalk, each awaiting the arrival of his artillery. While the main armies stood thus, almost in sight of each other, several skirmishes occurred between the pickets thrown forward on both sides, in one of which Colonel Dempsey, with two companies of his own regiment, encountered 200 foot and 60 horse of the enemy, only six of whom escaped; but the gallant colonel himself received a wound of which he died a few days after. This incident raised the spirit of the troops to a high pitch, and made them eager for a battle; and the king himself, much elated by the event, determined to abide the enemy in his present position. But the Irish leaders were not so favorably impressed, either with the condition of the troops, or the position which they occupied, and endeavored to dissuade the king from risking a battle under such disadvantages. They again urged him to abandon the capital, and to fall back on the defences of the Shannon, where, by instituting a desultory system of warfare, he could keep William in check until the winter set in, when, by the promised assistance from France, they could render his campaign as inglorious as that of Schomberg had been in the last. Every argument that could favor such a course was urged, and all the circumstances by which he was surrounded seemed to point it out as the best that could be adopted. A fleet was fitting out in France, of which his earnest friend, M. de Seignelay, would have command; a few days more would see it afloat, and on its way to destroy the fleet and transports of William around the coast of Ireland: it would also bring arms and ammunition in abundance, and by winter a powerful and well-disciplined army would be ready to take the field. These and many other arguments were urged, but all in vain. The king would not relinquish the capital without striking a blow for it; he became all at once as bold and intrepid as he had hitherto been weak and temporizing; rejected their remonstrance, and determined to risk all on a single battle.

This he tells in his memoirs, written several years later, and it is but just that his reasons for disagreeing, which are not wanting in plausibility, should be placed beside those of the generals. He held that the loss of the capital would end whatever prestige his name had with the French king; that it would entirely alienate the Protestants of Ireland; that it would throw the provinces of Leinster and Munster completely open to William, while he would be confined to one province, the smallest and poorest in the kingdom; and that his final defeat, though it might be protracted for a time, would be eventually certain. But, whatever were the merits of the different views, is now but speculation;—the king remained persistent.

On the 23d, William's artillery having arrived, he moved forward. The same day King James retired to Ardee, where he was met by his train, and drew up in a strong position in the direct route between William and the capital. William, still advancing, crossed the mountains between Newry and Dundalk, and, observing the situation of the Irish army, divided his own into two bodies for the purpose of flanking it, or forcing it into the plain, where his great numerical superiority would render victory certain. Seeing this, King James continued gradually to fall back; on the 29th, he crossed the Boyne, at Drogheda, and, drawing up his army on the heights of Donore, overlooking that river, he there awaited the enemy.

CHAPTER IX.
THE BATTLE OF THE BOYNE.

The Boyne, which finds its head-waters near Carbery, in the County of Kildare, takes a meandering course towards the west and north, until it enters Meath, through which it flows in a north-easterly direction through Trim, Navan, Slane, and Drogheda, four miles below which it falls into the Irish Sea. At tide-water it is navigable to Navan, a distance of nineteen miles, for barges of fifty tons burden; but at low-water, from Navan to Slane, it is a shallow stream, brawling over a rocky bottom of a few yards in width; and from that to Old Bridge it is fordable by horse and foot at almost every rood of its length. Below Slane, its course is due east for nearly a mile, when, dipping abruptly towards the south, it takes a semicircular sweep of nearly three miles to Old Bridge, and the curve so formed embraces its memorable battle-ground. The northern bank, for nearly half a mile back, is high and firm down to the water's edge, while the opposite one is low and sedgy, and the ground behind it broken, back to the base of Donore, which is over a mile from its mid-current:—the chord of the arc indicated is nearly two miles, and the distance from Old Bridge to Slane, in a direct line, is somewhat under three.

On the evening of the 29th, when James crossed the river, the distance between his rear-guard and William's advance, was about eight miles, and on the morning of the 30th the latter appeared, and halted his army facing the concave bend of the river, behind a line of hills which partially concealed it from observation, while awaiting his artillery, which was still some miles in his rear.

With that promptitude which characterized all his movements since his arrival in the country, he immediately ordered an examination of the river from Old Bridge to Slane, and proceeded himself with a detachment of cavalry to reconnoitre the position of the royal army. While so engaged he was struck by a cannon-shot that grazed his shoulder and drew a little blood. This caused a report of his death to be spread throughout the camp, and created the greatest alarm among his followers; but, calling for a napkin, he stopped the blood, and, putting on another coat, passed through the ranks to restore the confidence of his soldiers, and then completed his reconnoissance.[24] Towards noon he moved his army forward

---

[24] The many conflicting statements of this trifling affair are set at rest by a letter which may be seen in the Dublin *Nation* for May, 1865. It was written by Lord Meath—who was present at the battle,—is dated July 5, 1690, and is a rare specimen of epistolary correspondence. Enlarging on the affair, Pinnock, in his Catechism of Irish History, says: "Burke, an Irish gunner, having grazed the arm of William with a cannon-shot, and having taken a fresh aim, on which he might depend, James desired him 'not to make his child a widow.' It

to the river, when, his cannon having arrived, he established his batteries along the heights, ordered a heavy cannonade to be kept up against the Irish centre, and, retiring within his lines, summoned his generals to receive his plan of action.

It was the intention of William at first to cross the river at Slane during the advanced hours of the night, and falling on James by surprise, to strike his left, and turn it from the road to Dublin. The Duke of Schomberg, with characteristic caution, would have opposed this proposition, on the ground that though James's army appeared small from the English line of sight, he might have large reserves behind Donore. But the duke was again rebuked by the prince, and notified to retire, which he did, deeply mortified, and received his orders afterwards in his tent, with the querulous remark, that "they were the first that had ever been sent him!" Bating this, the utmost harmony pervaded the council of William, and confidence reigned supreme throughout his camp.

But, notwithstanding the discourtesy shown by William to the Duke of Schomberg, the advice of that old veteran had its due weight in his council; the determination to assail the Irish left during the night was abandoned, and the following plan of action was adopted: Of the 40,000 men of which the prince's army now consisted, about 13,000, composed of the Dutch Guards, the Enniskillen infantry, and the Brandenburg and Huguenot regiments, under the command of Duke Schomberg and Caillemotte,[25] formed his centre, opposite to the same division of the royal army. His right, 10,000 horse and foot, under Count Schomberg and General Douglas, respectively, was extended in the direction of Slane; and his left, about 12,000 strong, comprising the Dutch, Danish, and Enniskillen horse, and the British and Scotch infantry, was drawn up towards Old Bridge, and to be commanded by himself in person. His immense train of artillery, variously estimated at from fifty to sixty pieces, including several mortars, was portioned out to each division, the weight of it being placed against the Irish centre; and his reserves, about 5,000, were stationed in the low ground to his rear, within easy supporting distance of his right and left, and not more than a mile from either. The Count of Schomberg was to open the battle at daybreak by forcing the Pass of Slane, and turning the Irish left; when this should be accomplished, the duke was to cross at the centre, and, carrying the intrenchments opposite, press them back from the river; biding these results, the prince himself would cross at Old Bridge, and, flanking their right, cut off their retreat to Dublin. Thus, by a general movement, the royal army would be completely overthrown, and the war terminated by a single blow:—the chances of defeat had no place in his calculation.

---

is also asserted, and with apparent truth, that having seen his own troops overcoming those of William, he cried out repeatedly: 'O spare my unfortunate subjects!' and having turned the tide of battle against himself, by gross mismanagement, he fled precipitately to Dublin, leaving his Irish subjects behind him." Inadequate artillery, and gross mismanagement on the part of the king, were, no doubt, the causes of the final result of the battle; but such exclamations, even by this "most Christian king," would be either too saintly or too infamous, and on his own authority the statement is here rejected. It was he himself that ordered the battery down to fire at William. (See Berwick's Memoirs, vol. ix., p. 396.)

[25] Caillemotte was a brother of General Ruvigney, and Count Schomberg was a son of the duke of that name.

As William had the advantage of ground—that is to say, the northern bank of the river was steep and firm down to its margin, while the southern side was low and broken—James had thrown his army well back towards the hill of Donore, and during the interval had made the following disposition: His centre, about 8,000 men of all arms, was arranged in two lines; one, comprising the musketeers and pikemen, under Major-General Dorrington and the Marquis de Hoquincourt, was placed in the intrenchments along the river, and the other, composed of the exempts, under General Nugent and Taafe, Earl of Carlingford, in the broken ground behind it. For the support of these the infantry regiments of Tyrconnell, Parker, and Gordon O'Neil, and the dragoons of Lords Clare and Dungan, were held between a small village and the hill of Donore, as the ground nearer to the river was low, and commanded by the enemy's artillery. His right wing, about 3,000 men, of whom but eight battalions were infantry, rested near the town of Old Bridge, opposed to William's left, under the command of Lieutenant-General Hamilton and the Duke of Berwick. His left, composed of the French troops under the Duke de Lausun and M. de la Hoquette, stood about a mile from his centre, in the direction of Slane; while that important Pass, which, he tells us in his Memoirs, he expected to be William's first point of assault, and which lay three miles from his centre, by the course of the river, was entirely neglected until late at night, when, at the urgent request of his generals, it was occupied by Sir Neale O'Neil and his regiment of dragoons. A strip of moor-land, extending from Old Bridge to the Pass of Slane, ran behind his right and centre, traversing the base of Donore round to the southeast; and behind this, but well drawn up against the hill, he held a reserve of nearly 3,000 infantry and cavalry, the former under Sir Charles Carney, and the latter under Sarsfield and Brigadier-General Maxwell.

How little soever conversant in military affairs, one cannot fail to see the almost insuperable disadvantages of the Jacobite army. Lying on the convex of the river, with an army scarce half the number of the opposing force; its supporting distance to the Pass of Slane treble to that of the enemy; the ground near the river unsuited to the action of cavalry, which was its main dependence; and its ordnance miserably inferior in number and calibre, it was barely possible to repulse the enemy, but almost impossible to turn a repulse into a victory. To an ordinary observation the chances of battle would thus present themselves: by intrepidity and superior valor, James might hold his ground until the return of tide, which would suspend it, or if the enemy succeeded in crossing without his ordnance, he might draw up all his force on the heights, and by one of those desperate and sudden efforts that man is sometimes capable of, hurl him back into the river. There was no other alternative between him and defeat; the vast numerical advantage of the Prince of Orange rendered the former improbable, and the lack of military ardor in the king himself was not calculated to evoke the latter.

With a will concentrated on the object of his mission, exultant in power, and personally brave and enterprising, William's plan was simple, bold, and aggressive. Weak in numbers, and straitened in resources, that of James was tortuous, cautious, and weakly defensive. Fortitude and military capacity he is said to have possessed, and they would seem not to have entirely deserted him on this occasion; but in that desperate daring which alone could wring success from the surrounding disadvantages, he was utterly deficient. His army was gallant, and even eager for the conflict, and a rival whose persistent malignity would have roused the meekest spirit, confronted him; but the blood did not course warmly in his veins at the devotion of the one, nor did vengeance steel him to action at the sight of the other. Trepidity was manifest in all his motions, and he had not even the self-control to hide it from his soldiers. The Pass of Duleek, in his rear, claimed more of his attention than the enemy on his front; for, while ordering the battle, he was devising a retreat, and had, in their sight, dispatched one-half his artillery in the evening for the defence of the capital. It therefore mattered very little how he disposed of the remainder—six pieces, on a line of four Irish miles.[26]

So stood the hosts on the night of June 30th, 1690, prepared to deliver battle on the dawn of the morrow; and, as darkness settled down and hid each from the view of the other, the feelings that swayed them may be easier felt than depicted. One feeling, that in such moments pervades every bosom alike, from the private to the king, must have been theirs in common—the hope to survive the carnage;—in all else their thoughts must have been as different as the causes they represented. The mercenary can have but one passion and one object—to slay and to dominate. The patriot has many, and all are sacred. The poetry of emotion is his, and over none does it exert a more boundless influence than over the race of which this king's army was mainly composed. The memories of the past, standing out like the immemorial hills; the voices of futurity coming up the long vista of time, and all pleading the reversal of a fate more cruel than Egyptian bondage: while clearer to the ear and nearer to the heart come the pleadings of kindred, and the anxious household lifting up their prayers to heaven for the devoted hearts that shield them from ruin, death—dishonor. All these speak to them, and a thousand fancies, taking the form of life, pass in solemn review, till the hardiest soldier, with moistened eye, and heart full to breaking, grasps his sword, compresses his lip, looks out for the dawning, and sighs for relief in conflict.

But did not the Irish of that day deceive themselves? This king, whose cause they had espoused, was not their king. His restoration would still leave their country an appanage of the British Crown, and his house was a name of woe and desolation throughout the land! Would her future, under it, be much brighter than her past? There was, no doubt, many a thoughtful mind in that Irish army that had all those misgivings; but this was not the time to indulge them. Nor should we of the present day be hypercritical. Royalty was then something more than a name, and we should not judge the events of the seventeenth century by the light of the nineteenth, nor the Ireland of untoward circumstances as the nation of her people's will. To the memory of this unhappy king this truth should be generously conceded.... He could have retained his throne had he violated his conscience. He

---

[26] Seeing the superiority of William, in numbers and artillery, he was now as eager to avoid as he had been before to court a battle. The French generals also wished to decline an engagement. The Irish declared themselves ready to fight. Under these circumstances, a kind of half-measure was adopted. It was determined to hazard a partial battle, and to retreat without risking a general engagement. To this strange determination James, in all probability, owed the loss of his kingdom.—(Taylor, vol. ii., p. 148.)

could have ruled the Irish people as his predecessors had done, and at that time they had no power to stay him; for the Catholic descendants of the Palesmen were firm in their allegiance to the English throne, and the native race was destitute of means to strike for separation. He had forfeited his crown and jeopardized his power, for right. He had emancipated them from a bondage servile to mind and body. He was the first royal champion of civil and religious liberty. He had offered them justice in his power, and appealed to their loyalty in his adversity. His cause was their cause. He was banished by his own people, outraged by his own family; he came to them in his bereavement, and to their honor, be it recorded, they did not forsake him! His very injuries threw a sacred influence around him, and as he sacrificed to justice, they paid him the homage of their blood!

Yet, in truth, he was not their king;—not the ideal king of the Irish race. That should be a native king; one infusing nationality through every hamlet in the land, and defending its liberties against a world in arms! Six hundred years had failed to eradicate the hope of such a king from the hearts of every successive generation, and every outrage of the invader only rendered it the more indelible. The place, too, was historic. Every hill and valley, from Drogheda to Clonard, in rath and ruin, bore ample testimony of their aspiration for native rule. Tara and Skreen, now plainly visible in the soft moonlight of summer, stood out in relief against the southern sky, and it is no stretch of the imagination to say: from that same Pass of Slane, the ancestor of Sir Neale O'Neil, had, nearly 900 years before, reconnoitred the Danish host and marked it for destruction. Many a chief and many a clan of his martial house had, since then, crossed the Boyne to do battle with the invader, but never a braver soldier than he, nor a more devoted following than that which now counted the moments by the reverberation of the enemy's cannon along its banks, and looked through the night for the eventful dawning.[27]

The night wore slowly away, and as its shadows were blending into the gray dawn of morning, the cannonade which had been kept up since the preceding noon from William's batteries ceased for a time, and the beat to arms was distinctly heard on the heights of Donore. It was promptly answered by a roll from the Irish camp, and the troops on each side were immediately in motion, and deploying down towards the river. An hour of hurried preparation now passed on, when the waters of the gentle river were again startled from their short repose by a heavy peal along the whole English line, the smoke of which having cleared away, William's left, the cavalry in advance, was seen doubling the curve in the river, and advancing steadily towards the Pass of Slane. The firing thus resumed, was now kept up incessantly from the English left and centre, and as the sun appeared above the hills, and both armies stood out bolder on the foreground, William himself, accompanied by Prince George of Denmark, the Prince of Nassau, and the

---

[27] Nial-Caille, the last monarch of Ireland, of the house of O'Neil, after having defeated the Danes and Normans in several engagements, was drowned in the river Callan in Kilkenny, while engaged in raising the country for their total expulsion. One of his attendants having fallen into the river, he was trying to save him, and in the attempt lost his own life. The crown of sovereignty passed from the house of O'Neil, and it was not until the reign of Bryan, more than a century after, that the Danes were finally extirpated.—(See McGeoghagen's History of Ireland.)

Duke of Wurtemberg, and surrounded by a grand cavalcade, was observed reviewing his army, and, by word and example, infusing hope and courage through all its ranks.

King James saw all that was passing from the heights of Donore, and as Count Schomberg and Douglas moved in the direction of Slane, he ordered de Lausun to move his troops in the same direction. Then, after seeing the remainder of his baggage on its way to Dublin,[28] whither the half of his artillery had already been sent, he stood to watch the issue of the day, with much composure of manner and much Christian resignation, but none of that military ardor by which a gallant general often imparts a spirit and energy to a small army that render it invincible in the hour of battle. Not so, however, with the Duke of Tyrconnell. Though bowed by age, and broken in health, he moved from rank to rank, exhorting all to bravery; and it is very questionable which felt most solicitude at that hour—that king for the fate of his crown, or that patriot for the cause of his country. As for Sarsfield, he had little to do in the affairs of that day; for both he and General Maxwell were in continual attendance on the king's person, and his attention, with the exception of one visit to his right, was entirely divided between the reserve on Donore and the French troops on his left. Hamilton and Berwick were at their post on the right, and well had it been for James and his cause had he tarried in Dublin and committed the marshalling of his army to those generals, and the issue of the day to the King of battles.

Apprised of the design of the enemy on his position, O'Neil had made such preparations as time allowed for his reception. Around the pass on both sides of the river he had drawn intrenchments, and as the morning dawned had thrown forward a small detachment to impede his progress. The ground over which he approached was favorable to defensive operations, being much broken and interspersed with hedges: these natural impediments, and the weight of his artillery, rendered his movements slow and irregular; the fire of the skirmishers met him at every step as he neared the pass, so that it was eight o'clock before he had forced them back within their intrenchments.

Here the fight was renewed with great stubbornness, and continued for two hours longer, when Schomberg, with the loss of two hundred men, forced the position, and the dragoons retired with the loss of one-fourth their number, bearing away the body of their leader, mortally wounded, and renewed the contest on the other side of the river. Schomberg immediately commenced to cross, and the king, apprised of the state of affairs here, sent Sarsfield, with sixty dragoons and a piece of artillery, to oppose him; but these succors only arrived in time to see the defenders driven from their intrenchments, and the troops of Schomberg drawn out on the southern bank to receive them.

All further attempts to check the progress of the assailants were now futile; the dragoons retired on their supports; the gun brought down by Sarsfield got "bogged," and had to be abandoned, and Schomberg, his artillery being got over, deployed by his right, on the outer side of the marsh, to turn the left of the king's

[28] On seeing this, the king gave orders for his left to move in the same direction, and sent the remainder of the baggage to Dublin. (Memoirs of Berwick, p. 397, vol. i.)

army. He had, however, scarcely got clear of the river, when the troops of de Lausun appeared on the inner side of the marsh to oppose him. The force of the latter was 6,000 men, within support of a reserve of 3,000; it was fresh, finely appointed, and the marsh at this place was narrow and practicable to horse and foot; but he showed no disposition to engage, although Schomberg halted and drew up to offer him battle. After some time the troops on both sides were put in motion, Schomberg still moving by his right, and de Lausun by his left in the same direction, the marsh gradually widening round towards the rear of Donore, until nearly a mile intervened, when an engagement became impracticable, and the Irish left was flanked.

In the mean time, King James, seeing that Count Schomberg had crossed the river, believed that the other division of William's army would also move in the same direction, and that the entire battle would be finally transferred to his left. He therefore determined to withdraw his own right and centre from the river, to the support of de Lausun, and with this intention he now proceeded to his right. There seeing that William's left and centre were still drawn up on the opposite bank, and being opposed in his design by Tyrconnell, he returned to his left, where Count Schomberg and de Lausun were still confronting each other. Posting his reserves on the right of the latter, and riding up to him, he ordered him to charge the enemy across the intervening ground; but the order was disobeyed, although Schomberg halted again and formed to invite an action. In this state of perplexity the king rode back to the reserves, placed the infantry at the edge of the marsh, supported on each side by his cavalry, with the foot dragoons filling up the intervals, and approaching M. de la Hoquette, *"whispered him"* to lead on the French infantry. The latter was about to comply with this *request*, when he was checked by de Lausun; at this time, Sarsfield and Maxwell, who had been out inspecting the ground in front, returned, and pronounced it impracticable to cavalry, it being traversed by two double ditches with a rivulet flowing between them. So the king was convinced, and de Lausun was relieved from his importunity. In this manner the two wings continued to manoeuvre the situation each moment growing more critical, as Schomberg neared the end of the marsh, where the road turned towards Duleek, and led on to the capital.

Thus, through some motive of de Lausun, never after explained, and through the absence of control in the unfortunate king, never forgiven, the French auxiliaries, and with them the Irish reserve,—a body of 3,000 men,—were neutralized; the Irish left was completely turned, and the remainder of the army, not exceeding 11,000, was left to contend with 30,000 under William and the Duke of Schomberg.

In the mean time a considerable change had taken place in William's left and centre. The Duke of Schomberg had discovered another ford in the direction of Slane, and when that pass was carried, had moved by his right to avail himself of the advantages it offered, while William had moved by his left somewhat nearer to the town of Drogheda. These changes necessitated corresponding movements in the Irish line. A greater extension was the consequence, and some regiments of its rear were extended to oppose the Duke of Schomberg; but still they offered a good front, and awaited the enemy in confidence.

It was well on to noon, and the tide was on the return, when the firing ceased on Duke Schomberg's front, and the Dutch Guards, accompanied by their band, detached themselves from the main body and moved down to the river. Here the music of the band ceased; the guards formed in compacted columns, twenty abreast, and commenced the passage of the river in the face of a well-directed fire.[29] When they had all got below the level of their own artillery, its fire was again directed against the Irish intrenchments, and compelled the men there to lie close in their works, until the guards got beyond the mid current and began to ascend on the opposite side, when they quitted their defences, and advanced into the river to meet them, and, as they closed, Major Arthur, of the Irish Guards, singling out the leader of the enemy, passed his pike through his body. This stimulated his men to action; a desperate conflict ensued; the Dutch Guards were held in check for a considerable time, and many fell on both sides, and were trampled beneath the current.

The Dutch Guards were the household troops of the Prince of Orange; were fighting under his eye, and formed a compact body of five thousand men, while the Irish were mostly raw levies, inferior in number, and indifferently armed with pikes and muskets. The result was doubtful for some time, until Major Arthur was wounded and conveyed to the rear; disheartened and borne back by the weight of numbers, his troops gradually gave ground; and the Dutch troops advanced and effected a landing. As they reached the firm ground above the river, they were charged by the dragoons of Clare and Dungan, and wavered; but Lord Dungan being slain, the dragoons became panic-stricken and retreated, nor could they again be brought to the charge. In this state of indecision the Dutch renewed their assault, and established a position in the broken ground behind the Irish line. The position was a strong one, and at once laid bare the intrenchments on the river, while it afforded a protection against the Irish cavalry; and here they remained during the succeeding events of the day, suffering severely, but defying every attempt to dislodge them.

William, who witnessed this, felt deep concern for the fate of his household troops. They had accompanied him in all his campaigns, and his care for them, in peace and war, was that of a patriarch for his household. From his point of view, their condition was now perilous in the highest degree, they being surrounded by the enemy on all sides, and in danger of total destruction before relief could reach them. To him, the movements of Schomberg, always slow and measured, seemed now painfully so; and, suspending his advance against the Irish right, he rode down to the centre, to precipitate the troops forming there for the relief of his famous guards. Two regiments of the Huguenot troops and one of British infantry were immediately formed, and, under the leadership of Caillemotte, commenced the passage of the river.

Hamilton, from the right of the Irish line, had followed these events with a feeling akin to that of William. He believed, like him, that the fate of the Dutch troops was sealed, could the reinforcements of the enemy be held in check or re-

---

[29] The water at this time was low, not reaching the drums of the band, which accompanied them. — (Haverty's History.)

pulsed; but he also saw that the intrenchments at the centre were partially abandoned from the effects of the enemy's fire on their rear, and that all now depended on intrepid action. He therefore detached two regiments of infantry from the right, to march close by the river, and throw themselves before Caillemotte, while he hastened himself, by a more circuitous route, with the cavalry, to sustain them.

The troops of Caillemotte advanced rapidly to the mid-current, where they were met as the Dutch Guards had been, and, like them, were forcing their way against the Irish infantry, when Hamilton reached the scene of action. As he appeared, the infantry opened to the right and left to make way, and, with unchecked impulse, he rushed to the onset. The effect was instantaneous. In a moment, the enemy were helplessly broken, trampled, and dispersed. Caillemotte, two colonels, and two lieutenant-colonels were slain, more than half his command were either killed or wounded, and the remainder fled to the opposite side, pursued by the victorious cavalry. As they pressed the fugitives up to their lines, the Danish horse were precipitated against them, but were instantly broken, hurled back in confusion, and closely pressed on the columns now forming under the Duke of Schomberg. Rushing on wildly, and crying out "Horse! horse!" in great alarm, they created a panic, which was near ending in a total rout; when William again appeared among them, restored order in the ranks, and the Irish cavalry leisurely retired.

William now collected all the infantry of the centre, while Schomberg, placing himself at the head of the cavalry, entered the river, and advanced with the same coolness and caution that had hitherto characterized all his movements. The Irish horse had just returned from the pursuit, and were drawn up on the river to oppose him. They did not wait for his whole force to get in motion, but as he approached the middle of the river, they bore down on him with their wonted impetuosity. The effect was the same as before. Schomberg and Walker of Derry were slain; dismay and inextricable confusion was the consequence, and all retreated to the northern side to reform. Taylor, in his short but life-like portraiture of this battle, says of the event just detailed: "Had James chosen this moment to place himself at the head of his troops, for one general charge, or had the French auxiliaries attacked the Dutch in flank, the event of the battle would certainly have restored his crown!" The poor king—he was at that very moment concerting a retreat on his left, outraged by his French general; and even his reserves were two miles from the scene of action!

This was the crisis of the day. The tide was now making fast; the water was nearly waist high in the river, and half an hour more would render a crossing impossible for that day. William could no longer delay his movements on the left, and so, ordering Sir John Hanmer and the Prince of Nassau to reform his demoralized troops at the centre, and lead them on for the relief of his guards, he hastened to the left to make a last effort to restore the battle.

Had Sarsfield and Maxwell now appeared with the reserves, and left de Lausun to watch Count Schomberg, the battle had been won, or, at least, suspended; for at this moment the balance leaned to the Jacobite arms, and delay would have been tantamount to a victory. During the approaching night, the division of

Count Schomberg, cut off from support, and lost in the intricacies of the ground behind Donore, could have been totally destroyed; there were three thousand troops within a few hours' march of the field, and the morning would have opened with fairer prospects of success.[30] But all these chances were lost by the fears of the king for his capital; no support appeared for the centre; and Hamilton, after performing prodigies of valor, was forced to retire again to the right, to oppose the passage of the Prince of Orange.

William, whose design through the day had been to strike the Irish army in the rear of its right, turn it from the direction of the capital, and form a junction with Count Schomberg, was now compelled to abandon that project, and lead his left to the support of his centre. For this purpose he marshalled a force of about 12,000 infantry and cavalry. The Danish and Dutch horse, bearing the standard of Nassau, were placed in the advance; after them came the foot, and the Enniskillen horse brought up the rear. Placing himself between the cavalry and infantry, he entered the river, the water rising to the flanks of the horses as they reached the mid-current. Hamilton, who had just returned from the Irish centre, watched their approach with great anxiety, until they began to ascend the southern side and had gained a surer footing; when, ordering his infantry to retire, he withdrew the cavalry also, to reform for the charge. William, on seeing this movement, believed that they were abandoning the field, and urged his cavalry more hastily forward. He was soon undeceived: the Irish horse had but withdrawn for greater impulse; in another moment they dashed forward; the Danes were scattered right and left, bearing back the Prince among them, and the flanks of his infantry lay completely exposed. The Irish cavalry had, for the third time that day, asserted their superiority.

William's situation was now desperate. His Danish and Dutch horse were scattered and swimming in the river; his infantry were hardly able to bear up against its current; the Irish cavalry lay on his front, and their infantry had opened with effect on his flanks. But he was equal to the emergency, and his gallantry at this trying moment would go far to erase a very dark record. Making his way to the head of his Enniskilleners, now about to advance, he asked promptly "What they would do for him?" They cried out with one impulse that they would follow where he led, and hastening forward after him, they threw themselves between their infantry and the Irish cavalry, now reformed on the bank above them. The sight of these troops, their own countrymen, protecting the foreign mercenaries of William, roused the spirit of vengeance in the breasts of the Irish, and, wheeling as before, they swept forward in one compacted mass. The Enniskilleners did not await the shock, but turned and fled across the river, deserting their general at his greatest need; nor could they again be rallied until the battle was decided.[31]

---

[30] This force actually arrived next day, and narrowly escaped being captured by the victors. Two of them were taken and hanged as spies, and the rest retired after the Irish army. Had these been in the battle, the Irish army would have been twenty-three thousand, according with the estimate of the Duke of Berwick.

[31] Taylor, after commenting in indignant terms on this conduct of the Enniskilleners, adds: "Their apologists say that they misunderstood their orders, and returned again. However this may be, it is certain that William, ever after, viewed this part of his force with

William, on being deserted by the Enniskilleners, again rode through his infantry and reformed their disordered ranks. The Danish and Dutch rallied, and formed round his person, and, with the desperate resolve to do or die, he pressed resolutely forward.

The scene along the whole line was now terribly grand and exciting. The entire left and centre of the English army were in motion, and, stirred to the highest daring by the danger of their Prince and the exigency of the hour, were pressing through the river simultaneously. Hanmer led the cavalry of the centre, and the Prince of Nassau the infantry, each vieing with the other for precedence. The latter was crossing at the ford lately attempted by Caillemotte and the Duke of Schomberg, and the former at one hitherto neglected, which lay nearer to Old Bridge, and offered more immediate support to the Prince of Orange. This disposition nearly connected the English left and centre, and caused another derangement of the Irish lines opposite. The Dutch Guards, too, who still held their lodgement on the side of Donore, rallied as their succor approached, and drew a portion of their fire from the compacted masses of Nassau on their front. Three regiments of the Irish Guards—those of Tyrconnell, Parker, and Gordon O'Neil—the exempts under Nugent, and a few squadrons of cavalry, were thrown against Hanmer, and, animated by Tyrconnell and Dorrington, were opposing a most deadly resistance; while Berwick and Hamilton still disputed the passage of William, and held him in check on the right.

But the balance of the day was inclining, and the fates were again propitious to William. Nassau pressed fiercely on. The Dutch Guards assumed the offensive, and their fire became destructive. The Irish generals exhausted every effort to animate their troops, but in vain. Attacked in front and rear by superior numbers, they at last broke, abandoned the river, and withdrew in good order towards Donore. The command of Nassau, on ascending from the river, were joined by the Dutch Blues, and both turned their attention to where the Irish Guards were still offering a stern resistance to Hanmer.[32] The position of these troops now became critical in the extreme, and a short time would see them either all slain or captured by the enemy. There was scarce an alternative, when Berwick arrived with a portion of the cavalry of the right, charged vigorously, and held the enemy in check until the remnant of these famous guards retired. This was the most destructive conflict of the day to the Irish; "for," says King James in his Memoirs, "the greater part of the exempts and brigadiers in both corps were killed, likewise the Earl of Carlingford, M. d'Amande, and several other volunteers that served with them. Nugent and Casanova were wounded in Tyrconnell's, Major O'Meara and Sir Charles Tooke were killed, and Bada wounded. In Parker's, the Colonel was wounded; Green, the Lieutenant-Colonel, Doddington, the Major, and several officers were killed; and in both squadrons there remained but thirty men unhurt."

Hamilton, with the remaining cavalry, no longer able to offer an effectual re-

---

contempt, not unmingled with hatred." (Vol. II., page 151.)

[32] Sir Jno. Hanmer crossed the river nigh a place where, the day before, the enemy had a battery of six guns, but now they were gone, as most of their artillery, etc. (Story's Imp. History, Vol. I.—The Boyne.)

sistance on the river, retired before William, who crossed, wheeled to his right, and pressed on towards his centre. As the English forces united, the Irish horse also converged, and formed on their front for the protection of their infantry, forming in line of battle on the hill. A series of conflicts now ensued between the Irish cavalry and the converging forces of the English left and centre, which are described by the annalist Story, as of the most desperate character: for more than half an hour, during which all "were completely enveloped in dust and smoke," neither gained or lost an inch; and when no longer able to withstand the overwhelming force against them, the Irish cavalry retired, reformed, charged the enemy again and again, "ten times in succession," and at last fell back to the flanks of their infantry, to make another effort to redeem the day. William advanced boldly on the position now assumed by the Irish army, but, astonished at the imposing front they still presented, he halted to array his troops, when the Irish infantry, taking advantage of this hesitation, bore down on him. The first and second line gave way; but their force was spent against the Dutch Guards, and they retired; the cavalry now charged again and broke the guards, but the wings closing on them, they were completely surrounded. A terrific struggle took place; General Hamilton was wounded, unhorsed, and captured; Berwick had his horse killed, but was saved by a trooper; Colonel Sheldon cut his way through at the head of the cavalry, and again reformed them on the front; and while the two armies stood thus, neither advancing nor receding, the order for a general retreat sounded along the Irish line.

While the events just described were transpiring on the river, Count Schomberg continued to hold de Lausun inactive, wearing slowly round by his right; and as the Irish centre retreated on Donore, he had reached the termination of the lowland, and thrown forward his cavalry on the road leading to Dublin. King James, on seeing this, got alarmed for the safety of the capital—should Schomberg get the start of him,—so directing de Lausun to defend the road, he issued an order for a general retreat, and, taking the regiments of Brown and Purcell as an escort, withdrew from the field and pursued his way to Dublin. On receipt of this order, "the Irish army retreated" from the hill, bringing off all their standards and artillery;[33]—they crossed the lowlands to the north of Donore;—and the Boyne was lost.

It was six o'clock in the evening. The infantry soon reached the town of Duleek, the French bringing up the rear, and formed in line of battle behind the river Nanny. The cavalry arrived soon after, and had just crossed the river as Count Schomberg drew up and formed on the other side. Both armies then remained facing each other for over an hour; the Irish, seeing that the enemy did not advance, began to retire, and Schomberg followed. The Irish halted and reformed again, in a long ravine, near the village of Neal; the enemy also halted, but did not attack; and in this posture night settled down on the two armies. It was now nine o'clock; the Irish resumed their march, and the enemy following no farther, they continued their way unmolested towards Dublin. William remained on the field. Some say that sorrow for the death of Schomberg was the cause of his not pressing the foe. It

[33] They brought off five pieces. The other got bogged near the Pass of Slane, and was abandoned.

might have been caused by a lack of artillery, as his train had not crossed the river. Perhaps he might have been apprehensive that the garrison of Drogheda would issue out and capture or destroy it in his absence, as they might have done during the latter events of the day; but whether it was one of those causes, or a combination of them, now matters but little; he had won the Battle of the Boyne, and it was enough for a day.

The principal personages killed in the Jacobite army were Lord Dungan, Taaf Earl of Carlingford, Sir Neale O'Neil, and the Marquis de Hoquincourt; in that of the Prince of Orange, the Duke of Schomberg,[34] Caillemotte, and Walker of Derry, who commanded a regiment of Enniskilleners. Besides these, several officers of distinction fell on both sides; among whom were two colonels, two lieutenant-colonels, in the division of Caillemotte, and Sir Charles Tooke, Majors Arthur and O'Meara, and the Chevalier de Vaudry, in Tyrconnell's. The number of officers of subordinate rank killed and wounded on each side was very great, considering the loss in private soldiers, which did not exceed one thousand in either. The number of the wounded in the army of William is not known, and, excepting Hamilton, there is no mention of prisoners being taken on either side.

Such was the Battle of the Boyne. Memorable for the extinction of the Stuart dynasty, for the politico-religious government it entailed on England, and for the wrongs innumerable it bequeathed to Ireland; but for nothing more memorable than as a well-contested and long-doubtful battle. It was one fought by twenty thousand men,[35] indifferently armed, with only six pieces of artillery, and under a king whose conduct would have disconcerted the best army in the world, from six in the morning until six in the evening, on a river fordable at every rood of its length, against an army of thirty thousand[36] veteran mercenaries, with experienced leaders, cannon at will, and a prince of great military skill and daring. From the beginning their temerity seemed almost madness, to the bravest and most experienced, and their king was besought to relinquish it. Yet three times through the day the battle seemed equally poised, and once victory was assuredly within their grasp, had their king but displayed one-half the courage and intrepidity of his rival. Through the loss of this field the future was foreshadowed. There the Irish army lost prestige abroad—and at home every thing but their manhood: yet seldom was that better vindicated than on that "ill-fated river;" and as they turned their last look on it, and saw the long lines of William winding up to Donore, well might they exclaim in their anguish, "Change kings, and we'll fight the battle again!" The kings were changed, but not for them. On that river their web of destiny was woven, and though they battled on bravely for a time, patriotic devotion and heroic sacrifice were in vain.

---

[34] Schomberg was shot by O'Toole, an Irish officer of the exempts, who took him, from the blue ribbon which he wore, to be the Prince of Orange. (Memoirs, 398.)

[35] If the French auxiliaries, six thousand, and the Irish reserves, three thousand, which performed no service throughout the day, save watching the movements of Count Schomberg, be deducted, the number actually participating in the action was only eleven thousand men.

[36] This force is exclusive of William's right, which consisted of ten thousand men under Count Schomberg and General Douglas, with ten pieces of cannon and two mortars.

CHAPTER X.

FINAL DEPARTURE OF KING JAMES—A RETRO-SPECT OF HIS CHARACTER.

The consequences of "the Boyne" are too well known for comment; what a reversal of that day's events might have done, it is painful to contemplate. A suspension of the battle for a week—even for a day—would have changed the whole complexion of the war, and turned the finger of destiny. The very hour that William drew up at Townly Hall, on the 30th of June, the combined fleets of England and Holland had been almost utterly destroyed by Admiral Tourville at Beachy Head: and as he crossed the Boyne next day, the combined armies of the League, under Prince Waldeck, had been overthrown at Fleurus by the French army under the renowned Marshal Luxemburg. While James was hastening to Dublin to quit his dominions forever, the fleet of Admiral de Seignelay was unmoored, waiting a favorable wind to sail for Ireland to destroy William's transports round the coast; the fleet of Tourville was riding triumphant at the mouth of the Thames, and "there were not," says Hume, "ten thousand armed men in all England." There, disaffection was on the increase, the Jacobite cause was gaining strength, and it was not easy to decide, even with the loss of the Boyne, which was at that moment in the more critical plight—the victor or the vanquished.

Had any nominal force been thrown into England at this moment, all had been at once recovered; for William, if indeed he could, would have to withdraw his army from Ireland "to save the larger stake," and that country, relieved of his foreign veterans, would soon rectify itself; or, if compelled to remain in Ireland, and continue the war for awhile, he would certainly lose the other two kingdoms, and the third would follow as a consequence. His affairs in Holland, too, were in an unpromising condition. The arms of France were everywhere predominant, and this was a matter of deeper importance to William, than even the loss of the English throne, which, 'tis said, he ambitioned only so far as it enabled him to cope with his proud and detested enemy, Louis XIV. Such a happy combination of events, dashed but by a single defeat, in which only about one thousand men were lost, would have imparted courage and hope to any heart, but that of this unfortunate king. But from the first to the last his course, if not leading to the ruin of a noble people, might be read as a great "Comedy of Errors." He seemed continually under the spell of some evil genius that lulled him to a sense of security, while leading him to destruction:—and from his refusal of the first generous offer of King Louis, through M. Bonrepas, while he was yet upon the throne of England, the series of mishaps and miscalculations through which he stumbled, seems indeed to mark out a manifest destiny.

At Salisbury, when deserted by his nobles, he had but to choose generals from the ranks, and pledging his army the estates forfeited by this treason, he could have created a revolution within a revolution, and held his throne at will as the sovereign of the people. If, instead of going to Ireland, where four-fifths of the people were unalterably attached to him, he had gone to Scotland, we are told that the whole country would have risen under Dundee; and William would have had two countries to conquer instead of one. On his arrival in Ireland, he weakened the strength of that country by sending 3,000 trained soldiers to the assistance of Dundee; under the advice of Secretary Melford, a Scotchman, and against the advice of Tyrconnell, who had seen the fate of the soldiers sent under Hamilton to England. He next disconcerted the arrangements for the surrender of Derry, and afterwards, through a weak punctilio, refused the second offer, and protracted the rebellion of Ulster until the arrival of Schomberg. Again, deaf to the entreaties of his generals, he virtually saved the army of invasion from total destruction, on the plea that winter and desertion would do the work of war, on the foreigners. As time advanced, and the war assumed greater proportions, his blunders became more glaring and more fatal. In the spring of 1690, he sent Lord Mountcashel, the best general then in the country, and 6,000 men, "the flower of the Irish army," to France, in lieu of 6,000 nondescripts, under the lead of de Lausun, a man, if not of dubious courage, of very dubious loyalty, and to sustain this equivalent in Louis' army, sent 4,000 more the same year. He fought the Battle of the Boyne against the counsel of his generals, and when fortune seemed to favor his army, he lost an offered victory by trepidity and indecision. And, now, to complete a series of blunders by one more fatal than all: instead of sending Tyrconnell, or some other statesman of diplomatic ability, to plead his necessities before his "brother of France," he formed the resolution of appearing in person at the French court, where the general rejoicing over recent victories could only render his forlorn condition the more marked, and his suit the more neglected. And, yet, through all, the people of Ireland loved him, and followed him with a devotion deepened and intensified by each successive misfortune. Her young men presented themselves in thousands, aye, in tens of thousands, at every call for new levies, but to go away and fold their arms, while their country was sacrificed! Such a country! and such a king! We read the history of La Vendée in vain, for an exemplification of the fidelity of the one; and there is no parallel in the category of royal refugees, save that of the fabled Lear, for the misfortunes and melo-dramatism of the other!

When he arrived in Dublin, he summoned his council, and communicated his intention of quitting the country to solicit aid from France. It is but justice to state that he says they were unanimous in their approval; that de Lausun was importunate in his persuasion to that effect, and that letters, lately received from his queen, were still more urgent, and that so his resolution was confirmed. Ordering that the army should rendezvous at Limerick, each colonel leading his men thither as he might, he committed the government of the kingdom again to Tyrconnell, and, after giving some salutary advice on the regulation of affairs in the city until the arrival of the Prince of Orange, he made an exposition of his principles, and of the hopes he yet entertained of establishing them; then, in a very simple and affecting address, he bade farewell to his friends, and left the city under escort of two regiments of the Guards, those of Brown and Purcell. From Dublin he proceeded to Bray, where he left those troops to defend the bridge there in case of pursuit, and continued his route to Wicklow, where he spent the night at the residence of a gentleman named Hacket; from Wicklow he journeyed to Duncannon, and thence to Waterford. The detail of this route in the "Memoirs" forms a chapter, highly interesting and suggestive to a writer of romance, although of little import to the general reader. It tells how on the way he was almost startled from his propriety at every step by Messieurs de la Hoquette, Famechon, Chamarante, and Merode, colonels in the French contingent, who had, no doubt, been sent by de Lausun to urge him to swifter flight; for this general had many intrigues of his own at the French court, and, as they were spoiling in his absence, he encouraged the king's departure as the surest way of procuring his own recall from Ireland. But, as the subject is irrelevant here, the curious are referred to the notes of Berwick's Memoirs, where they may contemplate the web woven around this unfortunate king by the general for whom he had made the powerful Louvois his inveterate enemy.

At Waterford he heard that the French ship De Lausun, of twenty guns, was moored at Passage, with a cargo of corn and supplies; and in this he sailed from Waterford to Kinsale, where, after a short delay, he embarked, and arrived at Brest on the 9th of July, escorted by the *fleet of M. de Seignelay, which he met on its way to destroy William's transports around the Irish coast*!

So ended the reign of James II.; and with it, virtually, the dynasty of the Stuarts. He died at St. Germains, in France, on the 16th of September, 1701, surviving his daughter Mary by seven years; and on the 8th of March, 1702, his death was followed by that of the Prince of Orange, who broke his collar-bone by a fall from his horse; surviving his much injured father-in-law only by six months. The son and grandson of the expatriate monarch, each in turn, tried to regain his inheritance, but the Hanoverian line prevailed, and with Prince Charles, "The young Chevalier," the grandson of the renowned Sobieski, the noblest and bravest of his race, the royal house of Stuart became extinct.

James was an ascetic and religious prince, sincerely devoted to the Catholic religion, but perfectly tolerant of the religious doctrines of others. A just man, generous in great things, and yet scrupulously exacting and punctilious in small ones; a king solicitous for the welfare of his subjects and the glory of England, but, above all, unalterably devoted to the principle of civil and religious liberty, which he endeavored to establish in his realms, but which the intolerant spirit of the times prevented. He was the generous patron and consistent friend of William Penn, and the fosterer and protector of the American colonies, which received his charters with adulation, and repaid them with ingratitude. He was the first and last sovereign of England that stretched out the hand of justice towards Ireland; and her people served him with devotion, and, notwithstanding his many military blunders, which justify their irony, they appreciated his motives, and their descendants recall with pity, not unmingled with reverence, the name of this much maligned king, who, in trying to ameliorate the condition of their country, became the victim of intolerance, and died a discrowned exile.

Two characteristics, seemingly irreconcilable, are attributed to him by his enemies;—that he was at once an "enthusiast" and a "bigot,"—and they may be accepted. His enthusiasm was that of a good, rather than of a great mind; but that he was a "bigot," in the repulsive application of that term, cannot be accepted from histories which are in themselves but tissues woven of the darkest intolerance. *"Enthusiasm"* and *"bigotry"* are terms much at variance; but when applied to his whole life, they are easily reconcilable, and not unlovely. He was a *bigot* so far as to be a firm believer in the doctrines of the Catholic Church, but not to the extent of prescribing them as the *panacea* for the sins of others, nor of making it penal not to believe as he believed: and he was an *enthusiast* in so far as he imagined that he could harmonize the discordant religious elements of the country to abide in peace and good-will, and establish a name and an era in the history of England to which all her people henceforth could point with gratitude and admiration. He was a *bigot* and an *enthusiast* just to the extent that Washington and O'Connell were bigots and enthusiasts, and no more. The good that he intended for his own kingdom died with him, but his principles were carried to the Western continent by the Irish emigrants, and established there.[37] He failed; not because his object was unjust, or his reforms unnecessary, but because an evil spirit, not yet cast out, rendered the hearts of his people obdurate and insensate. Two things, however, that should not be forgotten, are manifest from the history of that period and the century succeeding it: that Ireland is the precursor and exemplar of American liberty, and that James II. was the first, the only English king that had the true idea of popular government; the first that had the virtue to practise it, and was at once its apostle and its martyr.

---

[37] "In April, 1783, Mr. Gardiner, afterwards Lord Mountjoy, remarked in the Irish Parliament, in reference to the Irish Catholics, that 'England had America detached from her by force of Irish emigrants.'" (Plowden's Hist. Rev., vol. iii., p. 45.)

CHAPTER XI.

THE SURRENDER OF DROGHEDA AND DUBLIN— THE FIRST SIEGE OF ATHLONE.

After the departure of King James from Dublin, Colonel Simon Loutrell, then military governor, in pursuance of the royal order, released all the prisoners, and, assembling the principal Protestant inhabitants, surrendered the government of the city into their hands. Those parties having constituted a provisional governor until the arrival of the Prince of Orange, Loutrell withdrew the Irish garrison from the city, and marched to Leixlip, where he was joined by Tyrconnell and De Lausun, and took up the route for Limerick. In the mean time, the French troops had been partially disbanded. One half of them, under De la Hoquette, had marched towards Cork to avail themselves of transportation to France; and the other, under Brigadier De Surlaube, brought up the rear of the Irish army, and followed De Lausun to Limerick.

Berwick, who had remained for some days with a body of cavalry between Drogheda and Dublin, to retard the immediate advance of the enemy on the capital, soon after took up his march for the general rendezvous, whither he had been preceded by the other division leaders, and in a short time an army was assembled there exceeding by some thousands the force that participated in the Battle of the Boyne. This, according to the estimate of the Duke of Berwick, consisted of 4,000 cavalry, still in good condition, and 16,000 infantry, of which only one half were armed with muskets.

De Lausun, who had become quite disgusted with the condition of affairs to which he had so largely contributed since his arrival, now lost no opportunity of effecting his recall, by representing the Jacobite cause as hopeless. Arriving at Limerick, he at once pronounced the place untenable; commented on the forlorn condition of the troops; the dilapidated state of its defences; ridiculed the idea of holding it against the army of the Prince of Orange; and in the excess of irony, declared that "his master could take it with roast-apples." Sarsfield and Berwick thought differently. It was their principal depot of provisions and military stores; one of the few ports of entry that now remained in their possession, and being moreover the key to the defences of the river, its loss would be soon followed by the total subjugation of the island. They accordingly set their minds on holding it to the last extremity, and being joined in this resolution by the governor, De Boïsselau, they at once set about strengthening its fortifications. De Lausun, finding that his motives were understood, and that he no longer possessed the confidence or respect of the Irish leaders, withdrew his men, military chest, and artillery from the city, and encamped within view of it, on the Clare side of the river, where he remained an inactive spectator of the events that succeeded. But whatever were the motives of De Lausun, the strait to which the city was at this time reduced could hardly be underrated. The provisions of the garrison were quite inadequate to the maintenance of such a force for any considerable time; its ammunition was nearly exhausted, and there were only nine guns, and those of inferior calibre, on its walls. The late reverse had opened up all the country to the east of the Shannon to the arms of William, and on the southern side, round to Cork, there was hardly a fortress capable of offering a day's resistance. The forts of Kilkenny and Clonmel, in the interior, which had been dismantled during the war of the Confederacy, had been neglected during this, and could hardly retard his march from the sea-board longer than to comply with the forms of capitulation. Commerce, which had been hitherto carried on briskly between this city and France, ceased as the risks increased; the shipment of military stores was suspended; and operations in the field had become utterly impracticable. The treasury, too, was empty. The sum of 50,000 pistoles which the king left with Tyrconnell, was soon expended; the troops had become clamorous for pay, and private contributions were no longer to be obtained. The king's Catholic subjects throughout the eastern counties, were beset by the soldiers of William, and the king once departed, the entire Protestant population transferred their allegiance. Still every motive of pride and interest impelled the Irish leaders to more determined resistance, for there was now no alternative between success and total ruin. They had indicated the Shannon as the proper base of operations during the earlier stages of the war, and now that they were driven to it as a necessity, its defence became doubly imperative. Should they now fail to defend it successfully, their former importunities would be looked on as the effect of a weak and vacillating spirit, and the king would be more than justified in having rejected their counsel. All these considerations stirred them to renewed action, and the work of preparation was carried on with vigor. In consequence of their straitened means, one of their first measures was a reduction of the garrison. All the cavalry, and 8,000 infantry were retained for the defence; a few regiments were distributed at the different forts along the river up to Lanesborough, and the rest were sent to live on the country, subject to immediate service when called on.

On the day after the Battle of the Boyne, General Mellioneire, with 8,000 men, and a battering train, approached the town of Drogheda, still held by a Jacobite garrison of 1,300 men. The place was immediately summoned to surrender at sight, or expect no quarter. This was the order of the Prince of Orange, and that he meant to carry it out to the letter, there could hardly be a doubt. The history of this old town had furnished more than one instance of similar cruelty in his predecessors, and there was nothing in the antecedents of William to leave room for a doubt in favor of his greater humanity. The commandant of the garrison, however, interpreted the message literally, and so accepted it. The Irish army had disappeared; there was no hope of succor; and successful resistance to such a force, supported as it would be, if necessary, by William's entire army, was impossible. All these considerations, duly weighed, determined the conduct of the governor, and the garrison was accordingly surrendered. This removed the last enemy from

William's rear, and at once opened the way to the capital. But to the great surprise and vexation of its expectant inhabitants, he drew up his army on the ground he had won, and took a respite of several days' duration.

On the withdrawal of the Jacobite authorities from Dublin, a scene of riot and plunder took place there which threatened the safety of the city. The Protestant mob, in defiance of all legal restraint, had commenced to plunder the houses of the Catholic gentry. Among them, the house of General Sarsfield became an object for special violence, and was rifled and totally demolished. The infuriated populace fled to the suburbs, and threatened to burn the city. Fitzgerald, the governor, did all that he could to protect life and property, but the riot increased in violence, and the greatest consternation prevailed among "the better sort." In this emergency, a messenger was dispatched to William's camp for a force sufficient to suppress these outrages, but he turned a deaf ear to the entreaty, and continued unmoved in his present quarters. He is accordingly much censured by the contemporary writers of his own party, for this neglect of what they considered the primary duty of a king who had taken them under his special protection. But, all things considered, the Prince was not so much to blame in this connection. The troops by whom he was surrounded, when from under his own eye, were entirely uncontrollable. They had given proof of this before Carrickfergus. There the presence of Schomberg was insufficient to check their excesses, and now, had they entered the city of Dublin during this tumult, they would but add fuel to the flame; and in this light the conduct of the Prince might be looked on rather as an act of forbearance than otherwise. But the truth is, that William, at that moment, was disturbed by graver considerations than the safety of his good citizens of Dublin. His spies at the French court, and his friends in England, kept him duly apprised of all that transpired abroad touching his interests. Immediately after the surrender of Drogheda, he had received intelligence of the situation of affairs, both on the continent and in England, since his departure, and that intelligence was not very assuring. The career of Luxembourg; the defeat of Admiral Torrington, and the preparations of de Seignelay, had wrought a change in the sentiment of the English people, and his presence among them had become a matter of pressing necessity. His fleet of transports, which accompanied him along the coast, was now moored at Drogheda; his army was encamped there, and his ordnance and military stores were still at hand, and he remained there but to watch the current of events, undecided whether to re-embark at once for England, and leave Ireland to its fate, or to risk his hold on England, by advancing into the country to renew a campaign but just inaugurated. — A few days, however, decided his course.

King James tells us that his principal object in leaving Ireland at this juncture, was to obtain a force from the French king to make a landing in England. He also adds that he had assurances from his friends in England, that any respectable force thrown into the country at that time would wrest it from the dominion of William. But his flight from his only remaining kingdom at such a juncture, so displeased King Louis, that he utterly denied him his presence for several days; and when at last he succeeded in obtaining an interview through the mediation of the queen, he found that de Lausun's misrepresentations had so completely closed the ear of the king to his appeals, that he not only denied his request, but that he had resolved on recalling the force already sent to Ireland.

William was duly apprised of all this, and it allayed his apprehensions for the safety of England; so, after a few days' delay, he struck tents, turned his steps southward, and encamping his army at Finglass, entered the capital.

The Parliament which assembled to meet him, presented a marked contrast to that of the preceding years of this war. The latter was earnestly intent on securing the liberty of the country and the religious freedom of all the denominations, and on having them secured by constitutional enactments; while the total extirpation of the Catholic faith, and the immediate confiscation of the estates of those still in arms for their rightful sovereign, alone could satisfy the former. William adopted a half-way measure, and one which was more likely to subserve his own interests. The confiscation of course became necessary, not only to satisfy his new subjects of Ireland, but also to reward his Dutch and foreign mercenaries; and it accordingly received his sanction. But the extermination of the people did not suit his views. The population of the country was already greatly reduced; and besides, 'tis said that William was opposed to persecution for conscience' sake. However, it became necessary, if possible, to detach the people from their leaders. While their interests were identified, the success of his arms was doubtful, and accordingly, a proclamation was prepared, subjecting the leaders to all the penalty of rebels in arms, and offering an amnesty to the artisan and laboring classes.

The following extract, from an impartial historian of the times, will give a brief outline of the parliamentary proceedings of that period: "His first measures after his arrival in the capital were highly impolitic, if not unjust. He promised, by a declaration, to pardon and protect such of the lower sort as should in a limited time surrender their arms; but he excepted the gentry, whom he resolved to abandon to all the rigors of war and conquest. He issued a commission for seizing all their estates and effects, though no court of judicature was open to proceed against them. The commissioners executed their power with the utmost rigor. They even ruined a country which they endeavored to appropriate to themselves. Public misery, persecution, and confusion prevailed everywhere. The king himself was either not sincere in his offers of mercy to the vulgar, or he possessed no authority to restrain the license of his army. His declaration was disregarded, his protections slighted. Revenge, wantonness, and avarice induced men to break through every form of decency and every tie of faith. Despair animated the Irish to a renewal of hostilities, as submission produced nothing but oppression and injustice."[38]

Those measures were at the same time sagacious and cruel, and such as would have disunited any other people than those to whom they were now applied. They exempted the men of no property, but marked out all others for total ruin; and had there been no other principle at issue than the individual merits of William and James, it is hard to tell what their effect on the artisan and laboring classes might have been. But the clan system was not yet entirely eradicated from the minds of the people. Most of the private soldiery in the Irish army were men attached to their leaders by all the memories and ties which that system engenders, and the

[38] Macpherson's History of England, vol. i., p. 664.

wrongs of those leaders were resented as their own individual wrongs. It is true that this system was dying out; but this war, which was waged for the maintenance of a common faith, served also to revive the ties of kindred and of clan, and it is probable, that had James succeeded in re-establishing his power in England, the feudal system of Ireland would have been revived in many, if not all, its forms. Therefore, in leaving the men of estate no choice between ruin and success, William utterly failed in his object of detaching the people from their leaders. On the contrary, they clung to them with greater fidelity than ever; and drawn back behind the Shannon, as their last line of defence, they submitted their cause to the arbitrament of the sword, and set the enemy at defiance.

After a short stay in Dublin, William determined to press the real object of his mission. He reviewed his army at Finglass, and mapped out his plan of operations. His own command, and that of Duke Schomberg at the Boyne, were to proceed along the coast, and after subjecting the eastern counties to his sway, turn westward for the reduction of Limerick. In the mean time, General Douglas, who now commanded that part of the army which had been hitherto led by Count Schomberg,[39] was to proceed westward from Dublin, capture the fortress of Athlone, and then join the main army at Limerick.

The march of Douglas across the country was marked by the most revolting excesses, and scarce had he lost sight of the capital, when the people's eyes were opened to the sort of amnesty intended for them. Depending on the proclamation of William, those to whom it was extended at first remained in their homes, but found that its provisions were disregarded both by the general and his soldiers. The Protestant population fared no better than the Catholics, the houses of all were indiscriminately plundered and given to the flames, and themselves mercilessly slain, without regard to sex or condition. His march could be tracked by the cries of his victims through the day, and at night by the light of the burnings. In this manner he advanced through the most fertile and populous districts, spreading death and desolation as he went. A report of these barbarities spread through the country, and roused the spirit of revenge. The Rapparees inflicted some losses on his outposts, but there was no organized force then east of the Shannon capable of offering effectual resistance.

Athlone was at this time garrisoned by a Jacobite force of 800 men, under the command of Colonel Richard Grace, a veteran of the last civil war. The life of this soldier was a stormy and eventful one. He seems to have been one of those who, like Bayard, stand out from time to time among men, as an example of fidelity and heroism. A colonel in 1645, and a colonel still, he had spent the interval in war—France, Spain, and Ireland being each in turn the field of his adventures. Twice, in youth, he had successfully defended Athlone against the arms of Cromwell, and again he stood there, in his eightieth year, as vigorous and agile as any of his command, to defend its walls against the assaults of this sanguinary general.

Douglas advanced with all the assurance of certain success, and appeared before the town on the 11th of July. He was, however, surprised to find that the part

[39] This force at the Battle of the Boyne was 10,000 men. Its artillery was twelve pieces. It sustained little loss in that action, and was now supplied with mortars.

of it east of the river had been given to the flames, its walls demolished, the bridge broken down, and the castle on the western side in a formidable state of defence. He halted before the walls, and immediately sent in a herald to demand a surrender. The governor, roused to indignation by the atrocities of Douglas, flashed his pistol in the face of the herald, and, pointing to a red flag which he had hoisted, said: "These are my terms; these only will I give or take." The herald departed, and the governor retired to animate his soldiers for the impending contest.

On receipt of this answer, Douglas lost no time, but, erecting his batteries over against the castle, opened a heavy cannonade. The garrison replied with a spirit and vigor that astonished the besiegers: their guns were dismounted, their works demolished, and several of their men and their best gunner were killed. Again and again they trimmed their works and renewed the enfilade, but with a like result—the castle was impregnable to direct operations. Seeing this, Douglas ordered a detachment of 3,000, horse and foot, to force a passage of the river at Lanesborough, about ten or twelve miles to the north of the town, at the head of Lough Ree. On their arrival there they found the ford intrenched on the opposite side, and a strong body of troops drawn up to receive them; and after a vigorous attempt to force a passage, they were repulsed with considerable loss, and the project was abandoned. On their return they were beset at every point by those desultory bands that traversed the country, and harassed up to the camp, losing many men and horses on their way. The unsoldierlike conduct of Douglas now began to have its effect. He had marched as if to certain victory, devastating every thing in his path, and making no preparation for a sustained siege. Owing to his sanguinary character, the people, both Catholic and Protestant, now shunned his camp; his provisions and provender were soon consumed, and he had to send out foraging parties daily, to levy on the surrounding country. But these were ambushed at every available point by the Rapparees, who also burned and destroyed in their turn; so that his subsistence soon became precarious, and his situation more like one besieged than one besieging. In this critical condition, he determined to force a passage across the river at a ford below the town; but in this he was also foiled; for the governor, apprised of his intention, had it protected by strong earthworks, and the project was abandoned as desperate. For seven days the siege continued with unabated vigor on the part of the besiegers, but with a like result; every succeeding day rendered success more hopeless. It was now reported that General Sarsfield was advancing from Limerick with a strong force to raise the siege. Whether this report was true or false, the narratives of the times do not affirm; but Douglas accepted it as true, and shaped his conduct accordingly. Not deeming it prudent to remain any longer before the town, he decamped on the night of the 26th, abandoning his heavy baggage, and avoiding the highways, lest he might encounter the enemy on his way.

The condition of the Protestant population was now worse than before. Hitherto they had received ample protection, nothing more being required of them than to remain peaceable subjects. But on the appearance of this army they had declared for the Prince of Orange, and having forfeited their former claim, they believed that retaliatory measures would be instituted when the army of Douglas was withdrawn. They had experience enough to convince them of their folly, and to satisfy them that they were safer at the mercy of the rudest of their countrymen, than as the camp-followers of a general who had already violated all the rules of civilized warfare. But their fears outran their discretion; many of them followed the retreating army, and received the treatment which characterized the foreign soldiery of William throughout this war; while others, adopting the wiser course, remained in the town, and received the accustomed protection.

Douglas could not have taken a worse route than that which he now selected. The country through which he passed was studded with woods and thickets. Innumerable rivers traversed it on all hands, and immense tracts of bog extended across his line of march, rendering continual deviations from the direct course imperative. He was beset on all hands by marauding parties of the Rapparees, who took bloody reprisals, with that total recklessness of life which had now become characteristic of these homeless wanderers. He had lost four hundred men at Athlone. Several skirmishes are related in which he lost from fifty to two hundred; and though his entire loss cannot now be definitely stated, it could not have fallen short of 1,000 men. Followed and beset on all hands, both by day and by night, after a most harassing march of fourteen days he formed a junction with the Prince of Orange, who had reached Caherconlish on his way to Limerick.

The Prince and his general had very different results to compare. The march of the former had been one of uninterrupted success. Kilkenny, Waterford, Duncannon, Clonmel, and all the intermediate places, had surrendered in succession, without even a check to mar the conquest of the Boyne, while that of Douglas had been one of continual disaster,—showing the only reverses that the Prince's arms had sustained since his arrival in the country. But if their military exploits were dissimilar, their catalogues of crime closely assimilated; for the same wanton outrages marked the footsteps of the Prince and his general. As William advanced from Dublin, he threw out detachments on all sides that plundered and laid waste the country, and slaughtered the defenceless inhabitants. Roused by the excesses of his soldiers, the people set upon them wherever they were found in detached bodies; and, neither giving nor asking quarter, no day went by without its tale of wanton aggression on the one side, and deadly revenge on the other.[40]

---

[40] It is worthy of remark, that while Taylor represents the atrocities perpetrated by the soldiery of the Prince, under his own eye, as revolting as those of Douglas's troops, he endeavors to palliate in the Prince what he execrates in the general. This is to be regretted in a historian otherwise remarkable for candor and impartiality.

CHAPTER XII.

THE SIEGE OF LIMERICK.

The city of Limerick, at the time of William's invasion, consisted, as it does at the present time, of three distinct divisions, or towns. One of these was on the right bank of the Shannon, in the County Clare; one on the left bank, in the County Limerick; and the third on King's Island, which is formed by the branching of the river about a mile above the city. The part on King's Island was known as the Englishtown; that on the Limerick side was designated the Irishtown, and two bridges connected that on the Island with the other two sections, — one bridge leading to each.[41] Holding a commanding position between the most fertile portions of two loyal provinces, and standing at the head of ship navigation, the military advantages of this city could scarcely be overrated; but the well-known loyalty of the people, the great difficulties that beset the king, and the exhausted state of his exchequer, through every phase of this war, had caused it to be neglected; and its defences were not at all in keeping with its strategic importance. It had, according to the Duke of Berwick, on his arrival there after the Battle of the Boyne, "no other fortification than a wall without ramparts, and a few miserable towers without ditches." But the month that had since elapsed had not been wasted; the old walls had been strengthened, and such new works devised as were allowed by the means at the disposal of the generals. The troops worked with a will corresponding to the exigency, the people shared their means cheerfully with them; and the gallant defence made during the preceding war against the arms of General Ireton, imparted hope and courage as the crisis drew near. The cursory view of this period to which these pages are limited, will not admit of a more minute detail of the disposition which had been made to meet the impending contest, than the following imperfect summary: A covered way had been constructed round the wall, to protect the soldiers in passing from point to point; St. John's Gate — the principal one of the city — which opened towards the south-east, had been strengthened on the outer side by a redoubt and some angular palisades filled with earth, and on the inner side by a fort called "The Black Battery;" a bastion had been erected near the bridge connecting the English and Irish town; and an earthen fort constructed on King's Island, the guns of which flanked the counterscarp, and raked the eastern front of the wall as far as the main gate. A tower on the southern angle of the wall mounted three guns; the redoubt opposite St. John's Gate mounted two; there

[41] As the siege of 1690 did not affect that part of the city in the County Clare, there is no necessity for further allusion to it here, beyond stating that the bridge leading to it was called Thomond Bridge. The other was called the City Bridge. King's Island is about two miles in length.

were two on the bastion near the bridge, and the fort on King's Island, probably mounted two more.[42] Eight thousand infantry manned those works; some regiments of dragoons occupied the island; the rest of the cavalry were disposed on the Clare side of the river, some below the city, at Annabeg, and some in the direction of O'Brien's Bridge, above it, — the branch of the river that separated the towns was easily fordable, and there were many fords on the main channel between that and Kilaloe.

When the Prince of Orange reviewed his army at Finglass, before his departure from Dublin, it was 40,000 strong; and after his junction with Douglas at Caherconlish, it is estimated, on good authority, as "38,000 effective men."[43] The disparity in numbers between it and the Jacobite army was very great; but in resources, appointments, and artillery, it was still greater, and such as to leave little doubt of William's success.

On the 8th of August, this army appeared within view of the city, on the eastern side, while de Lausun, who had, during the interval, occupied the position already indicated, on the western side, decamped, and marched his command to Galway, whence he shortly after sailed for France. On the 9th, William approached the city slowly and cautiously, bearing the Irish outposts before him, and took up his position between St. John's Gate and King's Island, within cannon range of the wall. His lines were soon extended to the right and left; the latter position being occupied by the Danes, who are said to have expressed great satisfaction at the sight of an old Danish fort that had escaped the changes of seven centuries, and reminded them at once of the sway of their ancestors over the island—and, mayhap, of the king by whose valor their power had been eventually overthrown.

Tyrconnell was still commander-in-chief of the Irish army, but the military conduct of affairs within the city mainly devolved on Sarsfield and the Duke of Berwick; and as William sat down before their walls, the latter requested Tyrconnell to place the cavalry at his disposal, and that he would cross the Shannon, make a circuit of the country in William's rear, destroy his magazines and supplies up to Dublin, and so reduce him to the necessity of decamping. In referring to this proposition in his Memoirs, the Duke says: "As all the towns in the country were open, and without defence, I was morally certain of succeeding in my enterprise; and as to getting back, which was objected, the knowledge I had of the country had already suggested to me by what means it might be effected. I had no doubt of making my way into the North, and returning to our quarters by Sligo." But Tyrconnell, fearing to part with all his cavalry at such a critical moment, represented to him that it would leave the river between Limerick and Kilaloe exposed, and as they were the only protection against a flank movement of the enemy in that direction, he discountenanced the adventure.

[42] Story's map exhibits thirty-six guns and four mortars on the part of the besiegers, and but seven on that of the besieged. But as the fort on King's Island is represented to have caused great injury to William's right, it is certain that there must have been guns on it; hence the writer, and he thinks not without reason, has hazarded the assertion in the text.

[43] See Haverty's History of Ireland, page 643—giving a Williamite authority for this estimate. This work came to my notice too late to make some corrections which, to a critical reader, might seem important.

When William had made the necessary disposition of his forces, he sent a regular summons to the governor—de Boïsselau—for the surrender of the city, but to this a polite answer was returned through his secretary, to the effect, that he could not comply with the demand; that he was there to defend the city for King James; and that he was resolved to do it, in such a manner as to win the respect of his master, the Prince of Orange. William lost no time in putting this resolution to the test, and had soon made all the dispositions for a regular siege. His main body rested nearly opposite to St. John's Gate, with the Danish troops well extended, encircling the city round on the south and south-west; and his right towards King's Island, with a division opposite to the bridge that connected it with the Irish town. Batteries were soon constructed, bearing on those different points, and, establishing his headquarters in Ireton's tower, which commanded a view of the entire front, he opened a fierce and incessant cannonade. The spirited reply of the besieged soon convinced him that they had set their minds on defending their city to the last extremity, and that the siege would be protracted and desperate. The batteries on King's Island were particularly troublesome; the guns there being so well served, that they did great execution on his right and centre, and after a short time, the former was compelled to withdraw from the river, and the latter to shift ground and heighten its defences. Finding, after a bombardment of two days, that he had inflicted no serious damage, William relaxed his fire on the wall, directed his mortars against the interior of the town, and dispatched orders to Clonmel to hasten up his battering train and pontoons, which had been conveyed by the fleet to Waterford, and were now on their way to his camp.

This intelligence being communicated to the governor by a French officer who had deserted from William, Sarsfield conceived the bold design of intercepting the convoy, destroying the train, and compelling the abandonment of the siege. With this intent, he opened the matter to the deputy; but the latter, being in continual fear of disasters, discountenanced the project, as he had that of Berwick. But Sarsfield, insisting with great earnestness, Tyrconnell at last yielded his assent, and placed eight hundred horse dragoons at his command. From those he selected five hundred men, and having secured the service of some Rapparee guides, to whom all the by-ways of the country were known, he held them in reserve until night would favor his departure without the knowledge of the enemy. The exploit was both difficult and dangerous:—over thirty miles of country, traversed by innumerable small rivers, lay before him; two branches of the Slieve-Phelim mountains stretched across his route; and in order to avoid suspicion, and keep the enemy unapprised of his absence, it was necessary to shun the highways and traverse the least frequented parts of the country. The enemy's scouts were thrown out for several miles to the east; his cavalry were foraging in all directions through the day; and the least inadvertence would cause the failure of the undertaking, and cut him off from the city, or perhaps entail the destruction of his entire command.

Darkness had settled over camp and city as Sarsfield crossed the Thomond Bridge, and followed his Rapparee guides into the open country beyond. For some time he pursued his course northward, in order to avoid the road by the river, the cavalry of William being extended as far as O'Brien's Bridge; but when distance removed apprehension, he wheeled eastward at Fahy, urged his command to greater speed, and crossed the bridge of Kilaloe towards midnight. He then struck southward through Newport and Murruo, crossed the Dead River and its tributaries, and as morning dawned, ambushed in the mountain district, about two miles north of the route from Clonmel to Limerick. Here he threw forward his scouts in the direction of Clonmel, to watch the convoy and give timely notice of its approach; but the day passed on, and the night was somewhat advanced, when the lumbering train at last appeared, and halted at a short distance from the place of ambush. The men were now within seven miles of their own camp; the little chapel of Ballyneety, which stood near the roadside, offered a pleasant resting-place; and being in no apprehension of danger, they resolved to bivouac there for the night, and reach the camp early on the following morning. Having made their arrangements and lit their fires, they betook themselves to rest, and were soon wrapped in slumber around and within the walls of the ruin, when the Rapparees, who had watched them throughout the day, taking note of their numbers and disposition, repaired to the general and informed him that the hour had come, and the word was "Sarsfield." The assault that followed was a complete surprise to the enemy, who offered but an ineffectual resistance. In a few minutes over sixty of them were slain, the rest put to flight, and Sarsfield turned his attention to the main object of the expedition. The cannon, eight in number, were loaded to the muzzles and buried deep in the earth: around and over those were pressed the ammunition and ball: over them were laid the chests, wagons, and carriages: the tin boats were next destroyed and placed on top: a train was then laid, and the troop-horses, and all that was portable, were secured and started in advance: and last of all, Sarsfield, with his own hand, lit the train and retired. Then followed that terrible explosion, which is said to have shaken the earth for fifteen miles around, and startled the Prince of Orange in his camp. But, notwithstanding the precautions taken by Sarsfield, his movements had not been unobserved. An Irish Williamite, named Manus O'Brien, had met the detachment on its way towards Kilaloe, and divining that it was on some expedition of importance, hastened to the English camp, and requested an audience of the Prince. He succeeded after considerable delay, and communicated his intelligence; but the Prince, though suspecting at once the design of Sarsfield, looked on it as futile, and took no further notice at the time; yet, as the night waned, he sent out Sir John Lanier, with five hundred horse, to meet the convoy, and ordered the fords of the river to be well guarded to intercept the Irish troops on their return. The delay of O'Brien was providential. Lanier had got within a short distance of the place when he heard the explosion, and pressed on with the hope of intercepting the enemy, but only reached the ground as Sarsfield retired. Warned by the appearance of Lanier that it would be dangerous to return as he had come, he changed his course, passed to the east of the Keeper mountains, and holding his way through Upper and Lower Ormond, he, on the following evening, reached the town of Banagher,[44] a distance of more than forty miles, where he halted to recruit his men, and returned through Galway and Clare without the loss of a man.[45]

---

[44] McGeoghagen's History.

[45] It is stated by some of the annalists that he lost two soldiers, who fell behind, but

This event roused the spirits of the besieged army, and mainly contributed to its final success. It also raised the fame of Sarsfield among the officers of rank, and left him without a rival in the affection of the soldiers. Known before only as a dashing leader of dragoons, he was from that day forward the idol of the populace, and through every change, or good or ill, his name has been a household word with his countrymen in every clime. Nor were the fame of this exploit and the successful defence of Athlone long in reaching King James; they were the first good tidings he had received since his departure, and they gave him assurance to press his suit at the French court. In due time Sarsfield was promoted to the rank of Major-General, and eventually created Earl of Lucan, Viscount of Tully, and Baron of Rosberry.

By this feat, which happened towards the morning of the 13th, William's operations were greatly impeded; but ever provident, he was still the master, and, not like his rival, the slave of circumstances. At the end of another week, the loss was supplied by a train still more formidable than that destroyed, nor did their loss cause the cessation of hostilities for a single day.

Two of the guns found among the *débris* at Ballyneety were still fit for use, and with these, his mortars, and field-train, he continued the bombardment, and by the 17th, he had pushed his lines of circumvallation close to the walls of the city. Nor were the besieged less active or determined in their resistance; every foot of the ground was dearly purchased, and no day went by without a sortie of the most desperate character. One of these, which occurred between the 17th and 20th, was of so novel a character as to demand a passing notice. As William's lines approached close to the walls, the fire from within was so fierce as to compel the soldiers to lie close within their trenches during the night. Those opposite the sally-port, between the bridge and St. John's Gate, were occupied by two regiments: the Blue Dutch and the British, between whom no very friendly feelings existed. The Irish, to whom this was known, taking advantage of the darkness, made a lodgement in one of the traverses, and threw in a stealthy fire on the Dutch. The latter seeing no enemy, and observing the British by the flash of the muskets, believed the fire came from them, and answered it by a deadly volley. This was immediately returned, and the two regiments commenced a murderous fire on each other, while the Irish, as occasion offered, directed a volley at each of them. After several had fallen victims to their own stupidity, the real cause was detected by one of the English generals, and troops were brought up to correct the evil, and chastise the authors of it; but these seeing the place getting too hot for them, rushed from their ambush and reached the city with little loss. The affray between the British and Dutch was not easily reconciled. The confusion of languages baffled, for some time, all attempts at explanation, and hostilities continued until both regiments were placed under arrest, and fresh troops stationed in the trenches. The blunder created great mirth among the Irish soldiers, but the besiegers redoubled their vigilance, and surprise was thenceforth a matter of impossibility. The most serious engagement that occurred after this, took place about the 22d, and was forced by the besieged for the purpose of destroying William's heavy guns be-

---

the text is in accordance with the Abbé's account of this adventure.

fore they could be got into position. Issuing out in force, at mid-day, they assailed the enemy's centre with such vigor that they drove it from the trenches; the Prince, who was present, retreated towards his quarters; but falling in his hurry, he had scarcely arisen when a cannonball tore up the very spot on which he had fallen, and after receiving a serious contusion from a fragment of a rock, splintered by the shot, he was carried to Ireton's Tower, nor did he appear again until the final assault. But the sortie ended in the repulse of the besieged, and the guns were rescued and placed in position.

This was the last sally from the garrison. The siege was now pressed with terrible energy by the besiegers, and the besieged, no less determined, addressed themselves to resist the final assault which now appeared imminent. By the 24th, William's entire artillery had been brought to bear on every vulnerable point within range, while his lines of circumvallation drew closer and closer to the walls. Six batteries lay along his entire front, disposed, according to his historian, in the following manner: The first, of eight eighteen-pounders, bore against the southern angle of the wall, opposite to the Danish quarters; the second, of eight twenty-fours, against St. John's Gate and the Black Battery which stood within the city behind it; the third, of twelve field-pieces, against the sally-port which opened near the bridge; and the fourth and fifth, of four heavy guns each—the former against the bridge itself, and the latter against the bastion which stood near it on the left—while behind them a floor had been constructed for a battery of four mortars, which poured a stream of red-hot shot and shell on every prominent object beyond the wall. Day and night, the fire from all was sustained with unabated vigor, until the 27th, when the outer works, before St. John's Gate, were demolished, and a breach, two hundred yards in width, was effected in the wall, opening up the very heart of the city, when William slackened his fire and again summoned it to surrender.[46]

The besieged were now hard pressed;—the trenches of the besiegers were within two toises[47] of the palisades in front of the breach, and overlooked them, so that they had but to step over to find themselves on the level and unobstructed area around the city gate. The Irish fort on King's Island, which until now had thrown a slanting fire across the enemy's right, was dismantled and its guns removed to the Black Battery to defend the breach; the wall, along its whole front, was rendered untenable to the musketeers; and the cavalry were withdrawn across the river, for the guns bearing on the bridge threatened the destruction of their only line of communication. Still, the English town itself was impregnable, being situated on low ground, which could be easily inundated by a flood-gate on the main channel of the river; the English cavalry, too, had been withdrawn from the island, and the whole fury of their guns concentrated on the Irish town. Such

[46] The Duke of Berwick, at page 69 of his Memoirs, gives the width of the breach at 100 toises, or 600 French feet,—the toise being six French, or six and a half English feet—and as he was present at the siege, his estimate is here adopted. Moreover, the breach, as exhibited on a map in Story's Impartial History, lays bare a great portion of the city, and shows the disposition of the Irish troops within it, which a breach of thirty-six feet—the width generally accepted—could not exhibit.

[47] See preceding footnote.

was the condition of the garrison when de Boïsselau received the second summon from the Prince of Orange, and, believing that further resistance was useless, he consulted the Irish generals and advised them to accept an accommodation. But he was opposed by the general voice. The soldiers were unanimous for resistance to the last; the citizens appealed against a surrender; the women declared that they would rather be torn piecemeal by the artillery than be subject to the barbarities of William's soldiers. The general voice prevailed, and de Boïsselau withdrawing from the city, declined further responsibility.

The herald was accordingly dismissed with an indignant refusal to the Prince's message, when the bombardment was again renewed, and active preparations were made for storming the city. For this purpose William selected 10,000 men from the different regiments, and formed them into supporting columns, under leaders of approved valor and experience. Five hundred British grenadiers were to lead the assault; the Dutch and Danish troops were to follow, and be sustained by the Huguenots in turn, while the Brandenburgers, English and Enniskilleners, were to bring up the rear. Biding these preparations, the artillery was to keep up its fire along the whole line, and when it ceased, three guns, fired in rapid succession, was to put all in motion, and be the signal of assault.

Meanwhile the Irish generals had made the best disposition of their force to meet the impending event. The bulk of their infantry was divided into four columns: two drawn back on each side of the breach, so that each of the opposite columns could meet promptly in front or rear of the assailing parties; the musketeers were posted in every available position on the wall, and the guns of the Black Battery were loaded with grape to rake the breach as they entered. Farther back, near the square of the city, a body was held in reserve to support the battery, and to give succor wherever it became necessary, while Brigadier Talbot, with five hundred of the Guards, was posted on the right, to guard against any surprise from the enemy in that quarter. The streets were filled with citizens armed with every available weapon, and with groups of women, the sad spectators of the approaching conflict.

It was three o'clock in the afternoon when the fire of the enemy's cannon ceased along the whole line, and the assaulting columns, in their varicolored uniforms of buff, blue, and scarlet, moved down to the intrenchments as gayly as if on parade, and halted. The fire within the town also ceased, and an ominous silence settled over the scene, the combatants on each side, standing with bated breath, and as motionless as statues. An unusual drought prevailed,—not a drop of rain had fallen for three weeks;[48] the weather was intensely hot, and the sun threw a flood of unobstructed light upon dome and spire, while the river glided away through its autumnal foliage, as placid as if peace had returned and war should revisit it no more. Some time passed on, and suspense was becoming painful, when the signal: one! two! three! pealed forth. The British grenadiers were over the palisades in a twinkling, hurling their destructive missiles, and followed by

---

[48] William afterwards declared before Parliament, that the cause of abandoning the siege was the continual rain that kept his trenches filled with water, but the Duke of Berwick asserts that not a drop had fallen during the time specified in the text.

the Dutch Guards, while the cannon rang out again along the whole front, excepting the point of assault. So quick was the movement, that the Irish troops, though awaiting it, were actually taken by surprise, and the grenadiers had reached the breach before they met with any opposition. Here, they were checked by a shower of grape that did great execution; still they pressed on with a headlong impulse, mounted the breach, and passed the first line of guards drawn up to oppose them. But they were destined to go no farther; another storm of grape tore through their ranks, the Irish Guards closed in on them, front and rear, cutting them off from their supports, and assailing them with such fury that in a short time they were nearly all slain, only four or five escaping out of this gallant body, which was reckoned the flower of the English army. The Dutch Guards pressed boldly on, and under the eye of their Prince, performed prodigies of valor; several times they bore back the defenders from the breach, and were as often repulsed through it; but being continually reinforced from the other divisions outside, the Irish troops were gradually forced back into the city, where they divided right and left, still disputing every inch of the way. William now threw forward a Brandenburg regiment to storm the Black Battery, and, filling up the breach with his remaining columns, prepared to enter the city. While this conflict raged along the widening expanse inside, the fire of the enemy's batteries was unabated; the soldiers were driven from the parapets; the populace from the house-tops; the city was on fire in several places, and "it seemed," says an eye-witness, "as if the heavens were rent, and the smoke that arose from the town reached, in one continued cloud, to the top of a mountain six miles off."

The whole storming force was now engaged within the breach, and the way was literally strewn with its dead and wounded; but the besieged, despite the most heroic resistance, were gradually borne back by the heavy masses continually hurled on them, inspiring redoubled energy with every accession. The Brandenburg regiment had captured the battery, and, having seized the guns, were turning them against its defenders, who were retreating from it in apparent consternation. William, who now stood at Ireton's Tower, looked on in proud anticipation of success; the city seemed completely within his grasp, and pushing forward his last reserve, he viewed exultantly the engagement which was to complete his triumph.

It was now near seven o'clock; the sun was sinking behind the western headlands, and still the battle raged with unabated fury. Throughout the long hours of this sanguinary conflict, the populace, men and women, stood by in painful suspense, watching the tide of fortune as it stood or swayed before them, and now it became manifest that every effort of valor was exhausted, and the doom of their city at last was sealed. Oppressed by odds, their brave defenders were giving way, and the battery, the last obstruction to the advancing foe, was in the possession of the Brandenburgers. A wild cry of despair rung up from all; their last hope was gone: at this moment a terrific explosion shook the city to its centre; a dark cloud overspread the combatants, and clearing away, it was seen that the mine beneath the battery had been sprung, and the whole Brandenburg regiment had been blown to atoms!

Consternation seized on the besiegers; even the besieged, though expecting the event, were for a moment astonished, and each stood as it were paralyzed and watching each other in amazement. But the advantage was not lost; the men braced themselves again for the contest, the women rushed forward, calling on the men to follow, and with one impulse threw themselves in front of the enemy. The effect was electric; all caught the inspiration; generals, soldiers, citizens; all, with one desperate effort, hurled themselves on the masses of William, and bore them back bodily through the breach. In the mean time Brigadier Talbot, anticipating the result, led his men round the outside of the wall, and attacking the rear of the assaulting force with great spirit, put it into inextricable confusion; panic-stricken, they fled precipitately from the city, pursued to their camp by the victorious Irish—and Limerick was saved.

The loss of William in this day's action was 2,000 men and one hundred and fifty-eight officers killed, and his casualties through the preceding eighteen days are estimated at 3,000 more. The loss of the besieged is nowhere definitely stated; but in the final assault they lost four hundred killed and wounded,—a small number for so great a result. But, as if to give a mournful grandeur to the event, many of the noble daughters of the city lay side by side in death with the men whose sterner natures they had animated to victory!

After the battle, William sent an ensign into the town for leave to bury his dead; this being refused, he dismounted his batteries, withdrew his army, and prepared to retreat, for he could no longer continue the siege, as matters of a pressing nature demanded his presence in England, and should the news of this defeat precede him the consequences might be serious. His Irish adherents entreated him not to leave them with the conquest of the country uncompleted, and the leaders of his foreign army besought him to the same effect: but he turned a deaf ear to their entreaties. A deputation of the soldiers, both native and foreign, headed by the ecclesiastics, waited on him, and promised still greater efforts if he remained among them; but his resolution was unchanged. Annoyed by their importunities and chagrined by defeat, he gave vent to that exclamation which English historians have industriously suppressed: "Yes," said he; "if I had this handful of men who defend the place against you, and that you were all within it, I would take it in spite of you!"[49]—A censure so caustic, and a eulogium so grand, render comment unnecessary.

Before retreating he set fire to his hospital, in which there were many invalids; but the Irish soldiers issued from the city, suppressed the flames, and saved the wretched victims. It is hard to credit, even on the authority of historians distinguished for wide research and cautious investigation, an act of such cold-blooded atrocity; and yet his conduct, during his retreat, was of a character that would seem to corroborate it.[50] "The curse of Cromwell" was repeated, the peasantry were murdered, their lands laid waste, and their homes given to the flames; so that the fertile district between Limerick and Clonmel was a scene of death and

---

[49] McGeoghegan's History of Ireland, Preliminary Discourse, p. 24.

[50] Excesses of a savage barbarity, but upon questionable authority, have been ascribed to the king himself, on his retreat from Limerick. Disappointments might certainly have raised his resentment; at least the outrages committed by his troops contributed to

desolation. Committing the command of the army to the Count de Solmes, with Ginkle as second in command, he proceeded under escort to Waterford, whence, accompanied by Prince George of Denmark, and the Dukes of Ormond and Wurtemberg, he sailed for England.

Though the theme of many a glowing eulogy, William's campaign in Ireland was not such as to exalt his name, either as a statesman or a soldier. The victory of the Boyne, had he taken that advantage of it which a great military mind would not have failed to take, might have led to the total suppression of the war within a month; and his short sojourn among the Irish representatives of that day, marked only by pusillanimity and cruelty, shows him entirely devoid of statesmanship. If, without dividing his army, after his first success, he had turned aside from the capital, and pressed the rear of the retiring army, he could have gained some of the passes of the Shannon, or perhaps have anticipated the enemy at Limerick, and ended the war without another blow. The truth is, his career, in this connection, was a very inglorious one. His doubt and hesitation after the Boyne were scarce less remarkable than those of Schomberg, which he so severely censured. Through indecision and delay, he gave his enemy time to recuperate for that memorable siege which checked his career, jeopardized his chance of eventual success, and sent him back to his newly acquired kingdom, to be humiliated before his Parliament; divested of nearly all popularity, and humbled before his courtiers by an aspiring subject.

stain the annals of the times; but whether they proceeded from his orders, or his want of authority, was hard to decide. (Macpherson's History of England, vol. i., p. 664.)

CHAPTER XIII.

THE ARRIVAL OF THE DUKE OF MARLBOR-OUGH—THE SIEGE OF CORK AND KINSALE.

While the events just narrated had been passing in Ireland, King James remained at the court of France, endeavoring to win King Louis' consent to his favorite plan of invading England in the absence of the Prince of Orange. Having failed in this through the persistent opposition of the French minister, he turned his attention once more to his affairs in Ireland, and requested an expedition to sustain his arms in that country. But the misrepresentations of De Lausun had so warped the mind of this sovereign, that in this he was equally unsuccessful; and finding himself unable to awaken the interest of Louis, or to change the mind of his minister, he gave way to despondency, and remained a passive spectator of surrounding events. In this exigency the Duke of Tyrconnell determined to present himself at the court of Versailles, and plead the cause of his country. The successful defence of Athlone and Limerick furnished him with arguments that her cause was not yet hopeless; and the favor hitherto shown him by the French monarch, led him to believe that his suit would not be unfavorably received. So, having constituted a council of three lords-justices and sixteen senators, to conduct the civil affairs of the nation, and appointed the Duke of Berwick as deputy, with Sarsfield as his second in military command, he left the city in company with De Boïsselau, the late governor, and joined De Lausun at Galway, where he embarked for France on an important mission.

Scarcely had he departed from the city when the spirit of discontent became manifest in the council and among the leaders of the army. Believing, or affecting to believe, that the deputy was indifferent to their wants and grievances, and had abandoned the country to its fate, they resolved to send a deputation to France to represent their policy, and urged the Duke of Berwick to sanction their proceedings. He opposed the design for some time; but the excitement daily increasing, he was forced to acquiesce in order to restore the general harmony. "Accordingly," says he, "I summoned all the principal lords, as well of the clergy as the laity, and all the military officers down to the colonels, inclusive, to attend me.... I proposed to them the Bishop of Cork, the two Luttrells, and Colonel Purcell. My choice was unanimously approved, and a few days after I dispatched my deputies. At the same time I sent Brigadier Maxwell, a Scotchman, to explain to the king my reasons for appointing this deputation, and to beg of him not to suffer either Brigadier Luttrell or Colonel Purcell to return: they were the two most dangerous incendiaries, and I had chosen them on purpose to get them out of the way. When these gentlemen were got on board, they conceived a suspicion that Maxwell might be charged with some instructions relating to them, for which they proposed to throw him overboard, but were prevented by the bishop and the elder Luttrell. The first was a prelate of distinguished piety; the other was of an obliging disposition, and always appeared to me to be a man of honor. Notwithstanding Maxwell's representations, the king permitted these gentlemen to return to Ireland. Tyrconnell consented to it, but he had reason to repent of it after."[51] Such were the inauspicious signs, too plainly indicative of a divided interest, and such the difficulties that beset the deputy in this, perhaps, the greatest emergency of his country. But undeterred by the party intrigue of the hour, he addressed himself to the duty of his embassy with such tact and decision that he soon gained the ear of the French monarch, put the conduct of de Lausun before him in its proper light, propitiated the minister, counteracted the designs of the *cabal*, and obtained the promise of an expedition to Ireland proportionate to the importance of the cause and the necessities of the crisis. This success being communicated to the council in Limerick, had the most favourable effect; hope and confidence were renewed among all classes of the people, and activity and courage were soon manifest in all ranks of the army.

On the other hand, the intrigue and party strife that prevailed at the court, and in the legislative councils of England, were of a nature, not less serious, than those which menaced the success of the Jacobite arms. Since the accession of William to the throne, two factions had been gradually maturing there, and at this time had reached the acme of party strife and hatred. These, for convenience, may be termed the Dutch and English interest, which they respectively represented, while apart from both, and, perhaps, numerically as strong as either, stood the Jacobite party, watching the course of events, and determined to take advantage of their mutual animosity.

William, who looked to the elevation of Holland as a European power, and the humiliation of France as the primary objects of his life, had neglected his English partisans, and raised his Dutch and foreign mercenaries to the highest civil and military offices of the State; and this lost him much of his prestige among the parliamentary leaders, while the people, who had begun to look calmly on the condition of their country, saw it, after all, but a conquered province of Holland. The invasion had succeeded, but their liberties were more circumscribed: "Popery" was ignored, but prelacy was enslaved; the Parliament existed, but the people had no voice in its construction; the foreign legions revelled in the capital, but the English soldiers were disfranchised and conscripted for foreign service. The general discontent had become alarming, and to add to the growing disaffection, and give it point and purpose, the Princess Anne, the younger daughter of King James, be-

---

[51] The particular line of policy that brought this deputation to France, or the cause of Tyrconnell's future regret, is nowhere clearly indicated by the Duke of Berwick. But the treason of Henry Loutrell, during the subsequent stages of the war, is an accepted belief in Ireland and in her history. His secret correspondence with William and Baron Ginkle, and his attempt to surrender Galway, are well authenticated. After the war he received his elder brother's estate and a pension of 2,000 crowns annually from William, and was assassinated in Dublin in the year 1717—"nor could it ever be discovered by whom." (See Berwick's Memoirs, vol. i, p. 97.)

ing treated with studied neglect by both William and Mary, to whose elevation she had contributed by a plot unworthy of her station as a princess and her dignity as a wife, had become their bitterest enemy, and the recognized head of the English interest. To such a pitch had she carried her resentment, that on William's return from Ireland, she had raised up an English champion to humble his pride, by eclipsing his military fame, and the person thus put forward was Lord Churchill, afterwards the renowned Duke of Marlborough. Owing to this, the return of William was not hailed by any of those popular manifestations that mark the return of a conqueror to his country. On the contrary, the ordinary gratulations, things of everyday occurrence, were but coldly accorded to him by the people;—his parliamentary partisans scarcely deigning the formal acknowledgments of success, while the opposition declared that the victory of the Boyne was overbalanced by the defeat at Athlone and Limerick, and that the result of his expedition was degrading to the British arms. He endeavored to remove this impression by representing to the Parliament, and causing to be reported on the continent, that the heavy rains which had fallen during the siege were the cause of its abandonment, although many then knew, what the Duke of Berwick afterwards affirmed, "that not a single drop of rain fell for above a month before, or for three weeks after that event."[52] But the English party were not deceived by the device, the assertion gave point to their irony, opposition became more bitter and clamorous, and in order to humiliate him the more, it was proposed to send Marlborough,—"at his own request,"—to Ireland to redeem the disgrace by completing the reduction of the country. William, though knowing this to be a direct insult to himself and his foreign army, was obliged to acquiesce, for the conquest of Ireland was a matter of pressing necessity to both parties; each desiring it for the national safety, and yet each aspiring to that honor, as a means to the perpetuation of its power. The expedition was accordingly ordered; but, while Marlborough was making preparations for his departure, William sent the Duke of Wurtemberg to Ireland with secret orders to claim the command of the expedition on its arrival, by right of military precedence, and thus counteract the designs of his political enemies.

After the departure of the Luttrells and Purcell for France, and the restoration of harmony in the councils of the Irish Senate, Sarsfield and Berwick directed their attention to the military affairs of the nation, which were in a very disheartening condition. The defences of the city were repaired, the garrisons along the frontier were strengthened and reinforced, and detachments sent into the counties bordering on the Shannon, to co-operate with the Rapparees in levying contributions of corn and cattle for the support of the army. The sieges of Athlone and Limerick, following in such quick succession, had nearly exhausted all their military stores, and had the enemy chosen to make a rapid descent on the river fortresses immediately after the retreat of William, it is more than probable that the war would have been terminated by the close of 1690; for there remained but fifty barrels of powder within the city, "and there was not, in the whole country which remained under the control of the royal army, enough to double the quantity."[53] But the indecision of the enemy, after the withdrawal of the Prince of Orange, enabled the

[52] Berwick's Memoirs, vol. i., p. 71.
[53] Memoirs of the Duke of Berwick.

Irish generals to anticipate events, and to distribute a supply of military stores, which soon after arrived from France. Early in September, with about 3,000 infantry, seven battalions of cavalry and four field-pieces, they encamped at Banagher, a good strategic position, on the Shannon, about fourteen miles south of Athlone, resolved to take the offensive, in order to check the enemy, now extended from Clonmel to Enniskillen, and making stealthy approaches towards the frontier garrisons along that river. The town of Birr, in the King's County, about seven miles from their encampment, was the most advanced post of the enemy at this time, and the first to invite an attack. It was a place of much importance, as it threatened the passes of Banagher, Meelick, and Portumna; and being the principal depot of military stores and provisions for that district, its capture would have been of immense advantage to the army. Accordingly, on the 13th of September, Berwick appeared before the town, and had soon carried the outer works of the castle by which it was protected, but met with considerable delay from the inefficiency of his guns, which gave the enemy time to hasten up their reinforcements. In a short time General Kirke appeared with a regiment for its relief, but seeing the Irish cavalry drawn up on a hill overlooking the town, he retreated back to Roscrea, where he was joined by General Douglas, and with a force of 8,000 men and ten pieces of artillery, appeared again on the 16th, as the garrison was on the point of capitulating. Upon this, Berwick withdrew his guns from the trenches, and taking up a good position on the hills, about a mile from the town, he spent all that day and the next offering every inducement to battle, which the enemy as persistently declined,—each failed to draw the other from its chosen position. At last, on the third day, Berwick withdrew towards his camp, followed at a distance by the enemy, who advanced when he advanced, and halted when he halted, until his cavalry, making a detour of several miles, assailed their flanks, doing great execution, and putting their whole force in disorder, when they retreated precipitately, pursued up to their defences; and so the affair ended. A series of bitter skirmishes between the pickets of both armies succeeded this for a few days, when the enemy again moved towards Clonmel and Kilkenny, where there was a general muster to reinforce the Duke of Marlborough, who had effected a landing at Cork, and Berwick retired behind the Shannon to collect troops to oppose him; the garrisons at Birr and Banagher were withdrawn to their defences, but the Rapparees moved over the country at will, and harried it without fear of retaliation.

On the 21st of September, Marlborough sailed up the harbor of Cork, effected a landing at Passage, without any serious opposition, and took up his march for the city, the men hauling the cannon, he being unprovided with train-horses or cavalry. His force consisted of 8,000 infantry, six hundred marines, some ships of war, and a few transports; but being joined by the Duke of Wurtemberg and General Scravenmore with 4,000 infantry and nine hundred cavalry, his army was augmented to about 14,000 men, provided with all the essentials of a siege, and a co-operative fleet to assail the city from the water-side. On the 23d, he appeared before it in form; Wurtemberg, according to the secret orders of William, claiming precedence in command, and Marlborough demurring, on the ground that he was specially commissioned for this campaign. A warm dispute arose, one insisting on the privilege of rank, and the other on delaying the siege, and referring the question back to the Parliament. This delay being likely to hazard the success of their arms, by giving the besieged time to strengthen their defences and get in supplies, a compromise was agreed upon, by which they were to assume the command alternately. Marlborough's turn came first, and he gave the word, "Wurtemberg," and in acknowledgment of this politeness, the latter, when his turn came, gave the word "Marlborough;" but notwithstanding this outward exchange of military compliments, their mutual jealousy continued without affecting the progress of their arms.

The city of Cork, situated in a valley surrounded by high hills, was defended by a few dilapidated outworks, all of which, excepting the Castle of Shandon, which overlooked it on the northern side, were abandoned as the enemy approached, the troops retiring into the principal fortress, which stood on a low, marshy plain, between two branches of the river Lee, accessible only at low-water, but poorly supplied with artillery, and almost exhausted of provisions and military stores. The Castle, after repulsing an assault of the Danes, was also evacuated, and its troops withdrawn into the inner fortress, against which the entire force of the enemy was now directed. Its garrison, after this junction, amounted to 4,500 men — a force ample for a protracted resistance; but already on limited rations, and there were only five barrels of gunpowder within its walls. By the loss of Shandon it was exposed on three sides to the fire of the enemy's land batteries, and on the fourth, to that of his ships, which could come within short range at tide-water.

On the approach of the enemy, the governor, Colonel McElligot, had received orders from the Duke of Berwick to demolish the fort, burn the city, and retire with his command into Kerry; but having disobeyed this mandate, at the solicitation of the citizens, until too late, he determined to redeem his error by the gallantry of his defence, and hold out long enough to give Berwick time to hasten up succors to raise the siege. The enemy, having gained possession of the hills, opened a fierce cannonade on the city itself, and having levelled all the intervening houses, descended into the valley, opened on the citadel, and after a most spirited resistance of two days, silenced its guns, and prepared to carry its works by storm. The assault could only be made at low-water, and once each day was there assault and repulse, in one of which the Duke of Grafton[54] was killed while leading his regiment across the marsh. At length, after a desperate defence of twelve days, it surrendered on the 5th of October, on terms considered highly honorable; "but the ink with which the capitulation was signed, was not yet dry when it was violated in every particular." The Catholic people were stripped and driven from the city; the city itself was given to pillage; the Earls of Tyrone and Clancarty were wounded and grossly outraged by the soldiers and the mob, and the prisoners subjected to indignities and cruelties, compared with which death would have been a refuge. They were pent up within a loathsome fen, where, being denied food, they were necessitated to feed on putrid carrion; more than half of them died within a fortnight, from the diseases it engendered; one-half the remainder were murdered by order of one Captain Lauder, on the way to Clonmel, some time later; and of the survivors, few ever returned to report the inhuman deed.[55] Marlborough and

[54] He was, says Taylor, the most respectable of the natural sons of Charles II.
[55] Lesley's History of the Civil Wars, &c.

his English army, were even more barbarous than the Prince of Orange and his foreign mercenaries.

On the surrender of Cork, Marlborough turned his attention to Kinsale, which is about twelve miles distant by land, and sixteen by water, and which had, in the mean time, been invested by a portion of his land force and his navy. The town was defended by two forts—Castle Ny and St. Charles—named respectively the Old and New Forts; the former having a garrison of 450 men, and the latter one of 1,200; and both being better provided in guns and material than the fortress just surrendered. But the Old Fort had been blown up by accident on the 3d, causing the death of two hundred of its garrison and the capture of the remainder; so there was now but the New Fort to resist the united efforts of the army and navy of Marlborough. The defence, however, was a gallant one, and marked by deeds of great personal daring, both of the men and commandant; but, being cut off from succor both by land and sea, they capitulated on the 15th; being allowed to depart with their baggage and arms, and to join their countrymen at Limerick. As this fort was impervious to the enemy's cannon, and might have held out, while its provisions lasted, a suspicion of treachery attached to its governor, and it is intimated by more than one of our annalists that he must have been bribed by Marlborough, who was impatient of delay, as he had pledged himself before his departure from England to reduce both Cork and Kinsale within a month; but the accusation is not sufficiently authenticated by any, while it is liable to doubt, on the consideration, that a soldier base enough to accept a bribe would not have scrupled to turn over his command to the enemy, which might have been as easily accomplished. The loss of life, with the exception of those blown up at Castle Ny, did not exceed four hundred on each side, but the Irish army lost heavily in prisoners at Cork, few of whom survived their subsequent sufferings; and the loss of those two maritime stations to their cause was incalculable.

The Duke of Berwick tells us that during the interval, he had collected a force of about 8,000 men, and had got as far as Kilmallock, in the County Limerick, with the purpose of compelling Marlborough to raise the siege. But considering his force inadequate, he contented himself with watching the enemy, and when the expedition was finished returned to his quarters. The indecision shown by Berwick at this juncture, in view of his well-known valor and intrepidity, would favor the impression that he was unwilling to appear in arms against his uncle, and his explanation would seem rather to fix than to remove it. Eight thousand men, in a friendly country, under the command of such generals as himself and Sarsfield, who was also there, against 14,000 investing two strong fortresses, and extended over a line of seven or eight miles, seem not inadequate, and might have created such a diversion as would have at least protracted the siege; and any disarrangement of Marlborough's plans would have placed him in a very critical position.

With the fall of Cork and Kinsale, the campaign of Marlborough may be said to have terminated; he remained but a few days more in the country, and after planning offensive measures against the counties of Cork and Kerry, to be conducted by Ginkle, he returned to England after an absence of five weeks, and received the congratulations of the people and Parliament, to the great annoyance of the Prince of Orange and his partisans. He was thenceforth the great popular idol of the nation, and was soon after started on that military career that has placed his name among the greatest of England's generals. After his departure, Ginkle pressed the war in the south with great vigor. Scravenmore and Tettau, with a heavy force of infantry and cavalry, penetrated northward to Mallow, and, turning to the west, began to plunder and lay waste the country. But they were soon beset by organized bodies of farmers and Rapparees, and, by an assault, as vigorous as it was unexpected, were driven with great slaughter towards Bandon, where they were again furiously assailed by Colonel O'Driscoll, and, panic-stricken, fled back to their quarters.

CHAPTER XIV.

THE WINTER OF 1690.

Before his departure from Ireland, the Prince of Orange deputed the civil government of the country to two lords-justices—Porter and Coningsby—who lost no time in entering on the duties of their office. Scarcely were they installed in it, when a flood of proclamations was issued against the "papists" who lived within their jurisdiction; and all devised, with the most "diabolical ingenuity," to plunder and exterminate. One of these assessed the Catholic inhabitants to make good any losses sustained by their Protestant neighbors, whether arising from accident or from causes incident to a state of warfare; another proclaimed that no more than ten Catholics should assemble in a body, and that the priest of any parish, where a larger assembly should take place, incurred the penalty of transportation; a third declared that the families of such as had been killed or taken prisoners in the service of King James, should forthwith remove behind the Shannon, or be treated as enemies and spies; and a fourth, that any family having a member within the lines of the Irish army, should either procure his recall, or remove thither by a certain day. The Protestant population were also ordered within the English lines, and a general exodus from both sides of the river immediately took place. The sufferings consequent on this disruption, it is painful to contemplate. Thousands of the young and infirm crossed the river never to return to their homes, while the men were driven to swell the ranks of the Rapparees and wring their subsistence from the country.

In the mean time seizures and confiscations kept pace with the proclamations, until a million and a quarter of acres, valued at four millions sterling, were appropriated in advance of all legal proceedings. "The manner in which the lords-justices and the Castle party did their work," says Taylor, "is an edifying example of the mode by which the forms of law have been so often prostituted to sanction injustice in Ireland. They indicted the Irish gentlemen who possessed any estates, of high treason in the several counties over which they had jurisdiction, and then removed them all, by *certiorari*, to the Court of King's Bench in Dublin. By this ingenious contrivance, those who were to be robbed lost all opportunity of making their defence; indeed, in most cases they were ignorant of being accused, and the Irish government was saved the trouble of showing how the Irish people could be guilty of high treason for supporting the cause of their rightful monarch against a foreign invader."

Commissions were also issued for raising large bodies of militia, to be equipped and disciplined on the plan of the English army; and the northern Protestants, who were considered as well adapted to predatory warfare, were furnished with the arms of Schomberg's soldiers who had died, or who had been killed in the preceding year, and sent forth, under the name of Protestant Rapparees, against those of the same class who followed the fortunes of the Jacobite army. This was all fair enough in war, but it is worthy of remark that those who exclaimed most loudly against the moderate taxation of King James, as ruinous to the country, now voted away sums that would lead one to think they believed the resources of the country inexhaustible. The militia of the country in a short time became good soldiers, and did great service to William by holding the garrisons in the rear of his regular army, and recruiting it when necessary; but the "Protestant Rapparees" entirely failed in the object proposed, for, unable to cope with their wily enemies, they soon turned to plunder indiscriminately on their own account, and, instead of increasing the forage or supplies of the English army, they wasted wherever they passed, and caused a dearth which afterwards greatly embarrassed its movements.

Still the affairs of William were of a serious and perplexing nature, both in England and on the continent. Party strife ran high in the British Parliament, and the Princess Anne, whether touched by remorse or excited to revenge, was known to hint at the necessity of recalling her father to the throne, while the continued success of Marshal Luxemburg, since the battle of Fleurus, had reduced the "Allies" to great extremities, and threatened the very existence of Holland as a European power. Several times since his accession, William was compelled to pass over to the continent to reassure his favorite subjects, and to take counsel with the members of the coalition against the increasing power of France. His visits on those occasions were necessarily hurried and unsatisfactory; the successful termination of the Irish war, alone, could grant him a respite from his manifold cares, and accordingly Ginckle, who had succeeded the Count de Solmes in command of the army, was ordered to continue afield through the winter, and press it to an issue, either by treaty or by force of arms. To put the result beyond peradventure, his force was strengthened by accessions from every available quarter: the militia and northern reserves were called into service; several regiments reached him from Scotland; and the Dutch Guards, who had been recalled to England with the Count of Solmes, were replaced by a body of British infantry, the dragoons of Colonel Mathews, and the cavalry of the Count of Schomberg, until a force of over 50,000 men were at his command, while abundance of stores and ammunition arrived daily at every port from Cork to the capital.

Nor did the complete reduction of the country, judging from the relative numbers, the condition of both armies, and the territories occupied by them, seem an end either distant or difficult to accomplish. Three of the four provinces were virtually under the sway of General Ginckle; the coast from Kinsale, eastward to Derry, was under the control of his fleet; his army lay extended through the centre of the island, within a day's march of the Shannon, the possession of any pass on which would break the Irish line of communication, and open up the remaining province to the progress of his arms; and to this was his attention now directed as the speediest manner of terminating the war, which had become so irksome to his sovereign.

Warned by the reverse of the British arms before Athlone and Limerick, that an assault in force at any one point of the Irish line, would be attended with hazard and delay, he devised a simultaneous attack along its whole extent, as the more speedy and efficacious. It would keep the enemy, who were not half his number, divided among many garrisons, weaken them at some point, and give him the advantage of selecting that for his most determined assault, which should be found the least capable of resistance. For this purpose, he established his bases of operation at Cork, Roscrea, Mullingar, and Enniskillen; the first threatening that part of the southern province still in arms for King James, and each of the other three commanding one or more important passes into the still unconquered territory. That part of his army at Enniskillen was commanded by Kirke and Douglas; that at Mullingar, by Brewer, Lanier, Earle, and others; that at Roscrea and its environs, by Count Nassau and the Prince of Wurtemberg; and that at Cork, by Tettau and Scravenmore,—none of them varying far from 10,000 men, with strong detachments at several intermediate points, while he himself established his headquarters at Kilkenny, holding a strong reserve in hand, to be directed north or south as necessity should require. The campaign was to be first inaugurated by Tettau on the south and Douglas on the north. The former was to move against the interior of Cork and Kerry, and, wasting the country on his way, to threaten Limerick, in order to divert attention from the movements on the river above it. The latter was to proceed against Sligo, and, having captured it, to assail Lanesborough from the west, while Brewer, from his quarters at Mullingar, was to threaten it on the east. The investment of the latter place was to be the signal for a general movement along the whole line from Kilaloe, northward, when, if any one point were carried, the whole army was to concentrate round Athlone, which once reduced, Limerick should be evacuated, or the whole country westward to Galway left open to his march. The plan was well designed, the generals able and experienced, the army in the finest condition; and nothing was wanting to success but the time opportune for a general movement.

On the other hand, the fall of Cork and Kinsale were succeeded by a period of great distress within the Irish lines. The exterminating policy of the lords-justices had filled the province with a helpless population, enhancing the price of provisions and lessening the resources of the army. The brass coin of King James, in which the soldiers received their pay, was greatly depreciated within their own boundaries, while throughout the other three provinces it was decried, and had become utterly worthless.[56] A derangement of trade with France also intervened, and disasters followed each other in quick succession. A few days after the fall of Kinsale, a vessel freighted with salt and other necessaries, anchored under the guns of the fort, and the captain, believing it still held by the Jacobite troops, only

---

[56] The value of the brass money issued by the king in the early part of the war will be better understood from the following extract:

1 Barrel of Wheat, in Brass Money   £10   s.   d.

discovered his mistake when she was actually in possession of a boarding party from the enemy. Another, laden with ammunition and clothing for the troops, struck on a rock coming up the Shannon, and became a total wreck, and all on board perished. Almost coincident with those events; one Long, an English captain, who had been for some time a prisoner in Galway, aided by some disaffected inhabitants, made his escape, and seizing a French frigate of twelve guns, doubled the northern coast and reached Carrickfergus in safety with his prize. In the mean time the expedition promised by the French Government was unaccountably delayed, until hope seemed illusory, and the necessity of an accommodation with the enemy was intimated in the civic councils of the nation.

Through all these troubles Berwick and Sarsfield never faltered in their duty. The camp and the council alike demanded their attention. In both they seemed ubiquitous, and their exertions alone saved the Jacobite cause from utter prostration at this critical period. At length, after several weeks had elapsed, commerce began to revisit the coast; the immediate necessities of the army were relieved; the efforts of Tyrconnell were manifested in something more tangible than promises; arms and ammunition, as a first instalment of his good faith, arrived at Galway, coupled with assurances that the French king had at last accorded that consideration which the importance of their cause demanded, and appeals to their loyalty and patriotism to hold out until his arrival. The effect was soon observable: the despondence of the people gave way to hope; the discontent of the council was for a time allayed; and the generals turned their undivided attention to military affairs—Berwick to store the magazines, put the troops in order, and guard the different posts; and Sarsfield, with a few thousand available troops, to organize the Rapparees and direct their movements in frustrating the designs of the enemy.

Through the preceding events of the war, the Rapparees had played no insignificant part. The torch of the invader had rendered them homeless and reckless, and, thrown on their own resources, they took up this wild life, and wrung their subsistence from the enemy with a daring hand. From the Shannon to the eastern coast, wherever a tribute could be levied, or a British detachment ambushed, there were the stealthy Rapparees wresting a reprisal or wreaking a revenge. Neither toil nor privation seemed to affect them, nor could danger deter them from their purpose. Death, swift and certain, was their doom when captured, and that they dealt as swiftly and surely in their turn. Unable, through want of regular arms and discipline, to meet large bodies of the enemy in the field, they divided into small bands, and traversed the country in all directions. All the by-ways of the land were known to them; they came and went like shadows; and wherever they passed, there was a hostage or a victim. No position of the enemy, however guarded, was safe from them, and frequently in the dead of night, when his camp seemed most

1	Barrel of Malt, in Brass Money	9	0	0
1	Quart of Brandy, in Brass Money	3	0	0
1	Quart of Ale, in Brass Money	0	2	6
1	Pair of Men's Shoes, in Brass Money	1	10	0
1	Quart of Salt, in Brass Money	1	0	0

secure, the skies would be suddenly lit up by the blaze of his tents, and horses and other booty secured in the confusion, and borne with a noble disinterestedness to the headquarters of the Jacobite army. In fine, the Irish Rapparee was an Irish patriot, and a devoted one,—as brave and devoted as the Chouan of La Vendée. He fought without pay; suffered without murmur, and gave his life for a country that scarce holds his name in grateful remembrance.

Such were the men that Sarsfield now called to his aid, and for this purpose, he "let loose,"—says the English historian of the war,—"a great part of the army to manage the best for themselves that time and opportunity would allow them, giving them passes to signify what regiments they belonged to, so that in case they were taken they might not be dealt with as Rapparees, but *soldiers.*... Keeping a constant correspondence with one another and also with the Irish army, who furnished them with all necessaries, especially ammunition."

These soldiers now extended along the whole frontier, and in a short time established communication between the Rapparees and the regular army, while Sarsfield, with a small force, took the field, to profit by every diversion they might create in his favor.

Each army having thus adopted its plan of action, a furious desultory war soon raged along the whole lines, from north to south. The Rapparees, under the guidance of the soldiers sent among them, formed in two lines: one of these moved along between the English army and the eastern coast, harassing the militia in its rear, and ravaging the country up to the gates of Dublin; while the other hung around its encampments, interrupting communication, disconcerting its movements, destroying its forage, and driving large herds of cattle beyond the Shannon. Their courage and hardihood were surprising. They now attacked larger bodies of the enemy, and raids and skirmishes, terminating in loss of life on both sides, were of daily—almost hourly, occurrence. If the enemy lost less in men—as we are assured he did, on the testimony of his own annalist—he paid the balance in booty, for to this the attention of the Rapparees, even in the heat of battle, was principally directed. An instance or two of their manner of proceeding will better illustrate their service at this time than pages of general detail.—As the English army extended northward, pursuant to its design against the Irish quarters, the regiment of Lord Drogheda occupied Kilcormack Castle, in the King's County, as an escort to the supplies daily arriving and passing on northward. The forage growing scarce around that station, the commander, Colonel Bristow, billeted his men on Balliboy, a few miles distant, in a plentiful district, and scoured the country in all directions. After a few days the town was well stored with provisions for the winter, and the greatest vigilance was exercised against a surprise from the Rapparees, who were reported to be about in the neighborhood. From a steep hill behind the town, which commanded a view of the country around, a constant lookout was kept up through the day; and every evening, before retiring to rest, the hedges and brushwood were searched, and the guards doubled through the night. Notwithstanding all this vigilance, the Rapparees got within the lines and concealed themselves in the hedges around the town; where they remained three days without food, and exposed to the severity of the weather. At length, on the third night, when the very quiet that prevailed awakened suspicion, a lieutenant and twenty men were sent out, who beat up all the hedges, and even those where the Rapparees lay concealed, without detecting any sign of them; and retired for the night free from apprehension. In half an hour more the town was fired at both ends; this was a signal to the Rapparees at a distance, who flocked in from all directions. The soldiers were driven to the hill, where a fight raged all night between them and one body of the Rapparees; while another, in their sight, rifled the town, brought off a large booty of provisions and horses, and secured them before morning. The next day they attacked Philipstown, but were repulsed and driven through the country; when turning on their pursuers, they killed one hundred and twenty of them, returned and laid the town in ashes, and killed two hundred more, sent against them. No place was free from their assaults:—Clonmel, Cashel, Mountmellick, and Mullingar, were attacked by them in such quick succession, that the British soldiers were kept marching and countermarching to meet assaults either feigned or real, until the winter set fairly in, and the grand movement of Ginckle seemed yet as remote as ever.

The soldiers sent into the interior of Cork and Kerry also performed signal service to the Irish cause. Mounted upon the small surefooted horses of those mountainous districts, they traversed the country in all directions; organized the farmers and Rapparees; established lines for running the produce of the country to the general depot at Limerick; and then attached themselves to the forces of Colonels McCarthy and O'Driscoll, who still held the country against the incursions of the enemy. This Colonel O'Driscoll was a brave and intrepid soldier. He commanded a regiment of his own tenantry at the siege of Cork; but having no faith in English treaties, he refused to accede to the terms of Marlborough, and, at the head of his regiment of four hundred men, fought his way through the English lines, and reached the open country to the north-west of the city. Here he learned that his son, or kinsman(?), "young Colonel O'Driscoll," had been slain in an attempt to retake Castlehaven, which had been captured by the British; and that the country around was despoiled, and the people flying in dismay to the mountains. Burning with revenge, he marched rapidly along the line of the Bandon, passing through Ballineen and Inniskeen; scattering several English settlements as he passed; and turning westward, bore directly for Castlehaven, took it by storm, and put the whole English garrison to the sword. Other places were retaken in quick succession, his force increasing with each success; and being joined by Colonel McCarthy, they attacked the forces of Tettau, under Eppinger, Cox, and Coy, again drove them from the interior, and the reduction of the country was, for that time, abandoned.

By these and other movements, too numerous to specify in detail, the British general was kept in a state of alarm, and his object frustrated, until the last days of December. The 29th of that month was at last fixed by Ginckle for a simultaneous advance along his whole line, every thing being considered in proper train, and the enemy's apprehension being removed by the lateness of the season. Douglas, from Enniskillen, directed his march on Sligo. The regiments of Kirke, Lanier, Lisburn, Lord Geo. Hamilton, Brewer, "and several other regiments, with tin-boats for crossing the river," marched under Kirke and Brewer, from the north and east, against Lanesborough. A party of the militia was also ordered from Dublin, "and those in the country were ordered to be up on all hands." Drogheda's, Col. John Hamilton's, and others, under Bristow, were ordered from Birr to Lanesborough; and a strong force from Kilkenny and Roscrea were to attempt the river at Portumna and Banagher. Tettau at the same time was to renew his campaign in the south, by throwing a strong body against each of the counties:—"And now," says Story, "if they had been all pushed forward at one time, it had been a great advantage to our affairs next campaign. All things seemed to favor the attempt, especially the weather—better had never been seen for the season."[57]

On the 29th, Tettau was joined by Brigadier Churchill, Sir David Collier, Colonels Cox, Coy, and Matthews, with their respective forces, and on the 30th attacked and captured Scronolard. But the country for several miles around having been burned, and its provisions carried off, they were unable to penetrate farther, and retraced their steps after a series of assaults, in which they lost many men, and the campaign was pronounced impracticable for the winter.

The expedition against Sligo was not more fortunate. Douglas had scarcely cleared his quarters at Enniskillen, when he was met by the enemy, and after a succession of bewildering skirmishes for several days, he concluded to go no farther:—"as the ground was too difficult, and had been made more so." Then turning his steps towards Jamestown, he was forced to retreat after a severe encounter, in which he suffered greatly in men, and, harassed by the Rapparees, retraced his way to the north, "*giving out*" that it was no use to take Jamestown, as the country beyond it was too difficult to advance, even if the town were in his possession.

Nor were Brewer and Kirke up to time at Lanesborough. They found the "bogs" to the east all intersected by canals, which were fiercely disputed by the enemy, and when they at last reached the town, they found that the eastern half of it had been burned down, and the fort on the other side rendered impregnable:—"and after a few ineffectual attempts to cross the river, they also retired in despair."

The movements against Banagher and Portumna were also ineffectual; and the regiments of Bristow, Caulfield, "and others,"—about 2,000 strong,—which had been ordered to Lanesborough, by way of Mullingar, were attacked by 1,500 of the Rapparees and soldiers, and after a fierce fight of over five hours, were routed with great slaughter, and driven back on Mountmellick, leaving all their baggage and military stores in the hands of the victors.

Ginckle now drew in his lines, and retiring to winter-quarters, began to make extensive preparations for an early campaign in the spring. But he had scarcely retired when he was apprised of a designed attack on his whole line, and drew out his army to meet it. Nor were his precautions unnecessary; for no sooner had he made his disposition, than the Irish generals made a simultaneous advance against the principal posts approaching the river. But finding their movements anticipated on all hands, and some of their garrisons seriously threatened in their rear, they re-

---

[57] Story's Impartial History, 29th, 30th, and 31st of Dec., 1690, and Jan. 1st, 1691.

tired after a series of engagements that resulted in no advantage to either, and the British army also retiring, a temporary quiet succeeded. As it was hoped that this movement, which had been matured in secrecy by the Irish generals, would have resulted in great advantage to their cause, its failure filled them with indignation and alarm. They saw that they had been contending not only against the enemy on their front, but against treachery in their rear. A close inquiry revealed the fact that the English general had been in communication with members of the Irish Senate, and the treason being traced to Judge Daly and Lord Riverstown, they were arrested and conveyed in irons to Galway. These events ushered in the month of February: the *rôle* of the last year was repeated; active preparations along the English line, and great expectations along the other: but the Rapparees increasing in numbers and activity, continued their predatory warfare without cessation, "watching all opportunities of advantage," says Story, "killing our men by surprise in a great many places, but especially keeping correspondence with the protected Irish in all parts of the country. They stole away our horses, sometimes in the night, and often in the noonday, when our men least expected it; by which means they recruited their own horse considerably, and did us no small disservice; nor is it probable, unless they had made use of some such ways, they could have brought any body of horse into the field worth taking notice of in the succeeding campaign."

So ended this ominous campaign of General Ginckle. He began it with all the appliances of success:—a powerful army, a most superb artillery, supplies at will, and those powerful auxiliaries in the road of conquest—confiscation, extermination, and proscription, keeping pace with his military movements. It was directed against an enemy comparatively insignificant in number; wanting in every thing but courage, hardihood, and "good-will," and a disrupted population without arms or direct purpose. Yet day followed day, and month followed month, and still his object seemed farther from accomplishment, while his enemy grew bolder, more numerous, and more effective; until at last, driven to the defensive, he abandoned his purpose in despair, and retired with an army worn down by fatigue, and disheartened by continual disaster. Had the Irish generals, at this period, one-half the means at the disposal of Ginckle, there is scarce a doubt that their cause would have been crowned with complete success. But there is no use in idle speculation on what might have been; the events of the past are irrevocable, and the contrary is the record.

Such was the conduct of Sarsfield during the fall and winter of 1690; and it is to the admirable disposition of his force, and the capacity he displayed in conducting both the civil and military affairs of the nation at this trying period, rather than to the single affair of blowing up the enemy's train at Ballineety, that we are to look for the cause of his unbounded popularity, and the undying affection that his name still holds in every Irish breast.

No ample and digested record of that trying campaign, conducted by the Rapparees and soldiers, has ever been written, nor is it likely that it ever will be. The Irish historians pass it over by a few hasty allusions, and hurry from the Boyne to Limerick, and from Limerick to Aughrim, as if unwilling to more than glance at the terrific struggle for life and liberty that took place between them. What we do know of it, has to be accepted at the hands of a hired scribe, who, on his own acknowledgment, was obliged to alter and distort his notes which were taken at the time, in order to please his royal patrons three years later. But even from him, enough can be gleaned to show that there was manhood sufficient in the country, if properly directed, to restore the king his inheritance, and, that the only military mind capable of uniting and directing it to that end, was General Sarsfield.

CHAPTER XV.

ARRIVAL OF ST. RUTH—GINCKLE TAKES THE FIELD.

Towards the middle of January, 1691, three French ships entered the harbor of Galway, as an escort to the Duke of Tyrconnell, who, it was confidently believed, had succeeded in the object of his mission, and the tidings of his arrival were received with general manifestations of joy. To the soldiers this news was particularly gratifying. He left them victors, it is true, but victors over a city in ruins;—exhausted in military resources, worn out by fatigue, without clothing or pay, and living on the bounty of a greatly impoverished country. They had borne their privations with cheerfulness, restored and strengthened their city, maintained their flag against overwhelming numerical odds at every post of their frontier; and believing their services about to be rewarded, their enthusiasm knew no bounds, and they looked to his arrival in Limerick with the happiest anticipations. They had been led to expect a full arrear of pay, a complete outfit of clothing, arms equal to their need, and a powerful French auxiliary, that would enable them to turn the tide of war, and wrest the conquered provinces from the grasp of the invader. They were bright hopes;—the brighter for being so long deferred—but, like those of the previous years, they were doomed to cruel disappointment. It soon became known that the only money he brought was about £8,000, to be distributed as a present donation; that the clothing received was not only insufficient, but entirely unfit for wear—their old regimentals being preferable;—and that, instead of the expected auxiliary, he was accompanied but by Sir Richard Nagle and Sir Stephen Rice,—who had been sojourning in France,—and a few of those military adventurers that in all ages appear wherever hostilities in any cause offer a road to ambition. Furthermore, it was found that the Duke of Berwick, who had performed signal service to the cause, and who shared the popular favor with General Sarsfield, was ordered to France, and that the latter was to be placed in a secondary position to another French general,—the Marquis de St. Ruth,—who had been appointed to the command of the army. Serious discontent soon became manifest at this neglect of a general whose unceasing activity, through the darkest period of the war, had kept the army from entire dissolution, and saved the Jacobite cause from irretrievable ruin. Besides, it was believed that the experiment of placing French generals over native troops had proved too disastrous to be again repeated, and, notwithstanding the high military reputation of St. Ruth, the news was received with great disfavor, and in the army created a spirit of disaffection that it required but a breath to fan into mutiny. That Sarsfield himself felt deeply humiliated, we have abundant evidence in the records of the period; nor did the title of Earl of Lucan, nor the commission of lieutenant-general which was borne to him by the deputy, entirely reconcile him to his altered condition. The unbounded confidence reposed in him during the interval of Tyrconnell's absence, had invested him with almost plenary powers, which had been exercised with a discretion and ability that pointed him out as the man for the time; public sentiment was undisguisedly in favor of continuing those powers; and his own heart responded to the wish, for he saw there were elements of success around which he, and only he, could call into action. His humiliation was the greater on this account: that though irrevocably bound to serve his king and country in any position, however subordinate, it greatly impaired his future efficiency; and the new appointment was viewed by all as another fatal step in the downward tendency of the Catholic cause.

There was, however, a consideration which, when duly weighed, as no doubt it was at the time, must have lessened the poignancy of this neglect, and rendered it less intolerable. The Duke of Berwick had high claims to this appointment,—perhaps higher even than Sarsfield. He was the king's son, and had been Lieutenant-General since 1689: he was brave, and accomplished in the art of war; and there was no cause but his youth, why he should not have received it. That he ambitioned it, is plainly inferable from the tone in which he notices his "recall from a country so full of troubles," and from his disapproval of the manner in which his successor conducted the ensuing campaign. It would, in short, seem that King James, being a dependant on the good-will of the French monarch, had to bow to that will in resignation; that this new general was selected by Louis; and that Berwick, by his recall, was saved the indignity of being reduced to a secondary position.

The result of this last mission to France, becoming known along the English lines, gave rise to mirth and ridicule among the soldiery, who might well pride themselves on the timely consideration of their own provident monarch, who left nothing undone that could contribute to their comfort or efficiency. Wherever they met the Irish soldiers, as they did along the river during the month of February, they taunted them with their repeated disappointments. The effect on the weak and vacillating was soon visible. Desertions became of not unfrequent occurrence among the soldiers of English descent, but those of the native race clung more faithfully to their cause with every reverse; but the general depression soon passed away, and all murmurs and despondent thoughts were lost in the notes of preparation.

So frequently are the names of King James and his ally, Louis XIV. of France, linked with mismanagement and misadventure through the history of this period, that it would seem all the attendant misfortunes of the Catholic cause resulted from the weakness and indecision of the one, and the absence of timely support arising from the mistaken policy of the other. But though these were the leading, and perhaps the main causes of its ultimate defeat, it was also induced by the prejudices and follies of the Irish leaders themselves, as much as by the errors of either king, or of both together. We have already seen some of the evil effects of divided counsels, and of incipient treason in the senate: we have now to make a cursory allusion to a character hitherto unnoticed, who played no insignificant part in the closing scenes of the drama, and added a ludicrous page to a melancholy and tragic *dénouement*.

It had long been an accepted prophecy in Ireland,—one much akin to that of the "sleeping warriors" of Aileach,—that an O'Donnell, a descendant of the house of Tyrconnell, was one day to return from Spain, and free the land of his fathers from the English yoke, by a great victory to be gained by him at, or near Limerick; and this chief was to be known by the *Ball-dearg*,—or red mark,—on the shoulder, which, 'tis said, attaches to the true descendants of that noble house. It happened that at this time there lived in Spain, an O'Donnell, of the family mentioned, and known also to bear the mark that distinguished its true representatives, and him fame pointed out as the destined liberator of the country. Whether this personage ever entertained an idea of his wonderful virtue or not, until consulted by an Irish deputation in Spain, does not clearly appear from the records of the time; but that he *was* waited on, and awakened to a sense of his importance, there seems to be abundant testimony to warrant this allusion.[58] In the nineteenth century this infatuation of men intrusted with the destiny of a nation would seem almost incredible, but it was not the less true. It was a glorious destiny to be the liberator of the land of his ancestors; he heard the call, obeyed it, and arrived at Limerick during the month of August, 1690. It was the time of the siege, and he took part in its most stirring events from the 17th to the 27th, and, it is said, did good service in the memorable conflict that has immortalized that city. His appearance at such a time was hailed with acclamations of joy by the populace, and even the leaders of the army treated him with consideration. After the retreat of the Prince of Orange, he was furnished with a Colonel's commission, and empowered to raise troops from among the Rapparees, to co-operate with the regular army. Those of the north and north-west, scattered along the frontiers, at once flocked to him and acknowledged him as their hereditary chief: others sought his standard under the influence of the prophecy that attached to him, until he had a following, variously estimated at from eight to ten thousand men. But here his services ended. With this following, he established his quarters from Clare-Galway to Sligo, behind the Irish lines, and assuming the authority of an independent chief, instead of harassing the movements of the enemy, he levied on the surrounding districts, wasting the subsistence of the remaining province to support his infatuated followers.—

"In short, he was," says O'Driscoll,[59] "of a class found in Ireland and else-

[58] O'Callaghan's remarks on this subject are substantially as follows:—The import of his name, perhaps, marked him out to cooler-headed politicians, as a means of effecting much national good, by exciting the imagination of the people. Ball-dearg O'Donnell was accordingly sent for, to Spain, and arrived at Limerick, August, 1690. (See Greenbook, p. 242.)

[59] O'Driscoll's History of Ireland, vol. ii., pp. 288, 289.—There is a letter in the Appendix to Haverty's History of Ireland, which came into the possession of its author, "through the extreme kindness of the Editor of The Four Masters," after his work had gone to press, and which he regrets not having seen in time to change or modify the estimate which he had formed of O'Donnell, and adopted in his text. But seeing that the name of the writer of the *letter* is not given, and that the vindication of Ball-dearg, which it contains, though plausible, is not at all convincing, the present writer adopts the generally received opinion.

where. He was a great boaster, suspected to be a coward, known to be a knave; noisy, insolent, presumptuous, and corrupt.... He was afterwards known to have been in correspondence with both William and Ginckle, and treating for a title and a command in the English army." Yet he played his part ably; so ably, that he carried himself through to the end of the war; nor did he appear in his true colors to his deluded followers, or indeed to the leaders of the army, until the final result of the war, revealed at the same time, and in the same manner, the intrigues of *Ball-dearg* O'Donnell, and the treason of Henry Luttrell. Such was one of the many influences that helped to divert the strength of the country from the direct purpose of the war, and its evil effect cannot well be over-estimated. It placed a covert enemy in the rear of the national army; materially lessened the resources of a province already overburdened with a helpless floating population; and withdrew from the enemy's country, which the other provinces then virtually were, the most daring of those hardy Rapparee bands, that had hitherto wrung their support from it, and materially embarrassed the movements of the foreign army.

Though the appointment of the Marquis de St. Ruth was opposed to the public sentiment of the people and army, still they well understood that the countenance of the French king was indispensable to their cause, and resolved to make a virtue of necessity; all now daily wished for his arrival to remove the general suspense and disquietude of feeling. The enemy was known to be in an advanced state of preparation, and it was feared that he would open the campaign before a corresponding force should be ready to meet him. It was also hoped that as King Louis had this time made his own selection of a general, he would support him in all things necessary — arms, ammunition, and artillery, and perhaps a contingent of troops to sustain the national honor. The public mind now underwent another of those changes incident to a condition of war, markedly in contrast with that of the previous month. From the western headlands a daily watch was kept up, and expectation was on tiptoe for his arrival. But day after day, and month after month passed on, and still neither armament nor general relieved the fever of anxiety. At length, on the 7th of May, when all hope seemed to fail, a French fleet was signalled off the headlands of Kerry, and the next day, riding up the Shannon, it came to anchor off Limerick. It bore the Marquis de St. Ruth, with Generals d'Uson and de Tessé, and about one hundred French officers of different rank; but no money, and no military contingent. He came, however, well provided with the munitions of war, a good supply of arms, and an outfit of serviceable clothing. His arrival was hailed with general acclamations, the bells of St. Mary's chimed forth throughout the day, and the most solemn ceremonies of religion welcomed this devoted soldier of the Catholic cause.

Though considerably beyond the middle age, St. Ruth was still a man of vigor and activity. He was of a commanding presence, pleasing aspect; was nervous in address, and energetic in command; — the first passports to the confidence of the Irish soldier. He had but lately returned to Paris, after a successful campaign in

---

For, admitting many of the assertions of the letter to be true, there is no cause given for the absence of O'Donnell from the Battle of Aughrim. He was within seven or eight miles of the field during the engagement; it was, perhaps, the most momentous battle ever fought in the country, and whatever were his private grievances, he should have shared its perils.

Savoy, and was selected by Louis to command the Jacobite forces in Ireland. But fame, which preceded him there, had also told how the finer traits of his character were marred by a vain ostentation, a hauteur of manner towards his subordinates, and an overweening conceit in his own importance,—the very worst traits to win the confidence or esteem of the Irish officers of that period, on whom the conduct of de Rosen and de Lausun had left a very unfavorable impression; or that of the generals; who could not see the necessity for his appointment at all, when he came unsupported by an army, and without coffers to warrant the raising of one from the floating population of the country.

Preparations for the renewal of hostilities were now actively resumed along the lines, and the minds of the soldiers were diverted from all other considerations. Their "penny-a-day" went far, for the country still abounded in the necessaries of life, and the people shared their means liberally. The proclamation of non-intercourse between the British Islands and France, announced at once both in London and Dublin, only served as a spur to greater enterprise both by sea and land, and every succeeding day witnessed the arrival of trading vessels, bearing arms and munitions—while the love of adventure brought daily accessions to the ranks of either army.

After a hasty inspection of the frontier and the condition of the troops, St. Ruth directed himself to the work of reconstructing the army, and his first movement for that purpose tended to raise him greatly in the estimation of the soldiers. Notwithstanding the exertions of the Rapparees through the winter and spring, there was still a deficiency of cavalry horses, and to remedy this defect became a matter of the first necessity. He at once issued an order to the gentlemen of the surrounding country to assemble at Limerick to take counsel on the state of the nation, and for other purposes. They felt highly pleased at the courtesy extended; and in order to pay all possible respect to this champion of their cause, came armed and on horseback; making, notwithstanding the general depression, a most gallant show. The meeting was held on King's Island, the soldiers being drawn around it, to render the proceedings more solemn and impressive. After a spirited address in French, on the duty of allegiance and patriotism; and the sacrifice that all should be prepared to make for their country, he ordered them to dismount and surrender their horses for the use of the army. Remonstrance was useless, and any attempt at resistance would be less so, for the soldiers, closing in on all sides, showed them that the *émeute* was preconcerted. They bowed in resignation, seemed to relish the joke exceedingly, and were deeply impressed with his capacity to deal with coming events, while he extended to them the acknowledgments of his distinguished consideration.

The disbanded soldiers were next called into service, and on the 15th of May, the Duke of Tyrconnell issued a proclamation ordering the Rapparees to retire behind the Shannon and hold themselves subject to another levy. They obeyed with promptitude, and the required number being selected, the rest scattered or returned to their former haunts. But they were no longer able to perform any considerable exploit, and their after-fate was tragical in the extreme: prices were set on their heads; the trade became exciting and profitable: they died on the mountains and by the wayside, prowling like wolves, and fighting like tigers to the last.

While preparations went forward day by day within the Irish lines, it is necessary to revert to the other side, and note the progress of Ginckle's affairs since the suspension of active hostilities; and perhaps the fairest exposition that can be given, is the following extract from Story's Impartial History, about the beginning of February, 1691: "The king did as much as possible in the time, as any who have seen the country may know; for if Ireland were as well-peopled as the soil itself will bear, it may defy all the world besides. You cannot see a town but where there is either a bog or a river, or both," &c. Here follows a dissertation on the natural difficulties the English army had to contend with, and the wiles and wickedness of the Rapparees, that retarded their movements "the whole winter long," concluding with the following consolatory reflections: "As to our own army, our numbers are the same as last year (except two regiments that were broke); they are also much healthfuller, and better acquainted with the country and their arms; and to encourage us the more, the Parliament has granted his Majesty a considerable fund to carry on the war, and also to equip his fleet. Besides, we have now at least 12,000 of the militia in good order, either to defend the garrisons behind us or to assist our army upon occasion ... and more than all, we shall have a great many Protestant Rapparees from the North and other places, for the northern people are mostly armed ... so that we shall have no want of men."

Such was the numerical status of Ginckle's army at that period, and from that until the summer; recruits, ordnance stores, and clothing were poured in daily to every port in his possession. From the 30th of April until the 6th of June, "all hands" were at work in Mullingar fitting up every thing for the coming campaign: for instance—

April 30th. A large body of recruits sent into the County Kildare.—*Same day*, all hands at work making cartridges, &c., "though it was her Majesty's birthday."—*Same day*, several ships arrived at Kinsale from England, and the Charles galley and Assurance frigate landed at Waterford with four other ships under convoy, all loaded with cannonball, bombs, powder, and several other materials.—May 8th, five ships loaded with arms arrived at Dublin.—May 18th, Dragon and Advice land four hundred marines at Baltimore.—*Same day*, six English ships come to Cork with recruits and provisions, under convoy of the Smyrna frigate; and so on to the 6th of June.

Towards the end of May the different divisions of the British army were put in motion towards Mullingar. On the 27th, General Douglas marched from the North with a force of about 10,000 men, and encamped at Ardagh. At the same time Wurtemburg put his troops in motion from Thurles, taking the detached garrisons on his route, and replacing them with the organized militia. On the 28th, Major-Generals Mackey and Ruvigney arrived with their divisions and encamped outside the town. About the same time General Talmash and Sir Martin Beckman, the Chief Engineer, landed at Dublin with troops and a corps of sappers and miners, and set the great train of artillery—"such as had never been seen before in that kingdom"—on its way, and immediately started for the camp. And "to give them the more comfort," Ginckle received advice from Updam, who regulated the cartel at Breda, that the Irish soldiers released in lieu of the Dutch prisoners, were not to be returned to Ireland, but sent into the French service, and that the Irish officers would not be exchanged according to the rank they laid claim to.[60] Proclamations again became the order of the day, all tending to the same object—the "comfort" of the English troops, and inviting desertions from their enemy. On the 31st of May, Ginckle appeared in person at Mullingar. All his outposts were immediately called in, notwithstanding strong protests from the Lords-Justices to the contrary; for he had determined to put forth all his strength, as the arrival of St. Ruth filled him with apprehension, and he only yielded to their appeals so far as to give them some officers from the army to command the private companies which all the country gentlemen now enrolled for their own protection.

Ginckle immediately contracted the defences of Mullingar, drew out his troops, and sent orders to Wurtemburg to encamp opposite to Banagher and Meelick, being resolved to force the river at one or both of those places, and afterwards to invest Athlone on the east and west. But finding a portion of the Irish army well advanced towards Frankfort, he abandoned that design, the order was countermanded, and Wurtemburg was directed to take a more circuitous route to the eastward, and join him on his way to Athlone.

Ginckle drew out his army from Mullingar on the 6th of June, and halted at Rathcondrath, where he was joined the same day by General Douglas. Here he encamped for the night, and sent out a party to reconnoitre the fort of Ballymore, then held as an outpost of the Irish army. After a brisk skirmish with the pickets of the fort, this party returned, bringing in a wounded prisoner, from whom he learned the force and disposition of the garrison, and appeared before it at noon on the following day. The town of Ballymore lay on the direct road from Mullingar to Athlone, and a little to the right of it stood the fort on a peninsula, isolated from the mainland except at one pass which led up towards the town, and which was commanded by a ruined castle that stood at its outer entrance. The place had been in the possession of the English during the preceding autumn, but the country around it becoming too poor to subsist a garrison, it was abandoned, when the Rapparees took possession of it, and held it through the winter, as a rendezvous in their raids against Mullingar and the surrounding posts of the enemy. The place was of much strategic importance, being well adapted for either offensive or defensive warfare; but having been utterly neglected by the different parties occupying it through the last year, it was now in a dilapidated condition. The fort was of mud, mounting two pieces of "Turkish cannon on cart-wheels," with a garrison consisting of eight hundred soldiers, two hundred and sixty Rapparees,—four hundred women and children who had fled to it as a refuge,—and was commanded by Colonel Ulick Burke, who had orders to hold it to the last extremity, in order to gain time for the Irish army to anticipate Ginckle before Athlone.

Ginckle, impatient of delay, and not wishing to lose time in storming the

---

[60] From this we learn that William sent his Irish prisoners to redeem his Dutch soldiers from France, and that Louis used them to fill his ranks on the continent; while the Irish officers, who could not be induced to abandon their own cause, were left to languish in prison.

castle, into which Burke had thrown a sergeant and fifteen men, deployed to the northward, and, erecting his batteries, directed a heavy fire against the fort. But as the great body of the lake intervened, no impression could be made from that direction, and it was found necessary to reduce the castle, which commanded the narrowest part of the lake, and also the pass leading into the fort. It was accordingly stormed, carried after an obstinate defence of two hours, and the gallant sergeant hanged in sight of the fort, for an "obstinate defence of an untenable position." This obstacle being removed, eighteen guns and four mortars were brought to bear against the fort, until eight o'clock in the morning, when the firing ceased, and Ginckle demanded a surrender, the summons being accompanied by a threat, that if it were not vacated within two hours, the garrison would share the fate of the sergeant, which they had just witnessed. Colonel Burke denied its authenticity, asserting that Ginckle would not set his signature to such an atrocious order, and demanded the summons in writing. The form was soon complied with, the threat was repeated over Ginckle's signature, but leave was granted for the women and children to depart or share the fate of the garrison. Burke next stipulated for permission to withdraw the garrison, as the non-combatants were determined to share their fate; but this being refused, the firing was resumed on both sides, and continued without intermission until noon, when the Irish gunner being killed, and the sand-walls of the fort completely beaten down, Burke displayed a flag of truce to the assailants. Ginckle, greatly incensed by the obstinacy of the defence, refused to notice the signal, and the cannonade was continued until seven o'clock in the evening, when a storming party and boats being ready to cross the lake, Burke again displayed his flag, surrendered unconditionally, and Colonel Earl, at the head of eight hundred troops, took possession of the fort. The booty of the captors was considerable, consisting of four hundred and thirty sheep, forty cows, fifty horses, a quantity of oatmeal, the arms of the garrison, two pieces of artillery, *"but no powder."* The loss of life was inconsiderable on either side; the threat of the English general was not put in execution;—the men of the garrison became prisoners of war, and the women and children were sent beyond the Irish lines, in conformity with the usage of the times.

Ginckle made a pause of several days at Ballymore, awaiting his heavy artillery, and the reinforcements expected from the south. While here, he sent Lord Lisburn with 2,000 foot and five hundred horse, to attempt the river at Lanesborough, and another body to reconnoitre the defences of Athlone, and report the condition of the enemy. The former suffering a severe repulse, returned after a few days, and pronounced the place impracticable, and the latter reported that the Irish army must have arrived at Athlone, as they saw some troops of horse drawn up on the hills on the western side of the river. While here, also, General Douglas departed to join the army of William in Flanders, and part of his regiment were left under the command of Colonel Toby Purcell, to occupy Ballymore, which had undergone a thorough reconstruction, consisting of bastions, hornworks, a platform for a battery of eight guns, and a floor of mortars. At length, on the 18th, Ginckle's train having arrived, he moved forward to Ballyburn Pass, where he was joined by Wurtemburg and Count Nassau, with a force of 8,000 men, and the next day resumed his march for Athlone.

Though Ginckle's preparations had extended farther into the season than he at first intended, he had still taken the field considerably in advance of his enemy, and Ballymore had been reduced, and his march resumed, before St. Ruth had moved out of Limerick. Nor did the knowledge of this disturb the equanimity of the latter, nor disconcert his arrangements. Hearing that Ginckle's army had left Mullingar, he dispatched a regiment of horse for the defence of Athlone, with orders to its governor, Colonel Fitzgerald, to strengthen his defences and hold both sections of the town until his arrival; then sending a force under Brigadier Maxwell to move along on the east, and waste the country as he went along, he drew out his army, turned his steps towards Athlone, and moved by easy marches along the western side of the river. Maxwell performed this duty with characteristic promptitude:—he soon rendered the country, for several miles beyond the river, destitute of provender; drove immense herds of cattle within the Irish lines; and then making that skilful display of his force at Ballyboy and Frankfort, which diverted Ginckle's attention from the lower fords, he recrossed the river at Banagher, and moved towards Ballinasloe, where he anticipated the arrival of St. Ruth.

The two armies now approaching each other were quite as disproportioned as when they met in the former year upon the banks of the Boyne. That of Ginckle, exclusive of the garrisons left at Mullingar and Ballymore, must still have numbered over 30,000 men, while that of St. Ruth, after all his detachments had been called in, and the garrisons depleted to the limit of safety, was, according to the most reliable estimate, but 23,000,—horse and foot. In artillery, and all the appliances of war, the disproportion was still greater; while the arms and appointments of the English army were incomparably superior to those of its less numerous adversary.

CHAPTER XVI.

THE SIEGE OF ATHLONE.[61]

Athlone—*Ford of the Moon*; so called, it is believed, from its connection with some ceremony of Druidic mythology—stands on both sides of the Shannon, in the counties of Westmeath and Roscommon; that part of it on the eastern or Leinster side, being designated Englishtown; and that on the western or Connaught side, Irishtown. Its position is as nearly central as the formation of the island will admit, and the country around it is rich in historic and traditional reminiscences. It was the scene of many a stirring event during the sway of the native kings and chieftains, nor has it lost in importance since the era of the English invasion; for ages it marked the greatest western limit of the "Pale," and it is still the strongest fortress and most extensive military depot in the kingdom. At the period under consideration, the two divisions of the town were of nearly equal extent, and a portion of each was encompassed by a wall of considerable strength, beyond which the suburbs extended for some distance into the country. The portion of the English town within the wall, was little more than half a mile in length, its greatest width being somewhat over a furlong, and the Irish town was similar in every respect, but extended a little farther towards the north and south on the river. In the middle of the eastern wall stood the Dublin Gate, facing the main street and market-place, and opposite to it a bridge of nine arches, connecting the two sections, being the only line of communication between them. The eastern end of this bridge abutted on the bank of the river, but at the western end there was a drawbridge of about thirty feet span, and beyond it, but a little northward, stood the castle, or chief citadel, built in the reign of King John; enlarged and strengthened in that of Elizabeth, who wished to make it the seat of her Lords-Justices; and the town was incorporated in the reign of James I. This castle commanded the whole extent of the bridge, in a slanting direction, and, with adequate artillery, could render it impregnable; but in the approaching siege, as in all others through this war, the native army was deficient in this arm of the service, and had for the defence of this castle, and two bastions that protected the fords on the river, but six pieces of light artillery and two mortars. The wall of the English town was in a dilapidated condition, and incapable of any protracted resistance. On the approach of General Douglas, about ten months before, its suburbs had been given to the flames by its governor, Colonel Grace, and the houses within the wall levelled and left in the same condition as when the siege had been abandoned. The Dublin Gate and its barriers were of great strength, but another which opened towards the north, had

---

[61] Ath luin. *Anglice*, Ford of the Moon.

been breached by the artillery of Douglas, had undergone but slight repairs since that time, and was incapable of offering a day's resistance to the immense siege-train of de Ginckle. The present governor, Colonel Fitzgerald, in pursuance of the plan which had proved so successful in the former siege, had determined on the destruction of this section of the town, when, contrary to the general advice, St. Ruth resolved on holding both sections, and issued his command to that effect, as Ginckle was about to move from Mullingar; and for this important service, Fitzgerald had but 400 garrisoned troops, and a regiment of cavalry, which came to his aid on the same day that he received notice of the general's resolution. His position was therefore most critical and embarrassing.—To abandon the English town without a defence, would be contrary to the orders of his superior, and subject him to the gravest military punishment; to withdraw his cavalry from the protection of the river was inadmissible, as it would uncover the town on the north and south, in case they should be cut off by a flank movement of the enemy, and compel him to surrender without a blow. His only course was then to make the best defence at all points: to dispatch a part of his garrison to retard the enemy's advance, and gain time for the arrival of the main army, which was known to be approaching, and within a day's march of the town.

Fortunately, the country stretching towards the enemy was well adapted to defensive measures, being such that a small body of resolute men could throw great impediments in the way of an army like de Ginckle's, encumbered with baggage and artillery, and arrayed in all the panoply of war. An extensive sweep of marsh and bog lay to the north, both difficult and dangerous to infantry; to the south the country was broken and irregular; and the road along which the enemy approached was lined on either side with hedges and thickets, affording convenient shelter at almost every step of the way.—Such was the country through which the English army had to march, and determined to seize on every advantage that could, even for a moment, retard it; the governor dispatched about two hundred foot dragoons and grenadiers of his garrison on their perilous adventure.

Ginckle left his encampment at sunrise on the morning of the 19th, and throwing out detachments towards Ballinahown and Killinure, where the Rapparees were reported to be troublesome, he took up his line of march. At Bealin, about a mile from his camp, his advance-guard received a warm salute from the ambushed Irish pickets, and, falling back on the main body, caused some confusion; when, throwing out detachments to clear the brush on his right and left, he approached slowly and warily towards the town. The Irish Guards now disputed the ground with the most obstinate valor; every hedge and thicket became the scene of assault and defence; when they yielded a position to the overwhelming force of their assailants, it was but to renew the strife with still greater desperation at another; the nearer the enemy approached to the town the more deadly the conflict became; many, both assailants and assailed, lay dead by the wayside, and it was well on to noon, when, forced from their last intrenchment outside the wall, the latter retired within their fortifications, and the English army appeared before Athlone.

Ginckle, who, finding that St. Ruth's army had not yet arrived, determined to press his advantage, immediately set to work in the construction of batteries, and had soon two at work outside the walls of the English town: one of three guns to the north of it, over against a bastion, on the western side of the river, and another of five guns to the south, and both played fiercely all day without cessation. At six in the evening another of nine eighteen-pounders was opened against the northern gate, and all worked steadily until noon on the following day. It was then found that the last one had effected a breach of its own width, practicable for the passage of infantry, when the fire of the two first was turned on the interior of the town, a council of war was held, and it was determined to assault it in force that evening.

The Governor, anticipating the result, and seeing that section of the town no longer tenable, resolved on the destruction of the bridge, as the only means of protracting the siege. For this purpose, after withdrawing his artillery, he detailed a part of his force, while the rest were stationed behind the breach to check the assault, and gain time for the accomplishment of this work, which was now a matter of vital importance.

The order of assault was soon arranged by the British generals, and was to be substantially as follows:—Five hundred grenadiers, with triple the usual number of officers, and a corps of sappers and miners, were to be arrayed in two divisions to support each other and lead the advance. The first, after effecting an entrance into the town, was to turn to the right, while the other was to follow close upon its footsteps, and, at the same time, file to the left. That which took the right was to be supported by 2,000 picked men, under the command of Brigadier Stuart and Prince Frederick, and the other by an equal number under Colonel Brewer and the Count of Nassau. The first column was to make its way to the bridge, and, seizing it, cut off the retreat of the besieged; or, failing in that, to seek cover in the nearest walls and await the support of the other division, which was to gain the Dublin Gate, and throw it open to the army outside. Then all were to push forward and seize on the bridge and fords, if successful, to assail the Irish town immediately, and if not, to cover themselves with intrenchments along the river.—All preliminaries were to be completed at five o'clock; the moment for assault was to be announced by the firing of one signal-gun; the grenadiers, in the mean time, were placed under cover to the northward of the town; and the whole movement was under the direction of Major-General Mackey and Brigadier-General Vittenhoff.

It was now the evening of the second day: the army of St. Ruth had not yet appeared in view; its delay was unaccountable; for he had received timely notice of Ginckle's approach. The cannon from without poured an incessant storm of ball and bomb into the town, and the defenders behind their torn ramparts calmly bided their time, but knew not the moment of assault. The fate of the Irish cause was in their hands, and their determination rose with the importance of their trust. Their Governor having done all that a brave and intrepid soldier could do, committed the rest to the bravery of his soldiers, and the gallant old Colonel Grace, who now served as a volunteer, took his stand beside them, and in his presence no man dare turn his back on an enemy.

At five o'clock the fire of the northern battery suddenly ceased, and the peal of a single gun immediately announced the moment of action. The report had scarcely died away, when it was echoed by a cheer from the British grenadiers, as, springing from their ambush, they rushed headlong towards the breach. A French officer of Cambon's regiment first mounted it, waved his sword, and pointed onward, when the Irish soldiers rose from their cover, levelled their muskets on the advancing foe, and in a moment the gallant Frenchman and many of his immediate followers were numbered with the dead. Still they pressed on, and hundreds of them thronged the breach, when a second volley, more deadly than the first, swept through their ranks, and the defenders stepped forward and stood to confront the whole force of the assailants. The conflict now became desperate, but the result could not be long doubtful; overwhelmed by numbers, they were borne through the breach, and the enemy gaining the open space inside the wall, commenced filing to the right and left in pursuance of their purpose. The way to the right was narrow and tortuous, and, though pressed on by the weight of 2,250 men, their way was disputed foot by foot, and dearly purchased in that direction. But that to the left being less obstructed, the result was terribly ruinous to the defenders. At the end of an hour one-half of them lay dying and trampled among the *débris*, and still the rest stood and fought as resolutely as ever. At length the gate was gained, the assailants thronged by thousands into the market-place, and the strife was transferred to the street leading down from it to the river. Another hour passed on, and the defenders were borne back towards the bridge; its destruction was not yet completed; and to win it on the one side and maintain it on the other, became the work of life and death. The assailants rushed on in their fury, but were steadily resisted, and even for awhile repelled, their overwhelming numbers defeating the very object of their assault. At length the arch was sprung, the word was given to retire; the defenders rushed along the bridge; some of them succeeded in crossing it, but their assailants pressing closely on them, many were borne over the battlements, to rise no more. Further persistence was now in vain; the work was done; the arch had given way, and sunk beneath the waters of the river; and the enemy retired under an effective fire opened on them from the opposite side; the bridge was rendered impassable.

History has few parallels for the bravery and devotion of the gallant men who performed this act of self-immolation. Two hundred of them strewed the way from the breach to the bridge; but not a prisoner was taken, nor a color, to grace the enemy's triumph. This happened on the 20th of June. On the 22d a French lieutenant-colonel was found wounded and dying under the bridge; and, three days after, a pair of colors was found in the same place, under a heap of the slain, for which Ginckle gave the finder a reward of five guineas. Nor was it a defence without a purpose,—for valor is generally estimated by the end attained:—it saved the Irish town from the immediate grasp of the enemy, and was a fitting inauguration to a siege which, for heroic daring and unbending fortitude, has few examples in the history of warfare. They had done their work at the sacrifice of their lives; the siege was now about to be renewed between more equally matched forces; for, just as they had retired across the drawbridge, on the western side, St. Ruth's army appeared beyond the town, and he took speedy measures to stop the progress of the enemy.—Wauchop was placed in the command of the castle; d'Usson and de Tessé were installed as joint commandants of the town, and Fitzgerald retired to his former position in the army, as colonel of his few remaining veterans.

Ginckle having thus gained the English town, removed all his artillery within the walls, and a train of eleven guns and three mortars having arrived in the mean time, he spent all the succeeding night in the erection of batteries. By the next morning he had five of them in full play against the Irish town and its defences:— two above the bridge, two below it—and one of five twenty-four pounders and six mortars at the foot of the bridge over against the eastern wall of the citadel. He next sent orders to hasten up his pontoons, which were on their way from Mullingar, and, warned by the desperate resistance he had just met, he took his precautions accordingly, and sent a requisition to Dublin for additional reinforcements.

Nor was St. Ruth now idle on his part. Encamping his army in a good position about two miles from the town, he garrisoned the castle with fresh troops, threw up lines of intrenchment along the river, and at once opened on the works of the enemy. His guns were few and of inferior calibre, but they were worked with a spirit and vigor that soon caused Ginckle to shift two of his batteries from the river, while the fire from the castle swept the bridge and rendered any approach along it impracticable.

Ginckle soon saw that to silence the guns of the castle was a work of the first necessity, and to this end all his heavy guns and mortars were at once directed. The labor of the gunners on both sides now became incessant. Night brought no respite to the toils and dangers of the day. The weather was extremely hot; an unusual drought had prevailed, rendering the fascines as dry as tinder; and their continual ignition made the work of the soldiers more harassing. The skies were clear, and the evening twilight almost ushered in the dawn, while the glare of the batteries lit up the intrenchments and rendered the assailants and assailed continually visible to each other, while the fire of Ginckle's mortars, being directed on the houses beyond the castle, added perpetual conflagration to the other horrors of the scene. After a short time, a mill which stood in the middle of the river, to the north of the bridge, and into which the Irish had thrown a detachment of sixty-four men to keep up a fire on the broken arch, attracted the fire of the enemy. The passage which connected it with the bridge was soon broken down, and the building itself taking fire, the whole detachment—with two exceptions—perished in the flames. The wall of the castle crumbled bit by bit, a rent became discernible in the eastern wall, and gradually widening, the greater part of the front gave way, strewing the passage to the bridge, choking up the sally-port, and exposing the interior to the great guns of the besiegers.

Such was the condition of the besieged on the morning of the 26th, and all that day the bombardment continued with increased fury. Towards evening the bastion opposite the ford was beaten down so as to be passable to horse and foot, and the battery which protected it was completely silenced; the castle was deemed no longer tenable, and Ginckle contemplated an assault in force on the following morning. Preparatory to this, he resolved to try once more the passage of the river, in order to create a diversion on the Irish rear while putting his design in execution; and, having lately received information that a ford had been discovered to the north of Lanesborough, which might be easily crossed in the face of the small garrison stationed there, had dispatched a strong force to that place, with orders to approach it in the night, and having captured the town, to make a demonstration on the enemy's left, while he himself, with the main body, would storm the bridge and fords on their front. But the design was communicated to General Wauchop, and he immediately sent a regiment of cavalry to the assistance of Colonel O'Reilly, who commanded there, with orders to defend the place to the last extremity. The troops of Ginckle had started on their expedition on the night of the 25th, under direction of a guide, and, after making a wide detour to the north-east, approached the ford with great caution on the night of the 26th; but, arriving there, they found the opposite side strongly intrenched and the Irish cavalry drawn up to oppose them. They, however, tried to force their way through, but being routed with severe loss, they returned, and reported that it would take the whole army to cross there, so the project was finally abandoned. Nor was this his only disappointment. The morning of the 27th broke over a scene as startling as unexpected, for in its light he beheld that the Irish battery above the bastion had been repaired and strengthened, and that the castle which he expected to find abandoned had been put in a better state of defence than before. An opening had been made in the western wall, through which rocks and beams had been conveyed to the top of the breach, and firmly imbedded there, while its one solitary tower, the Connaught Tower, still commanded the broken arch, and displayed its flag as proud and defiant as ever. He was therefore obliged to forego his intention for that day, and direct his whole force to the total destruction of the citadel before risking an assault on the bridge. To the five batteries already at work two more were now added, and an incessant storm of shot and shell was directed all day on the castle and the houses beyond it. Three times during the siege the town had been set on fire; the population had fled to the suburbs, and nothing having life remained within the walls but the gunners behind their crumbling earth-works, and the soldiers laboring to check the flames extending in all directions.

St. Ruth, believing that the tower could not long withstand the terrible fire brought to bear on it, set to work in the erection of earth-works to answer the same end, and for this purpose he conveyed some guns outside the town, and erected two batteries—one to the north and the other to the south—both bearing across the eastern angles of the bridge. Their fire soon drove the English gunners from their batteries, and during the cessation of their fire two intrenchments were thrown up on a high ground to the right and left of the castle. The fire from these dislodged the English musketeers from the walls near the river, and from this forward the contest became a duel of artillery. Ginckle's heavy missiles still bore down all obstructions; the ingenious traverse and change of position were unavailing; nothing could withstand the heavy guns of the besiegers but the Connaught Tower, and that, though crumbling bit by bit, still sent its shot with the same precision as before. In this manner the conflict raged during the whole of the 27th. The bombs of the enemy became exhausted, but this brought no respite to the besieged. Immense blocks of stone, even more destructive than shell, were hurled into the Irish intrenchments, crushing their fascines to atoms, and breaking down all barriers. Towards evening a body of the besiegers, moving behind an improvised breastwork, stormed the bridge, gained possession of the broken arch, and secured themselves behind a strong breastwork. The defence was stubborn, and cost both sides dearly; "for," says the English annalist, "what we gained here was inch by inch, as it were, the enemy sticking very close to it, though great numbers of them were slain by our guns, and the service cost us a great store of ammunition." But ammunition was of small account with Ginckle. One hundred wagon-loads of shot and shell reached the camp that evening; thirteen squadron of wagon-horses were sent to Dublin for more, and two batteries were added to the seven that had been at work since the morning of the 25th. One of these was on a hill outside the wall, which commanded the western end of the bridge, and the other in a meadow to the south of it, which raked the passage leading from the Irish town to the castle. Under cover of these nine batteries the English reached the last broken arch, and secured themselves by a breastwork overlooking that of the Irish on the other side. Here the grenadiers of both armies now stood firing their muskets and hurling their grenades across the narrow space that separated them. At length the fascines of the Irish breastwork took fire, the whole was soon a sheet of flame, its defenders were forced to retire, and on the night of the 27th the English remained masters of the last broken arch of the bridge.

The situation of the besieged was now most desperate. The town seemed all but in the possession of the enemy. The bastion opposite the southern ford, about fifty yards from the bridge, was levelled, and practicable to infantry and cavalry. The ford itself was easily passable, for the river was unusually low for the season. The town was a heap of smouldering ruins, and the castle,—with the single exception of the Connaught Tower—was beaten down to the level of the besiegers' guns. Beams had been extended across the last broken arch of the bridge, the planking was partially set, while the fire of their forty-seven guns was fierce and active as ever. Still the Irish relaxed neither in courage nor intrepidity. Though but one gun alone sent an occasional response to the incessant roar of nine batteries, sweeping every foot of their intrenchments, "they worked like horses, checking the fire within the town; carrying fascines to fill their trenches;" and exhibited a courage and endurance "such as was never excelled by man." Such was the situation on both sides through the night of the 27th:—the one in the face of inevitable death trying to reconstruct their shattered defences, and the other in exultation preparing to force the river at sunrise the next morning.

The night passed on, and the morning rose bright and clear above the river. The besieged seemed to have exhausted all the means of defence. Some lay close in the cover of their trenches, and others drawn up behind the western wall of the castle, waiting for the approaching conflict. The enemy alone were at work. The planking was nearly completed across the last broken arch of the bridge. The fire from their right and left traversed its western end between their workmen and the besieged, and their grenadiers were advanced along the bridge waiting for the expected signal. At this moment a sudden commotion was observable in the Irish quarters, and a simultaneous shout rent the air, as eleven men, cased in armor, were seen to clear their trenches, and bear directly for the bridge. A silence still as death fell over the besiegers and besieged, and for a moment all seemed spellbound. In another the noble fellows had reached the bridge, and "with a strength and courage beyond what men were thought capable of," commenced to tear away the planks and beams, and cast them into the river. The amazement of the English soldiers soon gave way to the stern necessity of war. A discharge of great and small guns swept the bridge, and the devoted men passed forever from the earth! Undeterred by their fate, eleven more sprang forward to complete the work! Another peal rang out as before, a cloud of smoke enveloped them for a moment, and, clearing away, it was found that their work was completely accomplished, that the bridge was rendered impassable, and that two of the eleven had escaped within their intrenchments.[62]

Ginckle, greatly chagrined by his disappointment, withdrew his soldiers to their camp, called a council of war, and deliberated on the alternatives of continuing the siege, or seeking a passage at some other point of the river. The council continued far into the evening; the questions were discussed in all their bearings, and another assault was determined on for the morning of the 29th.

In the mean time it became necessary to gain possession of the broken arch which had been lost in the last assault, and to silence the battery on the Connaught Tower, or, which was the same, to destroy the tower itself. This tower stood at the north-western angle of the castle, and though it had cost more ball and ammunition than all the rest of the defences together, it had never ceased for a moment to annoy the enemy, even when all the earth-works had been silenced. Against this tower all Ginckle's heavy guns were now directed. Towards midnight its abutments gave way, and shortly after it fell forward in one solid mass, and lay stretched athwart the ruins. While this was going on, the utmost activity prevailed in the English camp. Pontoons were put in order, a close gallery was constructed of sufficient length to span the arch and protect the workmen inside it, while a company of Danish soldiers had examined the river, and established another ford practicable for twenty soldiers abreast, about thirty yards to the south of the other. Three hundred yards to the south of this had been selected for the bridge of pontoons, and the banks at both places levelled for a proper distance. The assault was to be made in three places:—at the bridge: across the newly-discovered ford: and over the pontoons, outside the town. It was furthermore resolved that every regiment should have the honor of participating in the movement, and the selection of the men for this purpose was confided to Major-General Mackey, who made the following disposition:—From every regiment he selected forty-three grenadiers, eighty-three private soldiers, three captains, five lieutenants, two ensigns, and seven sergeants—a force not less than 8,000 men in all. These he arranged in three divisions, and stationed them outside the eastern wall, "in great secrecy," until the proper time to show themselves. The way from the gate to the river was cleared of all obstructions, and ladders were placed against the walls, near the river, which were pierced for musketry, in order to annoy the enemy while the assailants were crossing it. The bridge was to be the first point of assault, and on its success those at the ford and over the pontoons were dependent. Three thousand men were to cross at the bridge, 3,000 more over the pontoons, and 2,000, composed of horse and foot, were to attempt the ford. The assault was to take place at <u>sunrise, until w</u>hich time all should be conducted with the utmost "secrecy and

[62] Of these twenty-two men, the name of but one is known to history: that of Sergeant Custume, or Costy, who headed the first ten, and who was, of course, among the victims.

circumspection." The soldiers were to carry fifteen rounds to a man, to have each a green bough in his hat, as at the Boyne; they were rewarded in advance by the distribution of large sums of money, and the word of the night was—"Kilkenny."

But, notwithstanding all the precautions of secrecy observed in the English camp, St. Ruth received timely information of the design, and had taken active measures to counteract it. When morning broke over the Irish town, Ginckle was both surprised and mortified to see that all his movements were anticipated. The drawbridge had been secured by a heavy breastwork, a new battery had been constructed opposite the ford, and another in a meadow outside of the town, commanding the point selected for laying his pontoons, and reinforcements from the Irish camp had been stationed at convenient positions to dispute the town, in case he succeeded in forcing the passage of the river. He was further disconcerted at finding that General Mackey's arrangements were not all up to time. The men stood to their arms at the appointed hour: the musketeers lined the walls along the river; the gallery was ready to be pushed over the bridge; but the pontoons, which should have been laid overnight, were found insufficient to span the river, and it became necessary to repair some old ones to supply the deficiency. As this had now to be done in the face of the enemy's fire, it became necessary to construct a battery to dislodge them, while the work of repairing and laying the boats was carried forward, and it was doubtful whether he should have any timely co-operation from that quarter. Still, as all the other movements were dependent on the result at the bridge, Ginckle determined to persevere, and at the appointed time the grenadiers and soldiers moved forward under the protection of their covered gallery. After great danger and difficulty it was forced over the English breastwork, where the grenadiers stood face to face to dispute the possession of the bridge, and the strife of the 28th was repeated over again, with greater desperation on both sides. While this was going on at the bridge, the fire of the English batteries swept the whole Irish line, and under the diversion Mackey made desperate efforts to complete the line of pontoons; but, despite of all, he was driven from the work, and forced to abide the result at the bridge. All now depended upon this: and the soldiers on both sides looked on with feelings wrought to the highest pitch of excitement. The Irish grenadiers suffered dreadfully, for the enemy's breastwork completely overlooked that on the other side, and their grenades wrought terrible destruction in their trenches. Four hours passed on, and still this encounter raged without cessation. The gallery was forced forward, as it were, inch by inch; the arch was spanned, and the work, as before, had nearly reached completion, when the fascines on the English side caught fire. The soldiers made great efforts to extinguish it, but in vain; the whole was soon a sheet of flame; and being no longer tenable, they abandoned their position and retreated across the bridge: the Irish grenadiers advanced and completed the destruction of the gallery and defences; and the bridge was again impassable. The failure of this assault at the bridge caused the abandonment of those at the other two points, and the English soldiers were withdrawn to their camp, none remaining but the usual guards, and the cannoneers behind their intrenchments. The firing of the cannon ceased for the first time since the siege had opened, and silence brooded over the scene of desolation.

St. Ruth was now elated with success, and enthusiastic in praise of the soldiers, who had displayed such stubborn valor in the defence of their old town. It was now, throughout its whole extent, a mass of smouldering ruins, over which the soldiers made their way with difficulty and danger, and the intrenchments along the river had been levelled and reconstructed so often that the earth around them had been rendered as dry as powder. He therefore issued orders to have a road opened from end to end behind the batteries next the river, in order to facilitate the deploying of troops from one point to another; to have the western wall completely razed, the houses within them levelled, so that the enemy should have no shelter if they should succeed in passing the river; and the area behind the castle cleared, so that his raw levies should be drilled there and trained to perform garrison duty. He next withdrew most of the trained soldiers from the works, and supplied their place with three regiments of recruits; and, expressing his belief that the enemy would retire without risking another engagement, marched his army back to camp, and gave a banquet, 'tis said, to which he invited all the ladies and gentlemen of the surrounding district.

Ginckle was greatly mortified at the failure of this last grand movement. It was made in force; each of the divisions had fulfilled its part of the programme. All the resources at his command had been brought to support it, and yet a signal failure at all points, and a serious loss of men, had been the consequence; and, as he had determined beforehand that on its result his advance or retreat should depend, he immediately called a council of war, to signify his intention to retire, and try some other point of the river, or open a defensive campaign on the ground already traversed. All the propositions submitted at the previous council were taken up and discussed: the continual failure of his plans; the spirit and endurance of the enemy; the impossibility of remaining any longer in a district stripped of forage and provender for several miles around. The expenditure of ammunition, too, had already outrun his most extravagant calculations. Bomb and ball had accomplished all that could be effected, for both town and citadel were now reduced, and still the enemy, so far from abandoning the place, had recently renewed their defences, and should the river be crossed, were ready to offer battle amid the ruins. Should he again attempt the passage, and succeed in crossing, success was to be purchased, but at a great sacrifice. Should he cross and not succeed, the total destruction of his army was more than probable. Should he attempt to cross above or below this place, he uncovered the capital, and the enemy would not fail to profit by the advantage. The disadvantages of taking the defensive at the beginning of the campaign, and the disgrace of retiring in the face of the foe whom the soldiers had hitherto been taught to despise, would have a ruinous effect on the spirit of his troops, raise that of the enemy, and exert a powerful influence on the action of the French monarch. Having canvassed the subject in all its bearings, he was himself in favor of trying another ford above or below their present position, where less difficulties were to be encountered, and submitted the whole subject to the deliberation of the council. The debate was long and earnest, and the majority supported the decision of the General-in-Chief. The minority were against retiring, and they were the ablest and most prominent of the generals:—Mackey and Wurtemberg, Ruvigney and Tettau, urged another assault, and offered themselves to head the soldiers in person, and be the first to cross the river. The deliberation was long, and the matter remained undecided, when the opinion of the majority was changed by one of those fortuitous events which seem throughout this war to arise continually in favor of the invader. Two officers who had deserted from the Irish army were at this juncture brought before the council, and proffered most important information. They represented the feeling of security that prevailed in the Irish camp; the prevalent belief that the enemy would retire and abandon the siege; the substitution of untrained soldiers in the trenches; and the withdrawal of the veterans. They told of the bad feeling existing between St. Ruth, the deputy, and general officers; the scarcity of ammunition; and of all things that could give weight to the views of the minority. The opposing opinions were at once reconciled, and a plan of action was forthwith adopted.

It was now determined to take the town by surprise; and the better to conceal the design, it was concerted to make a feint of retiring and raising the siege. Guns were to be dismounted; tents struck; the baggage placed on wagons in sight of the enemy; and the general appearance to be that of an army about to retire from its encampment. The soldiers selected for the last assault were to be withdrawn from view, and held in readiness outside the wall until the appointed hour. At the usual time of changing guard, which was six o'clock in the morning, the men who were to cross at the ford were to move down as if to relieve their comrades, when at an appointed signal, which was the ringing of the church bell, they were to cross and storm the opposite intrenchments. These being carried, they were to move to the right and left, to assist the other divisions which were to follow in quick succession, and pass over the bridge and pontoons simultaneously. Every thing seemed opportune for the attempt; every part of the plan was observed to the letter; and to create the proper ardor among the soldiers, still larger rewards were distributed than on the former occasion.

All through the evening the cannonade along the English lines seemed to relax its wonted spirit; farther on it ceased altogether, and it was observed that some of the guns were being limbered and removed from the river towards the camp. The *ruse* immediately had the desired effect. The Irish soldiers, believing that the enemy had actually commenced to retire, came gradually out of their trenches, and ventured down towards the river. The English soldiers, too, seemed to relax in discipline, and came down to meet them. Jest and repartee were bandied across the stream; the soldiers of Ginckle twitting those of St. Ruth on their miserable "penny a day," and the latter reminding the former that they had given "bad penny-worths" for the money which their general had lately distributed among them. So they beguiled the time; with the closest secrecy and circumspection on the one side, and a feeling of security and a total unconsciousness of approaching danger on the other. As the night wore on both parties retired from the river, and sought repose in the trenches, and a deep silence settled over the scene, only broken at intervals by the occasional challenge of the sentries as they met each other in their measured round. Nor was it in the unconsciousness of the Irish soldiers alone that fortune seemed to favor the besiegers. The orders which St. Ruth had lately given, on withdrawing his army from the town, had not been carried out. The houses were still the same shapeless ruins he had left them; the western wall was still entire; but a roadway had been cleared behind the intrenchments on the river, and all the defensive works to the rear of it had been defaced and levelled. This neglect was the consequence of a disagreement between St. Ruth and General d'Usson—the former wishing to have all obstructions removed, so as to give battle on the ruins of the town if the batteries on the river were carried; and the latter wishing to preserve the walls as a line of defence, in the event of such a conjuncture. It therefore happened that the work "went by default," or that the bad parts of it were executed and the more necessary totally neglected. However this be, a want of concord was manifest among the leaders; and when to these untoward events it is added, that d'Usson was absent from the camp, that three untrained regiments manned the defences, and that a scarcity of ammunition prevailed along the lines, the whole train of circumstances pointed to a manifest destiny, and—the reader may anticipate an evil one.

It was yet the gray dawn of morning; the same supineness prevailed along the Irish lines, and the same cautious preparations went on in the camp of the enemy, when Colonel Cormac O'Neil entered the quarters of General Maxwell. He came to demand a supply of bullets for his men; for, being on duty overnight, he observed certain signs on the opposite side that led him to believe that another assault might be soon expected, and wished to take the necessary precautions. Maxwell was at first incredulous, and answering the demand by one of those Scotch apothegms, so prevalent at the time,—"If he wanted to shoot lavrocks," O'Neil retired moody and discontented. As the morning advanced, however, that general himself saw reasons to convince him that the colonel's suspicions were well founded;—he observed that the bridge of pontoons had not been removed, that the batteries there and at the ford showed signs of having been recently repaired and strengthened, and that the guards along the whole line had been doubled through the night. He immediately communicated this intelligence to St. Ruth, and requested that a division of veteran troops should be immediately sent into the town; but the herald soon returned with the insulting reply that "if he was afraid, another general officer would be sent to take his place." So the morning passed on; the plans of the enemy were matured, and they awaited but the appointed hour to put them in execution.

At six o'clock the tattoo in the English camp announced the hour of changing guard, and the soldiers marched down leisurely, as if to their accustomed duty. In six minutes after the church-bell rang out its signal, the artillery opened along the whole line, and under its shelter the assailants dashed forward and entered the river. A body of sixty grenadiers, cased in armor, and moving twenty abreast, led the advance. They were headed by Captain Sandys, a soldier of great daring and intrepidity, and were closely followed by a strong supporting column of cavalry commanded by General Talmash and Colonel Gustavus Hamilton, and by 2,000 chosen infantry troops under the direction of Mackey, Tettau, La Mellioneire, and the Prince of Hesse. Simultaneous with this assault, which took place at the ford, other movements were directed towards the pontoons and the town-bridge, and the whole scene was again alive with military ardor and intrepidity. There never was a more complete surprise. The movement was so sudden and unexpected that the assailants had nearly gained the opposite bank before the alarm was sounded in the Irish quarters, or the soldiers who were lying asleep in the trenches could be aroused to a consciousness of their danger. As the grenadiers began to ascend they were met by a few hasty and ill-directed volleys from those on guard, which checked their progress for a moment, but they were pressed on by the thousands in their rear, and literally borne over the intrenchments, where they soon silenced all opposition. Some of the Irish soldiers fled to the shelter of the ruined houses, where they rallied and kept up an irregular fire on the enemy thronging into the town; but most of them were taken, and, being unarmed, were slaughtered where they stood. Having thus carried the works on their front, the assailants immediately filed to the right and left; some to aid in laying the pontoons, some in securing the drawbridge, and still others to mask the castle and cut off the retreat of its garrison. The road which had been opened by St. Ruth's orders, was now of the greatest advantage to his enemy, who moved quickly behind the intrenchments, cutting off the Irish soldiers; who, having no batteries in the rear to check the pursuit, were surrounded, overwhelmed, and cut down with little resistance. The bridge and pontoons being soon made passable, thousands rushed into the town, swearing as they stumbled over the ruins, and dealing death to their disarmed prisoners. One battalion of veterans, led by Maxwell and some Irish officers, made a stubborn resistance, and for a while checked the pursuit; but, being surrounded and assailed on all sides, they were slain, with the exception of the general and a few of the superior officers, who were secured as prisoners.

On the first alarm, information was sent to St. Ruth that the enemy was crossing the river; but he scouted the idea, and boasted that Ginckle would not dare it after his late repulse, while he lay so near with an army to succor it. Sarsfield, who was present at the time, replied that the undertaking was not too great for English valor to attempt, but still St. Ruth, either through real or affected disbelief, scorned all remonstrance, and remained immovable. In a short time, however, the fugitives from the town began to reach the camp; he was at last convinced, and, with a seeming indifference, ordered Major-General John Hamilton to take two brigades and drive the enemy again beyond the river. The attempt was made, and the fight was renewed with such determination that General Maxwell expressed his belief, to his captors, that the town would be retaken. But after a desperate conflict of an hour and a half amid the ruins, the enemy gained the western wall; to dislodge them became impossible to an over-matched force; the Irish soldiers retreated to their camp; and Athlone was lost.

The loss of life by which Ginckle gained possession of this town is variously estimated. Twelve hundred would perhaps cover all the casualties of the siege, but in addition to this he expended fifty tons of gunpowder, 12,000 cannonball, 600 bombs, and innumerable tons of stone, hurled from the mortars whenever the shell became exhausted. The Irish army, during the same period, accepting the highest estimate, suffered a diminution of 2,300 men, of whom 500 were slain, and 566 captured in the last surprise and assault. Its loss in officers was very great—too great for specification. Among them were the French adjutant-general, the two

Colonels McGuinness, Colonels McMahon and O'Gara, and the veteran Colonel Richard Grace, whose body was found amid the slain under the western end of the bridge, where it had lain since the assault of the previous morning, — and there could be no place more appropriate for the fall of that patriot warrior. The booty taken within the town is thus summed up by the English chaplain, Story: "A good store of plunder among the ruins, and a great many dead men in the castle, with about twenty barrels of powder, twelve hogsheads of meal, some wheat, and a great many other things."

But Athlone was lost to the Irish army, and its last line of defence was penetrated, not through lack of valor or capacity to maintain it, but through a want of vigilance, totally inexcusable among the superior officers, and a singular combination of pride and folly on the part of the general, strangely comporting with the importance of the cause. Up to this day, no city had ever been defended with more determined valor, and never was eventual success more apparent than on the very hour that it was captured "by the most complete surprise that ever was." The last sun looked down on the Jacobite army exultant in spirit and confident of success; the next saw it overreached by the enemy, outraged by its general, robbed of victory, and humiliated by defeat. The world had seldom witnessed such heroic sacrifice, such patient endurance, and enthusiastic devotion as those displayed by the Irish soldiers of that period; but the loss of this old town, through manifest neglect—a tampering with fate, as it were, so culpable in a general—roused a spirit of indignation in every breast, and denunciations loud and bitter were uttered against St. Ruth, now as deeply penitent and as lowly obsequious as he had lately been haughty and intolerant. But little time was left for vain regrets or useless recrimination. The presence of an enemy flushed with success, within two miles of their camp, banished every other consideration for the moment, and, yielding to the appeals of their generals, they prepared for the final contest. All that day, and far into the night, they remained drawn up on the site of their encampment, in momentary expectation of the enemy, and determined to risk a battle. But as the night wore on and Ginckle made no forward movement, they decamped and marched in good order to Milton Pass, a small village about six miles to the north-west, on a river which empties into the southern section of Lough Ree. There they remained until ten o'clock next day, when the infantry took up their march towards the south-west, and the cavalry, after remaining some hours longer to protect their rear, took the same direction, and disappeared from the sight of the enemy.

CHAPTER XVII.

THE INTERVAL FROM JULY 1ST TO THE 12TH.

From its central position on the principal river of the country, Athlone, at any period of the war, was of the utmost importance to either belligerent; its loss to the Irish cause was, at this particular crisis, a misfortune almost irreparable. It was the main link in that chain of fortresses which the Irish generals had early recommended as a base of operations, from which they could indefinitely prolong the war, and eventually roll back the tide of invasion. Their successful defence of it since the battle of the Boyne had tended to strengthen that belief, for, notwithstanding the incessant assaults of the enemy, not a link in the chain had been broken, and every attempt to sever it had resulted in his repulse or discomfiture.

Well has the Shannon been termed the "principal feature of the island:" nay more! in a military sense it is the key to it. Though most of its principal garrisons are approachable by roads at all seasons; yet, by reason of its high winter floods, rising towards the beginning of October, and scarce ever receding until the end of May; with its islands and adjacent callow lands completely inundated, it appears throughout its whole length a chain of extensive lakes, completely hiding its main channel, and greatly limiting the number of assailable points throughout the intervening period. The possession of Limerick, too, by the native army, deprived the invader of the advantage of any craft, save such as could be improvised in the interior, and against the action of cannon these were almost or totally unserviceable. There were, therefore, only five or six months of the year during which the invading army could prosecute a vigorous campaign along its environs, and with its garrisons in a proper state of defence, with the native army lying conveniently behind them, and the other three provinces open to its incursions at will, all the power of England alone were incompetent to the reduction of the country.

Deeply impressed with this conviction, the defence of Athlone had been tenacious, and desperate even to recklessness.[63] Other considerations, too, tended to heighten the importance of this siege. It was the opening event of the campaign; it was carried on under the eye of their new general, of whom fame had spoken so loudly, and above all, it was hoped that a successful result would remove all misgivings from the mind of the French monarch as to the wisdom of his advocacy, and prompt him to immediate and more effective intervention. But the fall of Athlone at once dashed all these bright anticipations. The mind of Louis, contin-

---

[63] The French officers chided their recklessness, and asserted that they had never seen such bravery displayed by the men of any nation.—Rawdon Papers, letters C. L. I. and C. L. II.

ually warped by the misrepresentations of de Lausen and Louvois, had from the beginning wavered on the sustenance of the war; the ill success of his generals had been hitherto attributed to the intractability of the native race; deceived by the subterfuge, he adopted the accusation, and would, it might now be inferred, refuse any further support to a cause whose fate was already foreshadowed. Nor could it be doubted that the error of St. Ruth, though too palpable for evasion, would have its palliation, while the brave men whom his pride and arrogance had cheated out of assured victory, would again be the victims of covert calumny.

It is no wonder, then, that the Irish soldiers felt the loss of Athlone with a grief bordering on despair, and the Irish officers with a rage strongly savoring of mutiny. To those it seemed as though they were to be perpetually the dupes of every adventurer in search of a reputation, and to these, that their dearest liberties weighed as nothing, and that their country was but as a diversion from the military chess-board of Europe, and they deemed the neglect of St. Ruth a crime scarce less detestable than covert treason. To all it was an overwhelming calamity, opening at once to the tread of the invader the province which they had so long and so gallantly defended, and which until this day they could proudly claim as their country.

It is extremely painful, after the lapse of nearly two hundred years, to revive the weaker traits of St. Ruth's most singular character: for it would be far more congenial, in view of his subsequent career, to revive in him a bright reputation than a clouded one. He came to the country in good faith; he gave his life as an earnest of his sincerity in her behalf; and his ashes lie with those of her best and bravest on their last great battle-field for civil and religious liberty. That he planned it skilfully and fought it well, all admit; that it was lost only by the "special interposition of Providence," is generally conceded. He was brave, intrepid, and collected, in that moment which tries true heroism, and his fate still awakens a sympathetic chord in the breast of every generous Irishman. It should be remembered, too, that his name was one of hatred to the French Huguenots of the time, who sold their services to every country at war with their lawful sovereign, and came to Ireland as the crusaders of *that religious ascendency* they failed to establish in their own. From them the English historians who have treated of this war, have taken their estimate of St. Ruth's character; and such of the Irish historians, too, as advocate "Protestant ascendency and the dependency of Ireland upon England." Deeply imbued with the hatred of French influence in the island, the dissertations of such chroniclers on individual character is persistently in accordance with that feeling. With them the character of Tyrconnell and St. Ruth are alike the subjects of bitter and unmeasured sarcasm; that of the one, because he is said to have first advanced the theory of a French protectorate over the country; and that of the other, simply because he was the servant of their enemy, and a Frenchman; and so much, if not all of their testimony in this connection, may be regarded as either studied falsehood or gross exaggeration.

On the other hand, this policy of Tyrconnell is that which most endears his name to the Irish race, and wins it the general approbation of the native historian. And the wisdom of that policy has grown on them, age after age, until it has at last settled into a faith, that they are to be one day freed by the armed intervention of the enemy of their oppressor. This, too, may account in a great measure for the sympathy manifested by our native historians for the misfortunes of St. Ruth; for, in treating of him, the calamities consequent on his errors seem to be forgotten, and faults that, if committed by a native general, would call forth execrations, are touched so delicately, that one can scarce know which to applaud or to condemn.

Yet, weighing all these, and many other extenuating causes, there still stands out testimony, abundant and reliable, that his errors were ruinous to Ireland, and that in him a great soul was clouded by a most inordinate vanity; that his conduct towards Sarsfield was unwise and untimely, alienating from him the heart of that devoted soldier, and destroying that mutual confidence so indispensable to success; that the position of Tyrconnell as commander-in-chief was a canker in his heart, and not as regarded military affairs only, but that he persistently denied him that courtesy and consideration due to his age, his services, and his position as deputy: but, above all, that through his folly he lost Athlone, and precipitated the country's fate, at a time when a strong hope pervaded every breast, when the army had reached a high standard of efficiency, and after he himself, exultant in its valor, had pronounced it invincible.

Resting his character on its antecedents at this particular juncture, no special pleading could shield it from obloquy. But following it to the end, and coupling his faults with the heroic efforts he made to redeem them, the heart, deeply touched by his vicissitude, cannot restrain its sympathy; and that his memory can thus hold the heart divided between love and hatred, between disgust and admiration, is still the great singularity of his character. At one moment it would seem that he held the cause he championed unworthy of his desert, and had concluded to let it go by default; while the next, he appears to be impressed with its importance, and is seen imparting hope and animation to all around him. Yet over all his arrogance and folly a native nobility of soul predominated, and well had it been for his fame, and for the country that holds his ashes, had some reverse of a less serious nature overtaken him at a period less critical in its history and in his.

But whatever were the foibles of St. Ruth, from his advent in the country to his retreat from Athlone, we have now to look on an entirely different character. There he had learned, though at a fearful cost, that his *name* had no fears for his potent adversary; that deeds alone were to be the test of high emprise; and that his folly had narrowed down the campaign, and indeed the whole war, to the last resource of fallen heroes;—death or victory. With this feeling, all that was vainglorious in his character at once disappeared; the mist was removed from his mind, and it shone out to the end of his short career, as that of a true hero in adversity. Unlike his French predecessors, he scorned to hide his faults behind the shield of calumny, he candidly acknowledged his error, and bitterly lamented it. He became courteous to his officers, affable to his soldiers, changed at once from the despot to the patriarch, and touched by his sorrows, as much as by their own calamity, they again rallied round him, and determined on a final throw for religion and liberty.

On the evening of the first of July he reached the town of Ballinasloe, about ten miles south-west of Athlone, crossed the river Suck into the County Galway, and drawing out his army along its western bank, determined to await the enemy and stake his cause on the issue of a pitched battle. Here the ruinous effects of his late reverse became painfully apparent. The army that a few weeks before had marched from Limerick twenty-three thousand strong, buoyant in hope and spirit, was now reduced to less than fifteen thousand men. The cavalry was still powerful and efficient, having suffered little during the interval, but out of nearly nineteen thousand infantry he mustered somewhat less than eleven thousand, and the *morale* of the men had also deteriorated.[64] Still, his determination was fixed, and his spirit rose, even as his difficulties multiplied. In order to remove the disadvantages of divided command, Tyrconnell now resigned his position as commander-in-chief, but determined to lend all his influence and power to recruit the army and follow its fortunes to the end. This self-sacrifice on the part of the viceroy produced a reconciliation quite beneficial to the cause, and satisfactory to the general, but the feeling between himself and Sarsfield, never cordial, now bordered on mutual hatred, deepening to the last, and at the last was fatal.

Being now invested with entire military control, St. Ruth caused the garrisons of the Upper Shannon to be dismantled, drew in his outposts, and made speedy requisitions for men and munitions. Jamestown and Lanesborough were at once abandoned; Shannon Bridge, Banagher, and Portumna were each reduced to a nominal garrison; Galway sent a regiment, and Limerick all that could be spared from its defences, which were few, for the enemy had still ten thousand regulars, and a strong force of militia in Munster, and a desultory warfare, fierce and incessant, raged throughout the counties of Cork and Kerry, down to the vicinity of Limerick. A requisition for troops was also made on the *Pretender, Balldearg,* now holding court between Tuam and Athunree, surrounded by a force variously estimated at between eight and ten thousand. But this redoubtable chief would neither furnish the required levy, nor make any movement to discomfort the enemy; preserving at once his masterly inactivity and his worthless person.

With his scouts and pickets well advanced towards Athlone, St. Ruth established his quarters in Ballinasloe, to await his reinforcements, and to give his troops that rest so necessary after the toils and privations of the last month.—That Galway was Ginckle's objective point scarcely admitted of a doubt; but then there were other routes to it, as practicable, though not so direct, as that on which St. Ruth had taken up his position, and he determined to hazard no further movement while the intentions of his adversary remained a matter of conjecture. Here, then, we will leave him to the duties now imperative: to recruit and resuscitate his army, and restore that spirit and discipline so necessary to the coming event, and return to take note of what was transpiring in the English camp.

Ginckle betrayed no undue haste in following up his adversary; although his previous movements were indicative of a persistency scarce admitting of a moment's cessation. Athlone being once in his possession, he determined to make it his base of operations against the remaining province, and to hazard no advance

---

[64] "In this retreat the Conough regiments grew very thin, so that the foot, by desertion and maroding, was reduced from 19,000 to about 11,000 men." —*King James's Memoirs,* Vol. II., pp. 455 and 6.

until he saw it in a proper state of defence.—With his army drawn up on the ruins of the Irish town, he awaited the disappearance of St. Ruth, and when no longer apprehensive of renewed hostilities, he withdrew it again across the river to its encampment. The burial of his dead claimed his earliest attention, and this day being the anniversary of *The Boyne*, the evening witnessed its first celebration in all the pomp and circumstance of war. Bonfires blazed on the adjacent hill-tops; the names of William and Mary were duly glorified, and peals of musketry and salvos of artillery continuing far into the night, "proclaimed their conquest to the vanquished Shannon." His sick and wounded were next sent to Dublin and placed under the care of the most eminent army surgeons, while all that could contribute to the comfort of the hale, became subject of immediate requisition. On the 2nd, Paymaster Robinson arrived at the camp with several "cart-loads" of specie, and the whole army received full arrear of pay, and further promises of reward and booty, while pressing demands were made on the Lords-Justices for reinforcements to fill up its ranks to the regular standard. After this day, magazines, stores of ammunition, food, provender, and liquors began to arrive hourly, and one-half the army, divided into relief parties, were vigorously at work clearing away the *débris* of the siege; repairing breaches, raising ramparts, while reinforcements, now pouring in from all available posts, were placed in their allotted regiments and subjected to hasty and rigorous discipline. The garrisons left in their rear, and those along the Shannon, which had been abandoned by the Irish, were manned with native militia, and four of St. Ruth's cannon were mounted on carriages and added to his already enormous train of artillery.

On the 4th, as the works approached completion, he sent out a party under one Higgins, "a converted priest," and a native of that locality, to reconnoitre the Irish position; but, being attacked by a picket-guard in the wood of Clonoult, fifteen of them killed, four taken prisoners, the rest escaping with their worthy leader, who was himself "sadly wounded." At length, on the evening of the 6th, orders were issued to the army to be ready at dawn next morning in marching order, and with fifteen rounds of ammunition to a man; and, on the morning, the whole army crossed the river and drew out beyond the town, where they again went into encampment to await Ginckle's final preparations.

The Dublin commissioners had not yet taken cognizance of the situation, and, as usual, after such events, were preparing another of those parchment manifestoes, which, under a specious verbiage, were meant to delude the people, and to affect their cause as fatally as bomb or bullet. It was a proclamation of *amnesty*, and began with:—"Since it hath pleased Almighty God," &c., &c.—It offered pardon to all private soldiers;—with pay for their horses and furniture,—who within three weeks would surrender themselves to the commander-in-chief; and to colonels who would surrender their regiments, and to governors who would surrender their garrisons within the same period; and to such of the inhabitants of Limerick and Galway, in particular, as would be instrumental in delivering up said places, pardon and *possession of their estates,—"where it could be done;"* and that all such soldiers, captains, colonels, governors, etc., should be received into their Majesties' service and pay; and that *"as soon as their Majesties' affairs would permit,"* a Parliament would be called, when they would endeavor to secure their protection from "religious persecution," etc.—It praised the mildness of the English Government,—as the proclamations of to-day do,—denounced the tyranny of France,—another favorite theme.—It was given at the Castle of Dublin, July 7th, 1691, signed by Porter and Coningsby, and ended with—"God save the King and Queen."

With this was issued, by way of supplement, an address from Ginckle himself; more brief and more pertinent, offering rewards to deserters from the royal army, who would renounce their allegiance, and take service under his standard. To soldiers serving without pay, as those of the Irish army had been for several months, this twofold inducement of amnesty and reward was a terrible temptation; but it had little or no effect. The defection caused by St. Ruth's misconduct before Athlone had already done its worst, and the desertion rather tended to O'Donnell behind them, than to Ginckle in their front. Others, preferring a middle course, had joined the Rapparees, and the rest, true to their antecedents, resolved to retrieve their cause in the field, or depart the country forever.

Of the manifesto of the Lords-Justices, it may be finally said, that had it been meant in good faith, it would have won for them a very fair claim to justice and humanity. But when it is known that all their proffers were illusory, and that their subsequent conduct was cruel beyond description; that the lands to which they had promised reinstatement had already been sequestrated beyond redemption; that the plighted faith of themselves, the general, and their sacred Majesties were wantonly violated; and that a hundred years of more than barbaric cruelty elapsed after their "Majesties *had* found it convenient to convene a Parliament;"—the character of all—Lords-Justices, general, and "Sacred Majesties"—is too infamous for a single epithet.

On the same day that those proclamations were issued, Captain Villers returned from a reconnoissance, and reported St. Ruth as still holding the passes of the river Suck, and apparently determined to dispute them. But it being deemed advisable to give these missives time for the desired effect, a further postponement of action was the consequence, and the interval was spent in endeavoring to repress the excesses of the army. All religious exhortations having failed, a stringent military code was adopted. This held forth at once the severest punishment for crime, and the most liberal promises of booty and reward to the men, and of "lands and livings" to the officers. This comported so strangely with the "amnesty," etc., of the Lords-Justices, as to render it entirely nugatory, by exposing their covert hypocrisy in the same breath in which their manifesto was announced.

The morning of the 9th dawned bright and sultry, but towards noon the unusual drought of the last month was broken by a violent tornado. Trees were uprooted, houses levelled; several men and horses were struck dead by lightning; and the march of the army was suspended until the morning of the 10th; when, having left Colonel Lloyd with his own, and half of the Douglas's regiment in command of the town, Ginckle advanced as far as Kilcashel, seven miles farther westward, and encamped for the night. Taking a strong escort of cavalry, he advanced towards Ballinasloe, and found that St. Ruth had decamped from his position. Crossing the river and advancing to the hills of Dunloe, he ascertained that St. Ruth was still in the vicinity, for his outguards were seen hovering along the hills of Garbally, and retiring slowly as he advanced without offering any opposition. Continuing still to advance, he at length beheld the whole Irish army drawn out in line of battle upon an opposite hill, when, after a close inspection, he ordered a map of the ground to be prepared, and returned to the camp; when the Irish pickets again advanced, and occupied the hills along the western bank of the river. From Kilcashel he advanced to Ballinasloe the next day, and halted opposite the ground lately occupied by the royal army, where he summoned a council and submitted the result of his reconnoissance for the consideration of his generals.

Deeply impressed with the importance of St. Ruth's position, this council had serious misgivings as to the wisdom of pressing an engagement while he occupied it, and the necessity of adopting a more circuitous route was urged. But the majority considering that they had advanced so far that they could not recede without danger and disgrace, a forward movement was adopted, and the plan of battle finally arranged. It was, however, determined not to disturb their present encampment, lest the movement should be attended with a reverse, but to leave two regiments under Colonel Foulke for its protection, and that none should be allowed to proceed any farther, save such as bore arms. Ammunition was then distributed, the pioneers and grenadiers were ordered to the heads of their respective regiments, and it was arranged that the whole army should cross the river at daybreak, and be formed in array of battle by six o'clock, on ground already selected about a mile beyond it. The soldiers revelled, yet rested on their arms throughout the night, while the generals matured their plan, and the pass-word was—"Dublin."

St. Ruth remained several days on the river Suck, in a state of uncertainty as to whether Ginckle would advance directly on him, or, by taking a north-westerly route to Galway, induce him from the ground of his own selection. While there his army was also recruited by detachments from all the available garrisons still under his control; and he soon found himself again at the head of an army of 20,000 men. This force, according to the most reliable estimates, consisted of 16,000 foot of all arms and 4,000 horse; and the artillery, which had been greatly reduced by the reverse at Athlone, was now but nine brass field-pieces. Of this army, it may be said that the soldiers and officers of the subordinate rank were almost exclusively of the old Celtic race of the island, while the division and regimental commands were held by men of the same race, and by descendants of the Palesmen who had remained faithful to their king and country; and that at this time all, with hardly an exception, were of the Roman Catholic faith.

Having waited until Ginckle's design was clearly indicated, he decamped on the evening of the 9th,[65] and retiring still farther westward, halted at the village of Aughrim, and as if he had already selected his ground, pointed to the hill of Kilcommodon, and announced that there he was determined to die or retrieve his

---

[65] As we find him, according to Captain Viller's report, at Ballinasloe on the 7th, and apparently determined to give battle there, it is reasonable to infer that he did not retire until after the storm of the 9th.

fallen fortune.

From its marked inferiority in numbers and ordnance, the Irish army here, as at the Boyne, was compelled to act strictly on the defensive, and few places in that section of country were better adapted to this purpose than that which St. Ruth had now selected.

The hill of Kilcommodon, now known as the field of Aughrim, is about three miles south-west of Ballinasloe, and is the most considerable of an irregular chain of hills extending from the western bank of the river Suck for a distance of several miles in the direction of Galway. Its position is such, that if a straight line be drawn from Drogheda, on the east of the island, to Galway on the west, none of those memorable battle-fields in its history—Drogheda, The Boyne, Athlone, Athunree, or Galway—will deviate more than a mile from it, while most of them will be directly under it; and Aughrim adds still another link to that long chain of classic associations. Notwithstanding the many changes that time has wrought since the period under consideration, the hill and the country around it look still as sad and gloomy as the thoughts they impart, and few of the old race ever pass that way without uncovering the head and offering a fervent prayer—for, together with being the last battle-field for religion and liberty, which is sufficient in itself to awaken a melancholy interest, it is also remembered by them as *the field of their unburied dead*.

The hill from north to south is about a mile in length, and has nowhere an elevation of more than four hundred feet. Near its southern extremity stood the church of Kilcommodon and the house of Urrachree,[66] the latter the more eastward and the more prominent feature in the events then pending; and at its northern extremity the village of Aughrim, and a castle of the same name, which, during the Cromwellian war, had been dismantled and untenanted. From its ridge to its base it was considerably less than half a mile of very gradual descent, and from the house of Urrachree to the Castle of Aughrim, along the middle of this declivity, nearly a mile and a half. Along its eastern base it was traversed by intersecting hedgerows, dividing its lower half into small fields of meadow and tillage; but from these up to its crest it was bleak, arid, and heath-covered. Outside of the hedges, and nearly parallel to them, extended a belt of marshy ground, of irregular width, scarcely exceeding a furlong at any point, through the middle of which flowed a small stream, irrigating it from end to end, losing itself in a large bog which lay on the north, and rendering the marsh difficult to infantry and impractical to cavalry. This marsh covered about two-thirds of the face of the hill, and lay closer up to Aughrim than to Urrachree, while outside of it the north-eastern side of the hill was further protected by a strip of moorland lying close to a bog, which protected it on the north and north-west. The road from Ballinasloe ran straight up to this moor, and diverged abruptly; one branch of it winding round by Urrachree, and on to Loughrea; and the other, running between the Castle of Aughrim and the northern base of Kilcommodon, led on to Kilconel, Athunree, and Galway. That by Urrachree ran all the way through firm upland; and excepting the con-

---

[66] Story calls this building the Castle of Urrachree; but the other historians style it a house, perhaps to distinguish it from the Castle of Aughrim, and to avoid repetition.

fluents of the stream that watered the marsh, the hill on that side presented no more than ordinary obstacles to an advancing foe; but that which led to Aughrim offered considerable impediments from the manner of its formation. It lay through a common between the moor and the bog; narrow at its eastern side, and gradually expanding into an esplanade, or field, of four or five acres, and narrowing again, in its immediate approach to the castle, until it became passable for only three or four horsemen abreast.[67]—In fine, it may be said that, from the centre to the extreme right, this hill was no more than ordinarily defensible; but from that point round to the extreme left, it was well isolated, and, with little trouble, could have been rendered impregnable; at least to cavalry.

On this hill St. Ruth drew up his army, and encamped along its ridge; selecting as the site of his own tent one of two Danish raths that stood near its summit, and which commanded a view, not only of the hill itself, but of the country for several miles around it. On the morning of the 10th he formed his line of battle; his right resting on Urrachree, his left towards Aughrim, and his centre on its mid-slope between his camp and the hedgerows. Each division consisted of two front and two rear lines; the former of infantry, and the latter of cavalry; and in this position, with banners displayed and pickets well advanced to the river, he was observed by Ginckle during his reconnoissance on the same evening, and this he maintained until the morning of the 12th, to indicate to his enemy that he accepted and awaited the battle.

Such was St. Ruth's disposition, and such the ground which he had selected to countervail the vast superiority of his enemy in men and resources; and how far his skill contributed to that result now demands a passing notice. The hedges which wound along the base of the hill were in themselves no unimportant feature of defence for his infantry. But as some regiments of these were hastily raised levies, he had them also adapted to the offensive action of his cavalry, on which, from its well-established reputation, he had been led to place most reliance. They were accordingly opened at proper intervals, so as to admit of flanking and direct charges, both of infantry and cavalry, against such bodies of the enemy as should succeed in crossing the marsh and penetrating beyond any of these successive lines; and this disposition embraced the whole of his centre, and portions of his right and left. In the squares formed by these hedges his musketeers were to be stationed, while above them, in the direction of his camp, squadrons of his choicest cavalry stood opposite to each direct intersection, while the remainder of the hill, from these up to the camp, was cleared from all obstructions to the deploying of succors to either wing of battle. For the defence of the Castle of Aughrim and the pass which approached it, which were on his extreme left, he selected two regiments of musketeers and foot dragoons, and placed a battery of two pieces on an elevation between the castle and Kilcommodon, so directed as to rake the pass all the way between the esplanade and the grounds around the castle. On the side of Urrachree, where the country was open, and the hedges more broken and diversified, he ran additional connecting trenches, and placed some companies of

[67] Some writers say only two abreast. But if Story's map be any thing more than a fancy sketch, the narrowest part of this road would have afforded ample room for six horsemen.

musketeers in the house and its outer walls, which stood considerably in advance of his main line on that side. The seven pieces of artillery which remained, after detaching two for the defence of the pass at Aughrim, were disposed in the following manner: On the north-eastern face of Kilcommodon, almost over against the castle, was constructed a battery of three pieces, so directed as to throw a raking fire across the pass itself, a portion of the marsh, and the esplanade beyond it, to prevent the enemy's enlarging there; and the remaining four pieces were placed on his inner right, and directed over a portion of the marsh and the road leading up to Urrachree. But before his centre there were no cannon whatever; either because he deemed it less necessary, or that he wished to invite the enemy's infantry to cross, where he was sure to break them by repeated cavalry charges, and overwhelm them by his more agile infantry while recrossing the marsh in disorder. His line being quite an extended one for the number of troops under his control, he had no reserve of infantry, but a choice body of cavalry was held behind the north-western side of Kilcommodon, out of view of the enemy, within convenient support of his right, and actually but a rear line of his left, and extreme left at Aughrim.

As the battle of Aughrim, together with deciding the fate of Ireland and the dynasty of the House of Stuart, had also an indirect bearing, of scarcely secondary import, on the military affairs of the continent, it has been a subject of much more critical comment than that ordinarily bestowed on military events; and the historians of each successive period, down to the present, have visited the disposition of St. Ruth's army with praise or animadversion, each, no doubt, in accordance with his own peculiar views of what should or should not have been done by a general. While all approve the selection of the ground, as manifesting a keen perception of what a defensive position should be, nearly all censure some one or other of the arrangements made for its defence. His design of letting the enemy cross at his centre and beating them afterwards; the placing of his cavalry reserve so far from his right; and his neglect of the Pass of Aughrim, which was by nature so defensible; have been the subject of severe criticism, and the whole plan, or that of allowing the enemy to cross at any point, has been compared by the Duke of Berwick, to a similar error of the celebrated Marshal Crequi, which had been attended by a great disaster. But as the cavalry reserve had not been needed on the right during the action, and as all the enemy's forces which crossed at the centre had been successfully repulsed, the testimony of the duke, who was not on the ground, and of all who sustained that view, may be dismissed without comment. But what does really seem defective in his plan of defence, was the neglect of the Pass of Aughrim, which could have been rendered, with little labor, impregnable to either infantry or cavalry; and in view of his very inferior artillery, this omission seems totally irreconcilable, excepting on the ground that he believed the force left for its defence entirely adequate, as indeed they should have been, had they looked in time to their appointments.

Of the ground, also, it may be said that subsequent writers have attached more importance to it than it really deserved. Whatever features the hand of time may have defaced, it could never have been more than ordinarily defensible, excepting on its northern extremity, where it is still hemmed round by an extensive bog. Its advantages are thus briefly summed up in one sentence by the English chaplain: "*Here* we had a view of their whole army, posted as before described, by which posture they had the advantage by at least 1,000 men"[68] — no unusual advantage in the selected site of a battle-field.

Of the generals who commanded the respective divisions of St. Ruth's army, or of the regiments that constituted them, little can be established from contemporary or subsequent historians, beyond this: — That Colonel Walter Burke and his brother, Colonel David Burke, held the Castle of Aughrim and its defences; that Lord Bophin, Brigadier Henry Luttrell, Colonels Simon Luttrell, and Ulick Burke commanded on the left; that Major-Generals Dorrington, H. M. J. O'Neil, Brigadier Gordon O'Neil, Colonels Felix O'Neil, and Anthony Hamilton, held the centre; and that Lords Kilmallock, Galmoy, Galway, Clare, and Colonel James Talbot commanded on the right. And judging from the positions held by those leaders respectively, and the regiments they indicate, it may be inferred that the Munster troops were on the right, the Leinster and Ulster troops in the centre, and that those of Connaught held the left and its surroundings.

In addition to those division and regimental commanders, the marshalling of the entire infantry was deputed to General William Mansfield Barker, and that of the cavalry to Major-General John Hamilton;[69] and the whole was commanded by the Marquis de St. Ruth and Lieutenant-General Sarsfield,[70] aided by Generals d'Usson and de Tessé, and other officers of established reputation.

Having completed his arrangements, and allotted every division its service, St. Ruth drew up his army and reviewed it in front of its encampment. Then, in an eloquent and animated address, he set before all the great issues dependent on the coming battle. He reminded them that, unlike the mercenary army of the Prince of Orange, they were about to contend for all that man holds dear, and for all that exalts and ennobles the profession of arms — their homes and kindred;

[68] That is, if all things else were equal, the position would be worth 1,000 men to the army occupying it, which would still leave an advantage of 9,000 men, at least, in favor of Ginckle, irrespective of his vast superiority in artillery.

[69] Some very reliable historians, — among whom may be instanced Taylor and O'Driscoll, — lean to the opinion that Sarsfield was not at the battle of Aughrim, but only adopt it as a probability. This opinion also gains credence from a tradition still received in that neighborhood: that, owing to an altercation with St. Ruth, on the evening preceding the battle, he withdrew his own immediate command to Redmount Hill, about six miles distant, in a south-easterly direction, whence he returned to the field next day, but too late to restore the battle. That the altercation occurred, and that each general threatened to place the other under arrest, is abundantly corroborated; but by the same testimony the presence of Sarsfield is also established. Story names him as second in command on the day of battle, and the weight of testimony sustains that belief. But, what renders it certain, beyond peradventure, is this simple fact: that had Sarsfield, through neglect or petulance, caused the loss of that battle, he would never have appeared in France. There he would have been held accountable by King James; and neither from him, nor from the French monarch, would he have received the consideration that was afterwards accorded him. On this consideration, if on no other, the former opinion is positively rejected.

[70] Richard, John, and Anthony Hamilton were brothers, as were also Ulick, Walter, and David Burke.

their country and its altars. The duty of allegiance to their king who had staked his crown to free them from an odious religious bondage, and the certainty of immediate and adequate succor from his own sovereign, should their arms be crowned with success, were set before them in language calculated to awaken loyalty and enkindle enthusiasm. His own services in the cause of religion were alluded to as an earnest of that sincerity in their cause which tended to awaken sympathy and establish confidence, and his troubles, and even his errors, since he came to the country, were reviewed with an earnest ingenuousness that removed all traces of discontent and restored general harmony. This address was delivered in the French language, and interpreted to the soldiers by their officers and chaplains in their native tongue, till every eye kindled with devotion, and every bosom glowed in the hope of anticipated victory. Then exhorting them to prepare themselves by those religious observances that should distinguish the Christian soldier, he retired to his tent to digest the thoughts that labored in his mind, and to shape them to purpose and to action.

The eve of battle had come:—that hour which best attunes the soldier's heart to sympathy and devotion; and many associations contributed to render that one more than usually impressive. It was at once the season of full moon and perpetual twilight, and the sultry glare of day was succeeded by that chastened yet abundant radiance that at once soothes and spiritualizes; and, above all, it was the Sabbath eve, which more than any other awakens the sacred memories of love, home, and kindred.—The crest of Kilcommodon, studded from end to end with the white tents of the soldiers, stood out in its isolation like a city of silver, while the castles of Urrachree and Aughrim on the front, and the churches of Kilcommodon and Kilconel in the rear, seemed as sentinels of the place, and carried back the mind to the ages of faith and chivalry. Nor was the scene passing throughout the encampment less characteristic of the time and the event.—From sunset until the hours that precede the dawn, the chaplains of the army knew no repose: the voice of prayer arose on all hands, and the soldiers approached the confessional to prepare for the great sacrifice of the Mass, by which the human ordeal of the morrow was to be inaugurated. Towards morning heavy clouds obscured the moon, and darkness deepened over hill and valley, until all became as drear and dismal as it had before been full of grandeur and celestial loveliness:—nothing was heard but the challenge of the sentinels on their rounds, and the occasional neigh of the war-horse; and nothing seen but the distant watch-fires where the pickets on the eastern hills kept watch above the camp of the enemy.

How commendable is the spirit of religion on such occasions! History, sacred and profane, delights to record this manifestation of the divinity in man. The Israelites never joined battle without offering sacrifice, and even the pagan nations always propitiated their gods on the eve of battle. And yet we find this instance of it in the Irish people made a subject of the lowest ribaldry, even by the reverend historian of William's army. Without, however, entering on a disquisition as to the efficacy of prayer, or what providence, or good or evil directs the destiny of nations, a precedent in point may not be considered inappropriate.

The battle of Hastings was to England what that of Aughrim was to Ireland.

Each established a new dynasty, and each accomplished the subjugation of the native race. That of the Saxon was but the work of a day; that of the Irish was an incessant warfare of centuries. The one was the extinction of Thanes and Heptarchs; the other of chieftains and princes.—And there were still other traces of similarity.

At Hastings, the Saxons revelled while the Normans prayed. At Aughrim, the Irish prayed while the English revelled. Yet the same historians who appreciate the devotion of the Norman, and indicate its efficacy, make it a subject of ridicule in the Irish, and couple it with defeat. Providence and faith are often too lightly used to link a defective argument, or to round a happy period. Few will now deny that the Saxons were a more virtuous people than their Norman conquerors, or that the Irish were not much more so than the heterogeneous mass that followed the Prince of Orange. If the Saxons bent to the yoke of a conquering race, and prospered under it, let them glory in their wisdom and servility; but that the Celtic race, through every vicissitude, spurned it, hated the connection, and have still an undying faith in their ability to sever it, constitute, it is believed, a truer nobility of character.

CHAPTER XVIII.

THE BATTLE OF AUGHRIM.

'Twas five o'clock on the morning of July 12th, 1691. A heavy fog obscured the rising sun, and passed like a moving curtain along the hills that separated the adverse armies now preparing for the stern arbitrament of battle. What a chaos of human feeling surged and swayed beneath it! On the one side, the love of home, kindred, and country, and the memories that come of ages of persecution; on the other, that of power, plunder, and confiscation, and the wantonness that exalts vice into virtue, and deifies usurpation. The maintenance of legitimate right, and the establishment of perfect civil and religious liberty, called forth the royal army, and marked its footsteps from the advent of this war to its close. An unnatural usurpation, and the ambition to dominate in matters civil and religious, heralded the other, and its course was marked by cruelty and proscription. Their causes were markedly dissimilar, and of the spirit which impelled them to battle, each army, in its various gradations, was a fair representative.

At early dawn, Ginckle, who induced the battle, was moving his men across the river, and forming them, according to prearrangement, on a level ground about a mile to the west of it, leaving still a span of two miles between him and his adversary. This was effected by eight o'clock, but an advance was suspended, owing to the heavy fog that lay over the hills, and rendered the manoeuvring of his army in the vicinity of the foe both troublesome and hazardous.

As the line in which it was now drawn up, was that in which it entered the field of Aughrim, and which it preserved through the action, until forced to re-form after a series of futile assaults against the Irish right, it is here particularly described, in order to avoid disconnecting repetition hereafter.

Two parallel lines, somewhat over two miles in length, a considerable distance apart, arranged in four divisions, each consisting of a front and rear line under the command of its respective brigade and regimental commanders, constituted his entire army and array of battle. Beginning at the northern or right flank, and passing to the left, each division, front and rear, stood in the order following:[71]

[71] The above description of Ginckle's line of battle is taken from a copperplate engraving in Story's Impartial History, second volume, to which he refers the reader, with the following remarks:—"It is to be observed that my Lord Portland's horse is not in this order of battle, because they came not up until after it was ordered; however, they had their full share in the action; and Colonel Foulke's, which were always to guard the train, but being then convenient for it, and the General resolved to make all the force he could, they had also their part both of honor and service in the action; and though Brigadier Stuart is there set

First Division, front:—Levison, Winn, Oxford, Langster, Ruvigny, and Villers; rear:—Cunningham, Winn, Lanier, Wolseley, and Byerly. The front line of this division was under the command of Lieutenant-General Scravenmore and Brigadier Villers, and its rear under that of Major-General Ruvigny and Brigadier Levison.

The Second Division, front, presents the regiments of Kirke, Gustavus Hamilton, Herbert, Lord George Hamilton, Foulke, Bellasis, and Brewer; and its rear those of Stuart, Earle, Tiffin, St. John, Lisburn, and Meath; the former commanded by Major-General Mackay and Brigadier Bellasis, and the latter by Major-General Talmash and Brigadier Stuart.[72]

The Third Division, front:—La Mellioneire, Du Cambon, Belcastle, Greben, Danish, Danish, Danish; rear:—Nassau, Lloyd, Prince of Hesse, Lord Cutts, Danish, Danish, Danish.[73] It is scarcely necessary to remark that the troops of this division were all foreign, being composed of Danes and Huguenots; the front line under the direction of Major-General Tettau and Brigadier La Mellioneire, and the rear under that of Major-General Count Nassau and the Prince of Hesse—a Brigadier.

The Fourth Division:—Nearly all foreign too, stood in this order; front:—La Forrest, Schested, Donop, Doncour, Monpouillon, and Eppinger; rear:—Schack, Nienhouse, Zulistein, Reedefel, Ginckle, and Eppinger; the former under Major-General La Forrest and Brigadier Eppinger, and the latter under Major-General Holstaple and Brigadier Schack.—The whole was under the command of Lieutenant-General Ginckle, now Earl of Athlone,[74] and the Prince, or Duke, of Wurtemberg.

Of this long array of names, none represented less than a regiment, while many of them stood in front of a brigade. For instance: Ruvigny's place represents two regiments; Cunningham's two; Stuart's three; Wolseley's four; Brigadier Ginckle's two; Eppinger's two; and so on to between sixty and seventy regiments. And taking the lower number, sixty, and averaging the horse and foot at 500[75] to a regiment, we deduce a force that cannot, by any legitimate computation, be set down at less than 30,000 men.

Of Ginckle's artillery perhaps no accurate estimate can now be given,—some

down, it is only as to his post, for he was then at Dublin, ill of wounds received at Athlone." He might also have added that Brewer's remaining force was called up from Mullingar, the safety of which was committed for the time to the militia, and that towards the evening, he was further reinforced by a large body of Enniskilleners.

[72] See the preceding note.

[73] The six Danish regiments of this division stood as indicated—three in front and three in rear—but their regimental leaders are not named on the map.

[74] Ginckle was honored with this title after the fall of Athlone; but whether it had been already conferred is a matter of little import.

[75] Story estimates the foot regiments to be each 705, the horse 286, and the dragoons 444, irrespective of officers; but many of them were actually double of those numbers; as an instance Eppinger's Royal Regiment of Holland Dragoons was 920; Portland's horse 480; several others exceeded the standard, and all had been fully recruited after the siege of Athlone.

historians rating it at over thirty pieces, and others as low as twelve; while Story, who was present at the battle, is unaccountably silent on the subject. This, however, is well attested by all:—that at Ballymore, before his battering-train arrived, he had eighteen field-pieces and three mortars; that at Ballyburn he was joined by Wurtemberg and Nassau, with a force of seven or eight thousand men, who, from the important positions held by them through the winter, must have had a park of artillery not less than eight pieces. And that the number was further increased after the siege of Athlone by four of the captured guns, which were mounted on carriages and taken to Aughrim. From the beginning to the end of the war he had cannon at will; and this is beyond a doubt:—that while he might have had over forty pieces, he had certainly not under thirty; and with this immense train, and an array of 30,000 men, computed at 23,000 foot and 7,000 horse, he stood between Garbally and Liscappel, awaiting but a favorable moment to advance on his expectant adversary.

It was really a formidable host, and wholly composed of veterans, both officers and men: of Dutch, Danes, and Prussians, who had seen service on many a continental battle-field; of French Huguenots, whose bravery is generally conceded, and whose undying hatred of their own sovereign, rendered that service the most acceptable which was found under his most deadly enemies; of Scotch, whose native hardihood is proverbial; of English veterans, who, while well fed, are not wanting in many of the soldierly qualities; and of Irish Protestants, now well inured to war, and who, if not the most brave, were certainly not the least zealous, for to them were chiefly to appertain the lands and livings of the country, which had now, even more than liberty or religion, become the wager of battle. With perfect harmony in his councils; with an army which, for numbers, appointments, and appliances combined, was never equalled in the country since its first invasion; with the prestige of a recent victory, and excited to the highest enthusiasm that promised reward or religious frenzy could inspire; Ginckle now approached that field whereon was to be decided the destiny of three kingdoms, the fate of one of the oldest dynasties of Europe, and the liberty or thraldom of a race coeval with European history.

On the other hand, the scene passing in the Irish camp, while no less inspiring, was highly characteristic of the people and the cause they advocated. 'Twas the dawn of the Sabbath morning, and its advent was solemnized by those religious observances, the preparations for which had been made through the preceding night. And those ceremonies being ended, the troops were drawn out in the same order of battle in which they had, for the last two days, been awaiting the arrival of the enemy. As they stood in their mingled uniforms of red and green, with colors advanced, and their old battle-flag, bearing the emblem of an early civilization, and standing out above the long line of tents that formed the background, they made a most gallant show, which the import of the hour and the associations of the day and place rendered deeply solemn and impressive. In this order they remained through the early hours, the deep calm of determination settled over all; but as the morning advanced the silence was at length disturbed by the stirring notes of preparation. The shrill tones of the trumpet sounded along the hill, and was followed by a long roll of drums, when St. Ruth, equipped in a splendid uniform, and bearing "a snow-white plume in his hat," rode along the lines, and in a few impassioned words impressed on all the significance of his address on the preceding day, to which the chaplains added their exhortations and appeals, that touched the springs of many a harrowing and many a hallowed memory. The effect was electric. The history of centuries passed before them: the solemn ceremonies they had witnessed: the attested chivalry of their leaders: and the gallant bearing of their general, kindled the fire of heroism in every breast; the silence was broken, acclamations loud and prolonged rent the air, amid which, St. Ruth retiring, took post on the crest of the hill, and, surrounded by his staff, looked eagerly for the enemy through the passing clouds that still intercepted the two armies.

The signs of approaching conflict now multiplied rapidly, and aids were arriving in quick succession to announce the slow but steady advance of the foe. At eight, his right rested on Garbally, and his left on the river of Clantuskar. At nine, his right was at Cahir, and his left beyond the river, still preserving an unbroken front, and tending a little southward. At ten, the Irish pickets, borne back over the last line of intervening hills, were seen descending into the adjacent valley, and falling back on their supports at Urrachree and Aughrim; and at eleven, the clouds rolling away, the midday sun presented the two armies to each other in all the stern magnificence of war! At this sight, a shout of fierce defiance rang out from the opposing hosts, and echoed far over the hills, when a silence more dread and impressive than the clangor of battle settled over both, the English army still moving measuredly forward.

Up to this moment St. Ruth had kept his whole force drawn out along the hill, presenting an imposing front, as an invitation to the enemy; but as Ginckle, still preserving the order indicated, commenced to descend into the plain, the suspense of the Irish army was at last broken, the word of command passed along the line, and all were at once in motion. Then succeeded the rolling tramp of squadron after squadron of the cavalry, hastening to their allotted stations, the matrosses wheeling their guns into position, and the leaden step of the infantry, moving down the hill and forming in their advanced trenches along its base.

The English army continued to move on until within a quarter of a mile of the morass, when it halted, while Ginckle, who accompanied his left wing, advanced to a steep hill over against the Irish right at Urrachree, which enabled him to make a still closer reconnoissance than he had made on the evening of the 10th. St. Ruth, at the same time, took his stand on the ridge of Kilcommodon, above his centre, whence he had a complete view of the entire English army; and thus, for some time, each general stood scrutinizing the ranks and disposition of the other.

'Twas as St. Ruth expected. The weight of Ginckle's army lay towards Urrachree, and he expressed much satisfaction that he had anticipated this movement, and had made a corresponding disposition to meet it; for the heaviest division of his army, also rested on that side, which he now saw was Ginckle's objective.

This pause was of short duration. It was now on to twelve o'clock, and Ginckle seeing the absolute necessity of possessing the Pass of Urrachree, before he could bring the weight of his left infantry against the Irish main line in that quarter, directed his first movement accordingly.

Two rivulets, coming from different directions on the extreme right of the Irish army, crossed the road in front of Urrachree, and rendered the pass at that point more difficult than the ground in front and rear of it. Between these streams a small cavalry outpost had been stationed by St. Ruth, rather with a view to invite than repel the enemy, and against this point Ginckle now directed a company of Danish dragoons, with orders to gain the pass and hold it until reinforced by the infantry advancing from the main line for that purpose. Apprehending no resistance from the few troops stationed there, the Danish horse soon cleared the distance between them, and quickening their pace to a gallop, advanced at the charge, until within a few rods, when, seeing the Irish still maintain their position, they suddenly halted; when the former, taking advantage of their indecision, sounded the charge, and advanced on them at a full gallop. The Danes did not await the shock, but, breaking in disorder, retreated off the field, notwithstanding the efforts of their captain to rally them, and returned to the rear of their infantry.[76]

Ginckle was deeply mortified at the unsoldierlike conduct of his Danish horse, and in order to remedy the mischief created by it, in the presence of his troops, Sir Albert Cunningham's dragoons, who entered on the right of his line, were now called up to his left, and 200 of them were ordered to advance beyond the stream, and, clearing the ground of all minor detachments in their way, to take post behind some hedges beyond it, make a lodgement there, and await the support of the infantry. Those troops were reckoned the best dragoons of the British service, and as they rode across the intervening slope of tillage, with swords drawn, and their steel caps and cuirasses glancing through the clouds of dust struck from the parched soil over which they passed, the Irish felt that the battle was about to open in reality, and caught its inspiration. As the dragoons neared the pass, where the little outpost stood to receive them, they halted suddenly, wheeled to the left, and took post behind a line of hedges until the front line of infantry was seen moving across the plain to their support, when they were again put in motion towards the pass. But during the interval, it was found that the Irish outpost had retired to the shelter of a hill in their rear, where, being reinforced by a company of Lord Galway's horse, they wheeled to the front and stood to invite the charge of the enemy. But as the British dragoons advanced across the stream, the Irish again wheeled round and retired, with the intention of drawing them farther from their supports. Deceived by the disparity of their force, or encouraged by this indecisive conduct, the English horse charged on them with great impetuosity. Passing the hill, they were saluted by a well-directed musketry fire, under which they wavered, and, at the same moment, the Irish battery on the right opened on the advancing files of the English infantry. This was instantly answered by the opposing batteries, which had now been brought into position along the whole line, and, to the stirring responses of their artillery, the cavalry on both sides rushed to the encounter. It was deadly and intense; the British bore themselves gallantly, but here, as at

[76] "These men," says Story, "ran away from a less number than themselves, though the officer behaved himself very well." — He might have said less than half their number. The Irish were but seven men; there were sixteen of the Danes.

the Boyne, they were no match for the Irish horse, and, despite the advantage of numbers, they were broken, after a brief but deadly struggle, and borne back over the stream, where many of them were unhorsed and sabred, despite the steel cap and corselet that protected them. The smoke and dust of battle soon cleared away, when it was seen that they had relinquished the fight, and retired as the Danish horse had done, while the Irish cavalry stood leisurely behind the stream to invite another onset.

This discomfiture of his favorite cavalry, by less than half their number, filled Ginckle with deep concern, and had not a less dispiriting effect on the troops that witnessed it. The possession of this point, according to the plan adopted, was of imperative necessity; so, in order to carry out his design, as well as to remove the depressing effect from the minds of his men, he now resolved to throw forward an overwhelming force of cavalry, to clear the ground up to the Irish main line, and make way for the heavy columns of infantry drawn up and ready for the action. For this purpose, the whole of Sir Albert Cunningham's dragoons were massed into charging column, and, led by himself in person, were to be hurled against the Irish squadron at the pass; while Eppinger, with his regiment of Royal Holland dragoons,—920 strong—was to make a flank movement, more to the right, and, by sweeping round the hill, take them in the rear, cut them off from their supports, and lay bare their whole right for the action of his infantry.

St. Ruth, from his position, saw with exultation the gallant conduct of his cavalry, and, anticipating the next movement of Ginckle, now moved down to his right to counteract it. He caused the advanced troops to fall farther back, ordered another squadron to their support, and gave them directions to continue a retiring movement until they should receive the order to charge. He next ordered Lord Galway to hold his horse, stationed behind the house of Urrachree, well in hand, until the enemy, in passing, should receive a volley from the musketeers within it, which was to be the signal for a simultaneous charge on both divisions of the assailants. By this arrangement Galway's horse were held completely out of sight until the appointed moment, while the other detachment, which alone seemed to invite the enemy, was not such as to awaken their apprehension.

Both of the English regiments moved briskly across the open tillage field that led down to the stream, and crossed it without any opposition, the Irish horse retiring according to orders, and forming under the shelter of their main line. After crossing the stream and entering the field beyond it, the assailants separated, Cunningham bearing directly for the opposing cavalry, and Eppinger wheeling by his right, scattering the few infantry pickets in his way up to the house of Urrachree, where he again moved by his left to flank the Irish cavalry, as directed. In passing this point he received the fire of the Irish musketeers, which caused considerable loss, and the smoke from which had scarcely cleared away, when he received the shock of Galway's horse on his right flank, and recoiled in confusion. At the same moment the other detachment closed with Cunningham's dragoons, and the entire forces on both sides were soon mingled in deadly conflict; the English burning to wipe out the disgrace of the previous encounters, and the Irish to maintain the prestige of a name borne unsullied through all the changes of this wasting war.

Along the broad plateau in front of Urrachree, hidden by the enveloping clouds of dust and smoke, excepting at intervals that rendered the flashing of their arms perceptible, this tumultuous mass of men and horses rocked and swayed in all the dread clangor of small-arms and cannon, mingled with the fierce neigh of the war steeds driven headlong to battle. At length some squadrons of the English horse, detaching themselves from the main body, were seen to approach the stream, re-form, and again rush to the conflict, while the whole mass, assailants and assailed, rolled steadily on towards the scene of the first encounter. Ginckle beheld this sign with amazement and concern, for he well knew its import. His troops were giving ground, and he immediately advanced the Portland horse—480 men—under the command of General Holstaple, to succor them, while St. Ruth, on his part, threw in the Tyrconnell Guards, under Brigadier James Talbot, to sustain his cavalry, and the conflict was continued with unabated fury on both sides. Other detachments were now successively thrown in from each side, as chance or necessity directed, until what first began in a skirmish between outposts, absorbed nearly the entire cavalry of the adverse wings, and, after a series of rencounters, which lasted for over two hours, the English horse broke and fled in disorder, the Irish horse were recalled from the pursuit, and the same little band that had invited those successive assaults, reined up behind the stream, as fresh and defiant as ever.

Ginckle lost heavily in those attacks. The dragoons of Eppinger and Cunningham were decimated; the Portland Guards suffered "severely in men and horses," and their leader, General Holstaple, with many of his officers, was slain. The loss of the Irish, though beset by twice their number, was insignificant. An infantry picket, stationed behind the hill, was scattered, and had a few men sabred by the dragoons of Eppinger; but Brigadier Talbot, one of the heroes of Limerick, in an encounter with the Portland horse, fell, covered with many wounds.[77] It was now past two o'clock, and the battle rested as it began, but the prestige of success, and the spirit it infused, remained with the Irish army.

---

[77] As none of the histories consulted by the writer alludes to the death of Holstaple and Talbot, save in recapitulating the loss on both sides, he deems it necessary to give his authority for placing it so early in the battle, lest his assertion shall be attributed to fancy, which should always be held in abeyance to historic truth. The following lines from Garrick's rambling play, "The Battle of Aughrim," it is hoped, will satisfy the reader. It is necessary to introduce it by stating that there was no general named Hostile in the English army, and that the renowned comedian only adopts it for the sake of euphony: Holstaple being a rough, and rather unpoetic name:—

> Lord Portland's horse approached the mortal fight
> With sword in hand to put our troops to flight:—
> This Talbot saw, and like a hero bold,
> Disdaining life, he scorned to be controlled;
> But, as a Mars, amid the throng he run,
> And there he stood, like marble to the sun,
> Till, being hacked and flanked on every side,
> By multitudes oppressed, he bravely died.

And again, after the retreat of the English, an Irish officer is made to say:

> Aughrim is ours, brave General Hostile's dead,

While Ginckle had been pushing forward detachment after detachment of his cavalry towards the Irish right at Urrachree, his own right wing and centre had moved into position along the edge of the marsh, and had brought their artillery to bear on the opposing lines beyond it. Their guns were disposed in six batteries:— two on the esplanade in front of Aughrim; two at the centre; and two against the southern slope of Kilcommodon.[78] Here, in the order already indicated, the troops stood observing the different changes of the battle raging within their sight; but, as the excitement increased, their order became gradually indistinct, until both lines mingled into one, which stood close up to the marsh, beyond which the Irish stood prepared to receive them. But, up to this, no movement was made by either, beyond the enfilades of their batteries; for the Irish plan was strictly defensive, and the enemy awaited the success of the movement on their left, which was to be the signal for their assault. In this state of expectation the first hour passed and the second, and still no order from the left reached them. The successive repulses of his cavalry had shaken the fortitude of Ginckle, and, despairing of success from a further persistence in his present plan of attack, he drew in his troops, ordered a suspension of hostilities, and called a council of his generals.

More favored by fortune in this particular than his adversary, the council was his tower of refuge, and had always been attended with happy results in the most trying emergencies. And the present was one of those on which depended, not only the result of this day's battle, but the success or failure of the campaign now favorably inaugurated. To this council he represented his fears for the final issue, should the battle be continued much longer, with the result of the last two hours. He had directed it according to the plan stamped by their general approval, and with that impetuosity that best suited the condition and character of his troops. But, notwithstanding their ardor and overwhelming odds, they had been repeatedly hurled back, with a valor and intrepidity that had damped their enthusiasm and restored the confidence of their opponents. As yet, the battle had been entirely between the cavalry, in which branch of the service he outnumbered his adversary two to one; and though all the cavalry of his right had been drawn into it, the Irish main line had not been approached, nor any portion of its infantry brought into action. And should he now, at this late hour, fling the whole weight of his horse and foot against the quarter in dispute, and even succeed, after a protracted engagement, in reaching the Irish main right, it was more than probable that night would close upon a suspended battle; in which case, the advantages would be in favor of the native army, and it were hard to divine what morning would bring forth to his own, remote from its encampment, and in an enemy's country. Impressed

---

> Who, even now, Lord Portland's horse did head,—
> Drove all before him, till a lucky ball,
> Shot with good aim from off the castle wall,
> Clove up his skull, etc., etc.

Nothing, perhaps, could excuse the introduction of this doggerel, save the name of the author, who lived at a time which enabled him to consult many of the real actors in the battle.

[78] If the dots on the batteries, as represented in Story's map, indicate the number of guns, there were thirty of them in all; and on his other maps they do indicate them.

with these views, and before the council had assembled, he dispatched couriers to Ballinasloe to order up his tents, being resolved to encamp along the valley, opposite to Kilcommodon, for the night, and renew the battle early on the following morning. The consultation lasted until four o'clock. The council was divided: some being in favor of the general's plan, and some for immediately renewing the battle; but finally, the latter course was adopted, on the advice of Major-General Mackey. This old veteran remarked that neither the English right or centre had yet been engaged, and it occurred to him that by a change of disposition, and by bringing up additional forces to the left, St. Ruth would be ultimately compelled to weaken his left or centre, or perhaps both, to sustain his right, when a simultaneous advance of the whole English line would change the tenor of the battle. The age and experience of the general, and the simple plausibility of his argument, prevailed; the order to bring up the tents was countermanded, and preparations were accordingly made to renew the engagement.

The British army accordingly underwent another transformation. The cavalry, which could not cross at the centre, were posted on the right and left wings. The left wing of infantry was further strengthened by some fresh regiments from the right, while 12,000 infantry were massed against the centre and inner left of the Irish line, to await the result of Mackey's experiment.

It was half-past four o'clock, as Ginckle moved forward his left wing of infantry, flanked on either side by his cavalry, determined to reach the ground in front of the Irish line. As they approached the stream which had been the scene of the previous encounters, two Danish regiments, consisting of infantry and cavalry, deployed to the left, along its outer margin, as if intent on turning the extreme right of the Irish position. This, which was a feint on the part of Ginckle, had the desired effect; for no sooner was it observed by the latter, than a corresponding force was detached to counteract it; and, as they continued to wear round in that direction, Ginckle hurled his main body to the assault, across the grounds of Urrachree.

This movement on the part of the enemy determined St. Ruth no longer to defer the battle; but by accepting his offer to confine him to the Irish main right, and prevent any discursive movements which should result in weakening it: so, withdrawing his cavalry, he threw forward his infantry to his first line of defence, and awaited the enemy in confidence. As the British advanced, their cavalry was also withdrawn, and thus, as if by mutual agreement, the ground was completely cleared for the action of the infantry on both sides.

The front line of the English left, consisting of the Huguenot regiments of La Mellioneire, Cambon, and Belcastle—about 2,500 men—marched boldly across the ground, followed by the other regiments in close succession. As they approached within range, they were met by a deadly fire, but still they pressed on with characteristic valor, delivered their fire in return, and were soon at close quarters along the first line of intrenchments. The disposition made of the ground here by St. Ruth, greatly tended to equalize the disparity of numbers, and the Irish troops were quick to seize on every advantage that offered; so that the enemy soon found they had to contend with men no less daring and intrepid than themselves. Every hedge-row soon became the scene of assault and defence. A deadly and protracted struggle now took place; the soldiers on both sides resting their muskets on the separating hedges, and literally discharging them into each others' bosoms. The Irish, after defending one of those lines with the greatest obstinacy, would suddenly retire on another, when the enemy, thus drawn on, would find themselves at once taken in front and flank, and borne back rapidly to the first line, where the conflict would be again renewed and again repeated with a like result as before. This desperate conflict raged along the right for over an hour without cessation. Ginckle's last column had been pushed forward, and the result was still the same;—every inch of ground won by their successive assaults, was again disputed, and again recovered. The Huguenots suffered dreadfully. Every advance into the inclosures thinned their ranks; and less and less able to penetrate this wing, the battle culminated on the outer line,—"until," says a Huguenot actor in the scene, "there remained only one course to adopt,—which was to perish and sell our lives dearly:" and, in this emergency, Ginckle called up two regiments of infantry, and the cavalry of Lanier and Ruvigny from his right for the final test of his experiment.

St. Ruth witnessed this intense struggle with varied emotions of hope and fear. Up to this hour he entertained grave doubts of the steadiness and discipline of his newly raised infantry. But as he saw column after column of Ginckle's veterans hurled on them and steadily repelled, his apprehensions were removed, and he felt and expressed a full assurance of victory. As yet, his whole line was intact, for he had not displaced a single man from his left or centre. But as this last reinforcement was called up, it became manifest that Ginckle was absolutely committed to turning his right at whatever cost, and he was at last compelled to order some fresh infantry from his extreme left to its support.[79] This gave Ginckle the desired opportunity, and he hastily availed himself of it; for while these troops were marching from the left to the right, across the hill of Kilcommodon, he ordered his centre to cross the marsh, and assail the main position of the Irish.

The whole English infantry were now put in motion. The regiments of Earle, Creighton, Brewer, and Herbert, sustained by those of Foulk, Stuart, and others, were to cross at the main centre, where the marsh was narrowest, and where the hedges approached nearest to it, to make a lodgement in the first line, and await the support of their cavalry. Those of St. John, Tiffin, Lord George Hamilton, the French, "and other regiments," were to pursue a similar course against the inner left; while the cavalry under Talmash on the right, and Lanier and Levison on the left, were to force a passage at Aughrim and Urrachree, sweep round the base of the hill to their support, and endeavor to bring on a general engagement.

The regiments of Earle, Creighton, Brewer, and Herbert, moved forward, crossed the marsh without opposition, formed on the other side, and advanced up the sloping meadows of Kilcommodon without firing a single shot. As they

---

[79] Those troops who were ordered from the rear of his left, were, either by design or inadvertence, sent from the front of that position; and on the concurrence of this and a subsequent blunder, historians have based their accusations of treason against Brigadier Henry Luttrell, who, it is said, received the order.

approached the first row of hedges, the Irish infantry received them with a destructive fire, and retired on their second line with a steadiness and precision that might have awakened suspicion of preconcert. But the feint was taken for an actual retreat; the ardor of the assailants was excited, and eager to avenge the fall of so many of their comrades, they rushed forward on the second line, which was temporarily defended, and yielded in the same manner. Exasperated beyond endurance, they now lost all caution, and pressed hotly up the hill until they reached the last line of hedges, where the effect of their rashness at once became apparent. The infantry that had lured them on by this feint retreat, now suddenly appeared on either flank, pouring volley after volley into their devoted ranks, while above them, on the hill-side, stood the Irish cavalry, reined back and ready for the onset. The ground over which they had passed was difficult and dangerous, and files of infantry lined the way down to the marsh to intercept their retreat; no cavalry support appeared on their right, for as yet the Pass of Aughrim had not been attempted; and on their left, towards Urrachree, the sounds of battle seemed to recede, as if their arms had met with a reverse in that quarter. Colonel Earle, who took in the situation at a glance, advanced to the front, exhorting his men that "there was no way to come off but to be brave," ordered them to re-form, and endeavor to reach the line which they had so imprudently abandoned. The troops, obedient to the command, halted, closed ranks, and commenced a retrograde movement; but it was now too late; for at the same moment the Irish cavalry charged fiercely down the hill; and, unable to withstand the shock, they were helplessly broken, hurled by repeated charges into the marsh, across which they retreated in utter confusion, hotly pressed by the infantry, and borne back to the level of their batteries.[80] Their loss was very severe. They had advanced to the assault over 3,000 strong. One-third of that number in killed and wounded strewed their way back. Colonel Earle, after being captured and rescued three times, escaped severely wounded; many officers of note were slain; and 400 soldiers, with Colonel Herbert, remained prisoners in the hands of the victors.

While the battle stood as described on the right and centre of the Irish line, the regiments of St. John, Tiffin, Lord George Hamilton, some French "and other regiments," were directed against its left. This division was led by the Prince of Hesse, and he had orders from General Mackey, who commanded in that quarter, not to pass the first line of hedges, but after establishing a position there to hold it until supported by the cavalry, which, under the command of Talmash, and supported by some regiments of infantry, were moving round towards the extreme left of the Irish, and forming on the plateau in front of Aughrim, with the intention of assaulting the pass leading up to it. The strength of this position, the narrow way which led to it, and the guns bearing across it from the hill, were such as to render the movement slow and hazardous; and the attack of the Prince of Hesse which depended on its result should necessarily be so regulated as to keep time with it. Talmash drew up his command on the common, and after directing his batteries,

---

[80] Some historians allude to the *"sounding"* of this marsh, and *"wading"* through it; but the fact is: that it was but a rushy bottom, difficult in no place, save at the stream, where it was impracticable to cavalry; for we find the Irish charging and recharging the enemy three times across it.

of which there were two, against the opposing force of the Irish, opened a fierce cannonade, while he formed his troops, both horse and foot, for the assault. In the mean time the Prince of Hesse had crossed the marsh, and approached the enemy's left on Kilcommodon. Meeting with no opposition, and scarcely apprehending any, so closely did the Irish there lie in their trenches, he advanced rapidly to possess the seemingly abandoned trenches, until within a few yards of them, when their sudden appearance, and a succession of well-directed volleys, warned him of his error. This unexpected salute checked the onward movement of his troops, and for a time they wavered as if about to retreat. But the ardor of the impetuous Prince being excited, he rallied them again, and under his order to charge, they rushed forward with increased fury and entered the lines of the enemy. This afforded the latter the opportunity sought, and no sooner had the assailants advanced to a proper distance, than they were taken front and flank, turned, as at the centre, and driven back on their supports, now being pushed eagerly forward by General Mackey, who, after several attempts to check their retreat, dispatched orders to Talmash to suspend his assault on the Pass of Aughrim, and lead back the infantry to the support of his broken division. Under this order fresh succors were deployed from the English right, but Talmash himself, unwilling to abandon his design, remained with his cavalry and a portion of the infantry, to carry out his projected attack.

The assault against the inner left of the Irish line was now renewed, that against the extreme left was begun, and the contest raged along the whole left with the utmost obstinacy, assailants and assailed being so completely "enveloped in dust and smoke as to be invisible to the bystanders." At length, after nearly an hour of the most intense excitement, during which the intermingled mass rolled with varied success across the fallow-fields between the hedges and the marsh, the English broke and fled across it to the protection of their guns, one regiment alone, of all that crossed to the attack, holding a position in the hedges, near the extreme left, whence the Irish troops had been withdrawn, and even this was in imminent danger of total destruction.

It was now near sunset, and the shadows began to deepen over the scene of conflict, when St. Ruth, from the ridge of Kilcommodon, surveyed the situation beneath him. On his right, where the battle commenced, the successive assaults of the enemy had been broken and repelled; from being assailants they had become the assailed; and driven far back from his outer line, had thrown up temporary intrenchments, behind which they continued to return the fire of his infantry, while they endeavored to withstand the repeated charges of his cavalry, careering on their flanks. On his centre he was completely victorious. The terrible repulse of the enemy's infantry there, and their consequent loss, had filled them with consternation and dismay, and though heavily reinforced, and urged forward with every threat and suasion of command, they could not be brought to attempt a second assault, but stood, a discomfited and disheartened host, under the shelter of their cannon, which alone disturbed his line in that direction. On his inner left the sight was no less inspiriting. There, the columns under the Prince of Hesse, after being, for the third time, bloodily repulsed, were floundering back through the morass in utter disorder, though Mackey stood on its outer edge, urging forward still fresh arrivals from the right, and doing all that a brave and intrepid soldier could do to retrieve an apparently lost battle. From the first, Ginckle's chances of success depended on his ability to turn the Irish right, or to bring on a general engagement along the whole line, when the immense numerical superiority of his army, with its proud array of field officers, could scarcely fail of success. To this end, all the energies of his mind, and all the resources at his disposal had been constantly directed; but, up to this hour, all had signally failed. Favored by the happy disposition which he had made of his ground, St. Ruth had so handled his army as to disconcert every attack, and defeat his enemy in detail. Everywhere he had cause to fear that the least inadvertence would be fatal, yet every thing moved with precision, every plan answered his expectations, and now, at every point, he stood secure and successful. His cavalry had sustained its wonted reputation, had borne down every opposition throughout the day, and its reserve stood fresh and eager, within immediate support of the only point undecided. His infantry, which had sustained the brunt of the battle, since its renewal after the early cavalry rencounters, stood now, on all hands, firm, defiant, and victorious. Two thousand three hundred of the enemy strewed the valley from Aughrim to Urrachree, while, up to this moment, his loss was quite insignificant. Victory seemed completely within his grasp; a grand future opened before him, and, perhaps, wrapt in one of those bright visions that sweep the mind on the wing of thought:—a people freed; a kingdom restored to its legitimate sway, and his own sovereign rendering him the meed of glorious service; he doffed his hat to those around him, and exclaimed in the ardor of enthusiasm:—"Now, my children, we will beat them back to the gates of Dublin."[81]—words which, though not realized, are worthy of grateful commemoration, indicative at once of a patriarchal spirit, and an exalted heroism.

Through all, the activity of the opposing generals was incessant. Ginckle was everywhere, aiding and animating his men, and sharing the danger and fatigue of the private soldier. On the other hand, St. Ruth had followed every movement of the battle, and was found at every point where aid or encouragement demanded his presence. Two horses had broken down under him during the fatigues of this eventful day; and now, mounting a third, a powerful gray, which stood ready to his call, he rode down to the left, to congratulate his infantry on their victory in that quarter. Here he beheld the last regiment of the enemy's infantry, abandoned to their fate, afraid to attempt a retreat across the marsh, and defending their temporary lodgement with the last efforts of despair. Dismounting from his horse, he approached the gunners, and with his own hand giving direction to one of the three guns bearing on the enemy's lines, returned to his staff, and remounted. His attention was then directed to the movements of Talmash, who, at the head of the English cavalry, and supported by a compact body of infantry, was approaching along the defile that opened up to the village and castle of Aughrim. Inquiring casually what the enemy meant by moving in that direction, he was answered that they intended to force the Pass and succor their infantry beneath him. *"Then,"* said

---

[81] "A boast," says Taylor, "which the special interposition of Providence alone prevented him from accomplishing * * * ten minutes more would have completed the destruction of the English army."—Vol. ii., page 180.

he, *"we have won the battle."* Considering the difficulties to be encountered, and the force stationed there, he deemed their destruction certain; and, after watching their steady advance for some time, he exclaimed with mingled feelings of admiration and pity:—*"They are brave, 'tis a pity they should be so exposed!"* Then forming his guards to charge down the hill, and dispatching orders to call up his reserve of cavalry to confront the force of Talmash, he addressed his staff, now ranged around him, saying:—*"They are beaten, let us beat them to the purpose!"* They were his last words,—for scarcely were they uttered, when his head was shattered by a cannonball, and he lay a corpse on the hill of Kilcommodon, while his horse ran wild and riderless across the plain! Amazement seized on all around him. The cavalry arrived and halted on the hill-side. His attendants approached, threw a cloak over the body, and bore it to the rear, whither it was followed by his guards and the members of his staff. The charge that was to decide the battle was suspended. The Irish infantry, unaware of the death of their general, still held their ground. The cavalry stood waiting the order to charge, and nothing was wanting to complete the victory but that expected word; but it never came. Meanwhile, Talmash beheld the confusion and the hesitancy of the Irish troops on the hill, and auguring that something was going wrong there, pushed on with greater rapidity. The fire from the Irish lines and the castle opened on him, and twice he was repulsed, but still renewed his efforts. It was now the crisis of the day, and so was it felt by assailants and assailed. Colonel Burke, who had command in that quarter, pressed the enemy closely and successfully. The cavalry were held in check, and unable to advance; but the English infantry, moving along the northern margin of the marsh, began to break through in battalions and companies. They too were checked, and for some time held immovable. At this trying moment Burke found that his supply of musket-balls was exhausted, and a fresh supply was urgently demanded. It arrived; it was opened; but by some fatal blunder, or treacherous design, it was found that cannonball had been sent instead of those demanded.[82] The effect is easily foreseen. The soldiers still fought as men seldom fight. They exhausted their last shot, and all means being gone, they cut the round buttons from their coats, fired them, and discharged even their ramrods at the enemy, and then in rage and despair stood to offer their bodies as a last resistance, and died fighting where they stood. The Pass was carried; the castle grounds were gained and barriers thrown up there to impede the Irish cavalry, while Talmash, after passing the defile, moved round by his left, and succored his devoted soldiers. The English infantry at the centre now crossed the marsh in force and formed to carry the left and centre. At this sight a wild and piercing cry of *"treason"* rang along the Irish lines. The infantry was left to struggle alone, and the cavalry, without a commander, retired to the crest of the hill and formed for a last effort to redeem

---

[82] It was found, on examining the ammunition with which they had been supplied, that while the men were armed with French firelocks, the balls that had been served to them were cast for English muskets, of which the calibre was larger, and that they were consequently useless.—*Haverty's History of Ireland*, page 661.

This would seem the more probable version, although that in the text is in accordance with general authority. This book was not seen in time to alter the text: but the effect was the same.

the day. It was useless. The infantry did all that men could do, and disputed every inch of the ground up to their camp, where, they made a last desperate stand, until surrounded by horse and foot of the enemy, when they broke, and, under the protection of their cavalry, retreated off the field. The left and centre of the Irish army being carried, the enemy turned their attention to the right, which, ignorant of what had passed, still pressed the foe beyond their lines, and were still victorious. But being now surrounded on all sides, and attacked front and rear, they were overwhelmed and literally cut to pieces; nearly all the infantry on that side being slaughtered where they stood.

The castle of Aughrim, which withstood the assailants long after the Pass was carried, was at length taken, and all within it put to the sword. Night closed over the scene of carnage. The Irish cavalry baffled in their design to support the infantry, which became intermingled with the horse and foot of the enemy, after aiding some time in the retreat, withdrew to the south-west and pursued their route to Loughrea, while the infantry crossed the bog to the west, and moved in the direction of Galway. The retreat of these portions of the army was regular and unbroken; but the fugitives were cut down without mercy; their cry for quarter was totally disregarded: and the slaughter of the straggling bands continued far into the night. In this butchery the Danish troops were conspicuous. Remarkable through the day only for pusillanimity, they became the "best pursuers," through the night, until a fortuitous circumstance put an end to the pursuit. While despairing and resistless they fled from the field which they maintained to the last, an Irish drum-major, who was lying wounded by the wayside, was ordered by the almoner of a regiment, named O'Reilly, to beat the charge. It was done, and on hearing it the pursuers halted, and believing the Irish about to rally, retired to the main body, and the vanquished pursued their retreat unmolested. Thus ended the disastrous day of Aughrim. Up to the death of St. Ruth, no pending battle was ever more prophetic of victory. After it none was ever so unaccountably lost in the presence of numerous officers of experience and ability. It would seem as if fortune held the balance of the day, to elicit deeds of unexampled heroism, and inverted it in the hour of victory to maintain her proverbial fickleness.

The loss of the British in private soldiers was 2,300; in addition to this, 200 officers of all grades were wounded, and seventy-three killed, including among them one major-general and five colonels—making in all nearly 3,000. The loss of the Irish as estimated by the victors was 7,000, including their commander-in-chief, and seventeen generals and officers of the highest distinction. The number of officers of subaltern rank was great, and far exceeded those of the enemy.[83] The spoil of the victors included all the guns and camp equipage of the vanquished; and their trophies, eleven standards and thirty-two pair of colors, were immediately

---

[83] Those were nearly all killed after the death of St. Ruth; for "up to that," says Taylor, "the Irish had lost scarcely a man." No insignificant number of them was put to death, after their capture, by order of General Ginckle; and for this brutal and unsoldierly order, Story offers as a palliation, the conduct of Henry V. of England, at the battle of Agincourt: —"*who, seeing the king of Cicilies appear on the field, ordered every man to kill his prisoner, contrary to his generous nature,*" —and among those so murdered in cold blood, was Colonel O'Moore, and that most loyal gentleman and chivalrous soldier, Lord Galway.

borne to London by "my Lord O'Bryan, as a present to her majesty," the Prince of Orange being then on the Continent.

The next day Ginckle encamped on the heights of Kilcommodon and buried his dead. The Irish slain, who strewed the hill and lay scattered over the country for miles, were stripped and left unburied, to be "devoured by the wild dogs and birds of prey." The country people fled the vicinity of the British army, and retired to the woods and mountains as their only refuge. The body of St. Ruth, according to the English annalist, was stripped and thrown into a bog. A more recent and better authority says, that "by tradition well attested, his ashes lie in the roofless church of Athunree, beside those of Lord Galway, who fell upon the same field of battle." There is, however, reason to doubt both, and the writer is aware that the people of the locality where the battle was fought, directed by tradition, point to a few stunted white thorns, to the west of the hill, towards Loughrea, beneath which, they say, rest the ashes of this great but unfortunate general.

It is painful to speculate on the cause that left the Irish army without direction after the death of St. Ruth. Many have endeavored to explain it, but all—as well those who doubt Sarsfield's presence on the field, as those who maintain the contrary,—are lost in conjecture, and none who participated in the battle and survived it, has placed the matter beyond speculation. So leaving that point as time has left it, what appears most strange in the connection, is the absence of all command at such a conjuncture. The disposition of the Irish troops, though dexterous, was simple. The day was all but won. The foiling of Talmash would have been the completion of victory. A force sufficient was on his front; a reserve more than ample to overwhelm him was on its way to the ground—nay, drawn up and even ready for the word. The few British troops that held a lodgement in the hedges at the base of the hill, were completely at the mercy of those above them. It required no omniscient eye to see this, nor a voice from the clouds to impel them forward, and surely no military etiquette weighed a feather in opposition to the fate of a nation. Any officer of note could have directed the movement, and many of experience and approved courage witnessed the crisis. Yet in this emergency, all the hard-won laurels of the day were tarnished, and land and liberty were lost by default! Nor can the rashness of St. Ruth, his reticence as to his plans, his misunderstanding with Sarsfield, nor the absence of the latter, justify the want of intrepid action among those present. This stands unexplained and inexplicable, nor will the flippant appeal to Providence, whose ways are too frequently offered as an excuse for human misconduct, answer here. The want of ammunition at such a moment, was, no doubt, of some import, but the concurrence of events too plainly indicates that Aughrim was won by the skill of St. Ruth and the gallantry of his troops, and that it was lost through want of decision in his general officers, at a moment the most critical in the nation's history.

Since writing the above, my attention has been called to Haverty's "History of Ireland," a work of much careful research and investigation, in which the loss of the Irish army is estimated at:—killed, nearly 4,000, and 526 of all ranks taken prisoners. This would seem the more probable, as Story doubts his own estimate, and in the end of the year, 1692, says, "time has informed me of some mistakes, though possibly there may be some as yet remaining."

But time passed on. Galway surrendered on honorable terms after an exchange of hostages. The passes of the Shannon were abandoned one by one down to Limerick, where the final stand was made, during which Tyrconnel, after years of faithful service, "died apparently of a broken heart." The city, though twice betrayed by General Clifford, made a most gallant defence, and its surrender wrested a treaty from the enemy, as glorious to its defenders, as its violation was infamous to the victors.—O retributive justice, how slow is thy finger on the dial!

THE END.

Lector House believes that a society develops through a two-fold approach of continuous learning and adaptation, which is derived from the study of classic literary works spread across the historic timeline of literature records. Therefore, we aim at reviving, repairing and redeveloping all those inaccessible or damaged but historically as well as culturally important literature across subjects so that the future generations may have an opportunity to study and learn from past works to embark upon a journey of creating a better future.

This book is a result of an effort made by Lector House towards making a contribution to the preservation and repair of original ancient works which might hold historical significance to the approach of continuous learning across subjects.

HAPPY READING & LEARNING!

LECTOR HOUSE LLP
E-MAIL: lectorpublishing@gmail.com

9 789390 387007